your ideas can fly high and around the world.

Challenge the news industry as a Media in Chapter 5.

Have fun **Playing in the MUD** in Chapter 9.

Through the Internet, your ideas can fly high

reate scavenger hunts and learn how to find information

our opinions through art or music? Then **Artistic Reflections** in Chapter 4 is the project for you.

Or have a virtual experience **Simulating Life** in Chapter 9.

secrets of **Predicting the Weather** in Chapter 8.

Experience the **Gallery of the Future** by exhibiting your art on the network in Chapter 7.

No matter which project you choose first, you are bound for an experience you will never forget!

playing in your head by accessing the **Musical Outlets** of the Internet in Chapter 7.

Jump-start your brain with new and interesting ideas for writing in **Writer's Corner**, Chapter 5.

For every kind of computer user, there is a SYBEX book.

All computer users learn in their own way. Some need straightforward and methodical explanations. Others are just too busy for this approach. But no matter what camp you fall into, SYBEX has a book that can help you get the most out of your computer and computer software while learning at your own pace.

Beginners generally want to start at the beginning. The **ABC's** series, with its step-by-step lessons in plain language, helps you build basic skills quickly. For a more personal approach, there's the **Murphy's Laws** and **Guided Tour** series. Or you might try our **Quick & Easy** series, the friendly, full-color guide, with **Quick & Easy References**, the companion pocket references to the **Quick & Easy** series. If you learn best by doing rather than reading, find out about the **Hands-On Live!** series, our new interactive multimedia training software. For hardware novices, there's the **Your First** series.

The **Mastering and Understanding** series will tell you everything you need to know about a subject. They're perfect for intermediate and advanced computer users, yet they don't make the mistake of leaving beginners behind. Add one of our **Instant References** and you'll have more than enough help when you have a question about your computer software. You may even want to check into our **Secrets & Solutions** series.

SYBEX even offers special titles on subjects that don't neatly fit a category—like our **Pushbutton Guides**, our books about the Internet, our books about the latest computer games, and a wide range of books for Macintosh computers and software.

SYBEX books are written by authors who are expert in their subjects. In fact, many make their living as professionals, consultants or teachers in the field of computer software. And their manuscripts are thoroughly reviewed by our technical and editorial staff for accuracy and ease-of-use.

So when you want answers about computers or any popular software package, just help yourself to SYBEX.

For a complete catalog of our publications, please write:

SYBEX Inc.
2021 Challenger Drive
Alameda, CA 94501
Tel: (510) 523-8233/(800) 227-2346 Telex: 336311
Fax: (510) 523-2373

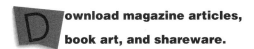

Internet
for Kids

Deneen Frazier

with
Dr. Barbara Kurshan
Dr. Sara Armstrong

San Francisco
Paris
Düsseldorf
Soest

Acquisitions Editor: Kristine Plachy
Developmental Editors: Brenda Kienan, David Peal
Editor: Laura Arendal
Technical Editor: Sara Armstrong
Book Designer and Art Director: Carl Wm. Kistler
Illustrator: Erika Luikart
Screen Graphics Captured by Deneen Frazier
Production Assistant: Emily Smith
Indexer: Matthew Spence
Cover Designer: Ingalls + Associates
Cover Illustrator: Eldon Doty

SYBEX is a registered trademark of SYBEX Inc.

TRADEMARKS: SYBEX has attempted throughout this book to distinguish proprietary trademarks from descriptive terms by following the capitalization style used by the manufacturer.

Every effort has been made to supply complete and accurate information. However, SYBEX assumes no responsibility for its use, nor for any infringement of the intellectual property rights of third parties which would result from such use.

Photographs and illustrations used in this book have been downloaded from publicly accessible file archives and are used in this book for news reportage purposes only to demonstrate the variety of graphics resources available via electronic access. The text, caption, or screen shot for each figure identifies its source. Text and images available over the Internet may be subject to copyright and other rights owned by third parties. Online availability of text and images does not imply that they may be reused without the permission of rights holders, although the Copyright Act does permit certain unauthorized reuse as fair use under 17 U.S.C., Section 107. Care should be taken to ensure that all necessary rights are cleared prior to reusing material distributed over the Internet. Information about reuse rights is available from the institutions that make their materials available over the Internet.

NetCruiser® Program copyright ©1994–1995 NETCOM.

Library of Congress Card Number: 94-74625
ISBN: 0-7821-1741-4

Manufactured in the United States of America

10 9 8 7 6 5 4 3 2 1

For my friend Ramón,
  whose support and love
    always brings out my best.

And for the children
  who will discover
    a new world of
      support and love.

Warranty

SYBEX warrants the enclosed Companion Disk to be free of physical defects for a period of ninety (90) days after purchase. If you discover a defect in the disk during this warranty period, you can obtain a replacement disk at no charge by sending the defective disk, postage prepaid, with proof of purchase to:

SYBEX Inc.
Customer Service Department
2021 Challenger Drive
Alameda, CA 94501
(800) 227-2346
Fax: (510) 523-2373

After the 90-day period, you can obtain a replacement disk by sending us the defective disk, proof of purchase, and a check or money order for $10, payable to SYBEX.

Disclaimer

SYBEX makes no warranty or representation, either express or implied, with respect to this software, its quality, performance, merchantability, or fitness for a particular purpose. In no event will SYBEX, their distributors, or dealers be liable for direct, indirect, special, incidental, or consequential damages arising out of the use of or inability to use the software even if advised of the possibility of such damage.

The exclusion of implied warranties is not permitted by some states. Therefore, the above exclusion may not apply to you. This warranty provides you with specific legal rights; there may be other rights that you may have that vary from state to state.

Copy Protection

None of the programs on the disk is copy-protected. However, in all cases, reselling or making copies of these programs without authorization is expressly forbidden.

Acknowledgments

I would like to thank the following people:

Dr. Thomas Sherman at Virginia Polytechnic University for providing me with insight into what we know about how kids learn and how to use online services to support this learning.

David Peal and Brenda Kienan for working tirelessly at Sybex to develop a high quality guide for kids as drivers on the Information Superhighway. The editorial and production team—Laura Arendal, editor; Bill Kistler, book designer and art director; Erika Luikart, illustrator; Emily Smith, production assistant; and Michael Gross, who wrote the NetCruiser appendix—for contributing their ideas and expertise toward creating the attractive book you hold in your hands.

Dr. Judi Harris, Professor at the University of Texas at Austin, for her significant contribution to understanding, developing, and archiving educational networking projects. Her research has helped me shape the framework of this book.

Several people—Caroline Wolfe, April Johnson, and Allison Weaver—for contributing their time and talents to help organize all of the details for many of the projects.

Naomi Hazlehurst for helping me develop the illustration ideas.

My dear friend Mara Kennedy for contributing ideas and writing to the book and hugs and laughs to the author.

Also thanks to the creators of all of the Internet sites I have used in this book.

I am especially grateful to all of the kids who reviewed my writing and tested the projects in this book. Their wide eyes and big smiles convinced me to continue with the book.

And finally, a sincere note of appreciation to Bobbi and Sara for their positive words and critical insights, which have made this a stronger book and me a stronger writer.

Contents at a Glance

Table of Contents

Foreword

by Senator Bob Kerrey

The chapters that follow are not so much an instructional manual as a tour guide for an educational journey that technology has made possible, a journey that can take our children bouncing across the globe at the touch of a button.

The Internet began two decades ago as an experiment at the Department of Defense and has blossomed into a massive network that links a vast and distant world, packed with vast and distant resources, into a global community. It is for us to choose how we use it and how we use the explosion in telecommunications technology that made it possible. We can choose—as we often have—to use the Internet and other telecommunications technology simply to entertain us. Indeed, experience tells us that if we let nature and the market run their course, better entertainment and easier shopping is what we will get from the new technological media.

I believe—and this book shows—that as adults we have a duty to bring our highest values and purpose to the technology revolution. Like the gardener whose back bends to the hoe used for 40 years, this technology will shape our spirit. We must decide what we want it to do. The fact that our children are more likely to use and understand this technology than we are does not lift from our shoulders the responsibility of planning how this technology is to be used. If we want our children to be more than better shoppers and/or game players, we need to act.

Action must follow dreams. My dream is that classrooms and living rooms will be networked together so that study in the home and study in the school become indistinguishable from each other. My dream is that we will build and operate public database servers containing curricula-relevant multimedia information. While the boundaries between the teacher and the student will blur in the best learning environments, the different needs of the teacher and the student must be considered when these servers are organized. My dream is that students will return to school in the Fall having completed and been given credit for doing course work online during the summer. Then our schools could become institutions that focus on complex and creative learning. That is my dream.

In the United States, education is the means by which all children— rich or poor—acquire the tools they need to rise as high as their dreams and effort will take them. Properly harnessed, technology will lift those dreams even higher by quite literally bringing the world into our living rooms. A research project for a civics class that once required a plane ticket to Washington, for example, can now be completed through the resources available on the Internet. A computer and a modem will transport students to the greatest museums in America and Europe without leaving their homes. Students who travel the Internet have the same access to Presidential statements and speeches as the reporters who travel at great expense in the White House press pool.

These things were once fodder for futurists and science fiction writers. Today they are reality. Today students in every corner of the United States who are studying the Civil War can access Matthew Brady's famed photographs of that conflict via the Internet instead of traveling to the Library of Congress in Washington. Of course, the real test of whether technology works goes beyond the test scores to the light in a child's eyes and the smile on his or her face when a new idea becomes a new concept learned. And while technology helps boost our test scores, I know firsthand that it passes the smile test as well.

To the children and students who read these pages, let me deliver an important message: The Internet and telecommunications technology are changing our world in profound ways. The way we communicate, work, and learn is fundamentally different, and you must be prepared for it.

A few years ago, you probably used computers in math and science classes alone. Today they are indispensable tools in learning to read, write, and study a variety of other subjects. And if you do not learn to use computers, you will be left in the competitive dust as changes take place —both in the classroom today and in the work force tomorrow.

When I graduated from high school, all a person needed to find a job, make a living, and support a family was a strong back and a willingness to work hard. Today the need for a strong back has been replaced by a demand for workers who can operate a computer and master mathematics. Those skills are no longer optional; if you don't have them, you can't make a living.

That might sound as though the world before you is tough, and it is. But there's good news, too. The Internet and other telecommunications technologies can give you more freedom, better information, and greater opportunity than any other generation has ever had. One of the great advantages of telecommunications technology is that it brings people and industries that are physically far apart electronically close together. Another advantage is that this exciting and emerging new field provides unprecedented opportunity for people like you who will lead our nation and our economy into the next century. The next pioneer of the Information Age may be the person reading this page right now.

The other piece of good news is that if you learn the kinds of skills that this book teaches, you will stand before a high-paying job market in which opportunity grows as quickly as technology changes. The Internet and computer technology give you the opportunity to travel as far as your imagination will take you. Now it's up to you to reach those heights. Your future depends on your dreams and the work you put into making them a reality. By reading this book and participating in the book's activities, you will be acquiring some of the skills you will need to make your dreams a reality.

Just as important: as you dream about where the Internet will take you, never forget that telecommunications technology will help you get where you want to go, but it won't drive you there while you sit in the backseat. The purpose behind education, and behind this book, is to give you the opportunity to prepare yourselves for the future. We want you to find a satisfying job. We want you to be an informed and contributing citizen. We want you to build your own family and network of friends who will support you through a life that could otherwise be lonely and unsatisfactory. We want you to be motivated and confident while being humble and respectful. And we want you to have fun. We can help give you the tools you need to accomplish these things, but it's up to you to get the job done.

Keep in mind that as much as we talk about the need to prepare yourself for the work force, learning is about much more than finding a job. The Internet can be a whole new means of discovery for you. It can help you acquire the information and perspective you need to connect yourself with those who preceded us and those who will come later. The information on the Internet, from history lessons to world maps to scientific research, can help you understand your place in the world.

The Internet can also help you be a better citizen, and that isn't an easy task in a democracy like ours. You have to work at it. You have to understand the facts behind the policies, and you have to know enough to reach your own conclusions. This book shows you how to use the Internet to become a better person and citizen in addition to being a better student and worker.

To the parents and teachers of the children who read this book, let me make a similar point. With our dreams for educational technology comes a warning. Technology is an exciting new treatment for our educational challenges, but it is by no means a cure. My friend Dr. Neil Postman—a skeptic of educational technology with whom I often disagree—is right when he says that any problem that cannot be solved without technology will not be solved with it. No computer can substitute for the loving guidance of a parent. No database will inspire a student like a teacher can. And most important, we must remember that computers do nothing more than carry information to our children. It is still up to us as parents, educators, and community members to address the larger, more challenging question of what information children need to learn.

Nevertheless, telecommunications technology remains vital to our children and their future. The computer and modem and the infrastructure that connects them with the rest of the world are as indispensable to our children's education as the textbook, and it is up to us as adults to see that our children have those tools. The three R's do not cut it anymore. In the knowledge-based world, the worker who cannot use the tools that create knowledge will not earn a wage sufficient to support a family. That worker will not look forward to the work day with anticipation, if work at that level is even available. He or she will have less control over his or her destiny than any other group of Americans. We must work together as parents, educators, and community members to see that our children have the tools for survival in the 21st Century.

Internet for Kids provides a wonderful start. Deneen Frazier is to be commended for understanding and showing us that the Internet is a valuable educational tool that will help our kids learn today and for the rest of their lives.

If our children can master the skills laid out for them in the ensuing pages, the doors to opportunity will be thrown open. The currency of power and opportunity in the 21st Century will be information, and when it comes to information, the Internet is a gold mine.

There will never be a substitute, nor should there be, for the real fuel behind the American dream: ingenuity, hard work, and risk. But telecommunications technology—especially as embodied in the Internet—will help the engine of the American dream use that fuel in new and exciting ways. So I encourage everyone—parent, teacher, and child alike—who turns to the beginning of this book: learn the Internet and use this technology to the utmost. Dream. Learn. Explore. As *Internet for Kids* shows, a whole new American frontier lies before us.

—Bob Kerrey represents the state of Nebraska in the Senate.

Introduction

What Is the Internet?

If you could take a picture of the Internet, you would see a spiderweb of connections between computers all around the world. With these connections, someone using a computer in Copenhagen, Denmark, can retrieve information from a computer in Chicago, Illinois, send information to a computer in Caracas, Venezuela, and validate information with a computer in Tokyo, Japan…all in about ten minutes. It's faster than flying, and you do it from the comfort of your own room.

There are several different Internet tools that you will learn about in Chapter 1. These tools let you travel across the spiderweb connections to find the computers that hold information about your area of interest.

Today, there are more than twenty million users in fifty countries, and this number doubles annually.

Why Write a Book for Kids about the Internet?

Before answering this question, ask yourself:

• Who likes using computers?

• Who is adventurous and curious?

• Who has the time and the energy to explore the vastness of the Internet?

• Who is the best teacher of technology?

The answer to all of these questions is YOU! Kids of all ages are familiar with computers and are not afraid to push buttons and try new things.

This book will give you some ideas about where to direct your curiosities and energy to learn new things, make new friends around the world, and contribute your ideas toward making the world a better place.

There are many books written for adults about how to use the Internet

for personal and professional reasons, but there aren't any (until now!) written for kids with ideas about how to use the Internet for learning and having fun.

Using the Book as a Guide

The Internet is far-reaching, and it changes too quickly to draw a map of it. This book will be your guide. It will direct you to a variety of resources that are interesting and fun. It will give you ideas for projects. Once you are familiar with the territory, you may not need a detailed guide but only specific addresses, which you can find in Appendix B in the back of the book.

This book is separated into nine chapters with each chapter describing a different type of project. The first chapter is about the Internet in general and should be very helpful if you are new to the Internet. It gives directions for using the Internet tools listed in the projects.

Chapters 2 through 9 include projects that help you approach the Internet with a particular goal in mind. For instance, Chapter 2, *Crisscrossing the Globe*, includes projects to connect you in different ways with people around the world and help you communicate with them. Chapter 8, *The World Is a Lab*, includes projects that use the Internet as a research tool and connect you to researchers with similar interests.

The order you choose to explore the projects in is up to you. A good way to start is to skim the table of contents and mark the titles that catch your interest. Read through the projects you marked and choose one to try first. You can always try others later.

Another way to approach the book is to think about what you're working on at school and find a project in the same area. The Internet is full of information you can use in your class assignments.

About NetCruiser

You can do the activities in this book with any software and Internet service provider you want. As an added bonus we've included NetCruiser, a popular Windows-based Internet service provider, at the end of the book. Appendix C tells you how to install and use NetCruiser if you choose to do so.

The Internet Is Always Growing

It is very important to remember that the Internet is dynamic, which means it is constantly changing and growing. What you find there today may be gone tomorrow.

So that you don't get stuck in any of the projects in this book, several different resources on the Internet are listed in every project. This way if one address doesn't work, you have others to try so you can continue to develop your interests.

If you see messages like ERROR or ACCESS DENIED, try another address. Many times, these messages indicate a problem with the resource you are trying to reach rather than with your computer.

Even with extensive checking and rechecking, some of the addresses listed in this book may be wrong or not valid any longer. Be patient and be sure to learn how to use the search tools described in Chapter 1. These tools will let you search the Internet for sites and information about your topic.

Advice for New Users of the Internet

Think about what happens when you go into a music store. Each time you enter, the displays change, the hot CDs of the week change, the sales change—but you still know you are in a music store and can search for and find what you need. The Internet is much bigger than a music store, but every time you go on the Internet, things may have changed. Don't let this discourage you. It just means there is more for you to explore.

Tip
Keep notes of new places you find on the Internet so you can remember how to get back. A three-ring binder will work well so you can separate your notes by the type of site (FTP, WWW, list server) or the subject area of the site (arts, science, fun & games).

Be a Pioneer!

You are one of the pioneers in the new frontier of the Internet. With this guide you can plan your adventures and join forces with other pioneers. You are at the controls to go anywhere you want. The most important thing to remember is to have fun!

A Note to Parents & Teachers

The Internet is a remarkable resource for kids of all ages. You can let them explore on their own or through suggestions. What kids learn and how they grow and develop will be a function of their experiences and yours, as well as their reflections on those experiences. The projects included in this book describe just some of the ways you and your kids can take advantage of what's available on the Internet.

One thing to remember about the Internet is that it is a public arena where a variety of opinions, behavior, and information exists. Given this environment, talk with kids about what they can do to identify appropriate sites and communicate with well-meaning individuals. Here's a list of suggestions to share with your kids:

- Use only your first name when posting notes and sending messages online and do not share your address or telephone number with anyone.

- You are in control of where you go on the Internet, so if you don't like what you are seeing online, quit or exit from that site.

- Respect the people on the Internet with whom you communicate. You can't see the people, but you are still responsible for what you say to them.

Keep in mind that there are both nice and not-so-nice people on the net, just as in the real world, and you may want to supervise what kids are seeing online.

During the first few journeys on the Internet, sit with your child in front of the computer and discuss what you see and how to make intelligent decisions while exploring these new sites.

Following are brief descriptions of the development opportunities the Internet affords kids.

Social Development

One common advantage often attributed to computer-mediated communication is that everyone becomes equal because all the visual and nonverbal conversational cues are missing. Internet speech does require some verbal skills and composition abilities.

This allows young to speak to old and shy to speak to bold in relative security and equality. Thus, kids can learn to discuss and debate with a wide array of people as they develop their communication skills.

Personal Development

The Internet opens access to a vast range of subjects, directions, and projects. Almost any whim or wonder can be pursued and discovered.

Open exploration that has the purpose of broadening background and understanding is valuable. All activity on the Internet does not have to be focused or intentional. It is good to reflect with kids on what they do and what they learn.

Cultural Development

Because of the easy access to people and information on the Internet, kids have great opportunities to discover things about themselves and others outside their cultures. Even if you live in an isolated community, you can learn about how others, both close and far, live their lives.

Because communication can be personal and relatively intimate, kids can find net pals—like pen pals—and share much about themselves and their cultures.

Intellectual Development

The Internet brings worldwide resources, including information, ideas, issues, and people, to your computer. Using these resources can contribute much to success in school. Even more significant is the gradual vocabulary, conceptual, and organizational development that can occur. As with most important developmental influences, the real benefits accrue over time.

Empower the Kids

Put the computer and this book in the hands of kids and watch them go. When kids are at the helm of a project and decide where to go and what to see, they will be in control of their own learning. They will be empowered to chart their own course for what to learn next.

Watch and let your kids have successes and make errors. This is how they will learn; by trying things out on their own and by talking about what they did that worked and failed. Be as willing to listen and discuss as you are to show and tell.

We hope this book helps you have fun and learn together.

Hello

The World of the Internet

The whole world is at your fingertips. Instead of using planes, trains, and cars to reach new destinations, you can use the Internet. Believe it or not, you can use your computer to travel across mountains and seas, to explore new places, meet new people, and learn about anything you want.

You are the pilot, navigator, and passenger. You decide where to go, when to go, and what you want to see. You plot your own course for travel.

The Internet is a collection, or *network,* of computers all around the world that are linked together. With an Internet account, which gives you access to all these computers, you can travel across the network to find the specific computer that has information or people you are looking for. The Internet has been around for a long time and has been used by scientists, researchers, and university professors. Now, it's available to anyone who is interested…like you!

As you learn how to navigate through the maze of networks, you will discover that the Internet is like a giant connect-the-dots that surrounds the earth, only the dots are computers. As you explore the Internet, you are actually circumnavigating the globe.

Because the computers are connected electronically, you can collect the best information from each and use it to help you achieve a goal— maybe you want to answer a question you have, meet people from India or Australia, or get more information about a recent hurricane. No matter what you are interested in, the Internet can help. On the network you can find written information, graphic images, sounds, and even digitized movies. Some computers on the Internet also have databases with vast amounts of information you can search.

This book has many different projects that will tell you how to move from computer to computer, to find and get the information you want, and how to do something with it once you've got it. Let your own personal interests guide you to projects; pick ones that sound fun or interesting to you.

The Internet is open 24 hours a day, so you can travel whenever you want. But before you jump on your computer, rev it up to warp speed, and dash around the Internet, check your equipment and directions. You'll enjoy the projects in this book much more if you take the time to prepare yourself and your computer for the world of the Internet.

The most important piece of equipment you need for every activity is YOU! The Internet is made up of computers, networks, programs and the *people* who use these things. Your unique personality and interests will lead you to cross paths with people who are experts, people who have questions, people sharing their feelings, people who speak different languages, people like you!

To Make the Most of Your Adventure:

- Use your imagination
- Prepare to explore new places
- Think of your mistakes as chances to learn something new
- Ask for help (and be sure to say thanks!)
- Show people the same respect you would if they were sitting right next to you

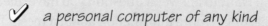
Let's make sure you have the right equipment. Here's what you'll need:

- ✓ *a personal computer of any kind*

- ✓ *communications software (available from your local computer store)*

- ✓ *a modem (recommended speed or "baud" rate: 14,400 or above)*

- ✓ *a connection to your phone line*

If you aren't already set up for this, you'll need to ask for your parents' help. They can speak with the local computer store and find out what additional equipment or software you may need. Be patient! It may take some time to get it working, but it is well worth the wait.

Note

When your modem is plugged into the telephone jack and you are connected to the Internet, if someone calls, they will hear a busy signal. You are already on the line, just as if you were making a regular phone call. If you have Call Waiting, you may get cut off from the Internet if your phone line rings. Check with your local phone company to find out how you can temporarily turn off your Call Waiting.

Your Ticket to the Internet

You have your equipment and a road map (this book) but you still need a ticket to get through the Internet tollbooth. The ticket is actually your own personal address on the Internet that you will use to get on and off the network. This address will be yours. No one else can use it, because you will also have a secret password.

To get an address and password, you have to establish an Internet account through a commercial network, a state network, a local university, or a private company. Check with your parents or teacher to see whether you already have access to an Internet account. Many states

give free access through a statewide network. If you do have access to an account, you will have to learn how to use it. If you don't have access, ask your parents or teacher to check the list of Internet Access Providers (IAPs) in the back of this book. These companies and networks offer a variety of services for a variety of prices.

When calling a company about Internet accounts, there are several questions to be sure to ask:

> ‽ *What is the price for setting up a basic account with Internet access?*
>
> ‽ *What services does a basic account include?*
>
> ‽ *What is the price to keep the Internet account? (There is usually a fee you pay every month.)*
>
> ‽ *Is there a local phone number to access the account?*
>
> ‽ *Does the company provide a user manual?*

How Do I Use the Internet?

With an Internet Account You Can

- Publish your own story in an online magazine
- Play games like Scrabble or Chess with people on the other side of the world
- Join forces with kids all over the world to conduct scientific experiments
- Become a regular character in an online play
- And much more…

The activities in this book direct you toward many different places and resources on the Internet that let you do many different things.

Internet accounts come with features that let you explore:

Electronic Mail	you can send e-mail to and receive e-mail from sites around the world
List Servers/Mailing Lists	you can be part of a number of people (a list) who receive information on a certain topic
Gopher	a menu-based system that organizes information for you to look at
Telnet	your computer connects through the Internet to another computer, and you operate the other computer remotely
Usenet Newsgroups	conferences or forums concerning a specific topic where you can see what others say and post your responses
FTP *(file transfer protocol)*	software that lets you download files from computers on the Internet
WAIS *(wide area information servers)*	software that lets you find and retrieve information from Internet computers
WWW *(World Wide Web)*	a browsing tool that lets you access information by clicking on high-lighted or underlined text or icons that are linked to other documents in other places
IRC *(Internet relay chat)*	area on the Internet where you can have real-time online discussions
MUD *(multi-user dungeon)*	area on the Internet where you can create a character and participate in an online role-playing game

Just as there are different kinds of software on the computer that help you do different things, different Internet tools are available. Word processors help you write on the computer, databases help you find and organize information, and games help you have some fun. Different features of an Internet account let you explore the Internet in a variety of ways. Several main features are described below.

Even if your Internet account includes only the most basic features of electronic mail, you will still be able to explore interesting places and experience exciting things online.

Note

Electronic Mail (E-Mail)

Through the Internet, you can exchange messages electronically with people all over the world. All day and all night, messages speed back and

forth. The cost is usually less than a long distance phone call and much faster than "snail mail," mail that travels through the postal service.

There are many different e-mail programs, each with a different way for doing similar things, such as sending a message, forwarding a message to someone else, or deleting old messages from your mailbox. For instance, in one e-mail program the command to create a new message is "w" for write a new message, and in another program it is "c" for compose a new message. Check the manual for the e-mail program you are using for a list of commands.

Most e-mail message headers look like the one in Figure 1.1, which is from the e-mail program called *Pine*. It is called the header (or sometimes the envelope) because it includes all of the necessary information to get your message sent to someone else. Headers will look different depending on the e-mail program that is on the computer you are using to access the Internet, oftentimes called the *host computer*. Let's take a look at the parts of the envelope.

Figure 1.1

This is an example of a message header (which is like the envelope) from one e-mail program.

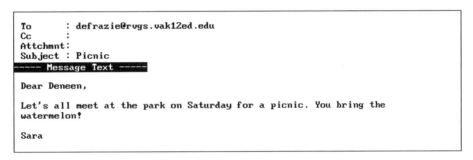

To:

This is where you will type in the Internet address of the person you want to receive your message. Addresses are made up of two parts separated by an @ sign. (This is called the "at" sign; it can be found above the number 2 on your keyboard.) An address might look like `dfrazier@pen.k12.va.us`. The first part, `dfrazier`, is a *user* name. It's the name of a *person*. Everything after the `@` sign identifies the *computer* where the person's account is located. The last three letters refer to the *type of organization* the computer belongs to. For example, `edu` means the computer is connected to the Internet through an educational organization, like a school.

There are six different endings that show the types of organizations where people have their Internet accounts:

com	commercial organizations
edu	educational organizations
gov	governmental organizations
mil	military
org	other organizations
net	network resources

Notice that there are no spaces between any of the parts of an Internet address and that some parts are separated by periods. When you give your Internet address to someone else, you'll read the period as "dot." For example, "My Internet address is 'dfrazier at pen *dot* k12 *dot* va *dot* us.'"

Cc:

This is a common abbreviation used in the business world. It means that you are sending a "carbon copy" of the message to someone else.

Attchmnt:

This tells the person reading the message that more information is "attached" to the message. "Attchmnt" is actually an abbreviation for the word "attachment" and means that there is another file that is a part of the message. To find out how to attach files in your e-mail program, check its instructions or ask someone.

Subject:

This is like a headline for your message—a brief phrase to say what your message is about. You will want to be as specific as you can in a few words so that the person receiving your message will pay attention and want to read it right away. For example, if you are asking someone if you can quote them in a report you are doing, you might put "Permission Request" in the subject to call attention to what you are asking for in the message.

Message Text

This is called the *body* of the message, and it's where you type what you want to say. Some e-mail programs limit the length of the message, but there is usually plenty of space to create complete and detailed messages.

If your message is an answer to someone's question, be sure you say this at the beginning of your message. Make sure the person has all the information needed to understand your reply.

Tip

Some e-mail programs don't "wrap" lines like word processing programs do. Instead, you must press Enter at the end of every line. Take some time to figure out how your particular e-mail program works.

A Final Word on E-Mail

Most e-mail programs will automatically include your Internet address in the message you are sending. This is helpful because then you do not have to type in your address (like the return address on a regular letter) every time you send a new message. Also, most e-mail programs have a "reply" feature, so you can send a message back to the person who wrote you without typing in any addresses.

E-mail is your personal connection to the Internet, which you can use to send messages to just one other person or to a big group of people. Check your e-mail instructions for how to set up your address book and group mail. You can make friends quickly on the Internet, and you may begin to receive many messages every day to which you can respond quickly and easily using your e-mail features.

List Servers/Mailing Lists

A *list server* (or a mailing list) is a special e-mail situation where messages are sent from one person to everyone who has subscribed to, or become part of, a group. When anyone in the group posts a message to the list server, you can send a message back to that person or to the entire list server.

To subscribe to a list server, you must first send a message to the computer that has the list server. When you subscribe, there are two important pieces of information you will need to include: the name of the list server and the address of the list server. For example, to subscribe to a list server called "Kidzmail" at the computer address `asuacad.bitnet`, you would send a message that looks like one shown in Figure 1.2. As you can tell from the list's name, kids who subscribe will be talking about their interests and issues.

Figure 1.2

When you want to subscribe to a list server, send an e-mail message like this one.

```
To       : listserv@asuacad.bitnet
Cc       :
Attchmnt :
Subject  :
----- Message Text -----
subscribe kidzmail Deneen Frazier_
```

Leave the subject line blank and only put one line in the body of the message that includes the word "subscribe," followed by the name of the list server, followed by your full name (not your Internet account name). Note that each of these is separated by one space. You will find many lists in this book that you can join, and they're all free!

You can usually tell what people who belong to a list server will be writing messages about by the name of the list server. For example, in the "Kidzmail" list server, kids are writing about their interests. There are so many list servers that you can find one for just about anything you like to talk about: movies, sports, you name it.

Getting a List of List Servers

There are several lists of operating list servers available through the Internet. These are very long files and will take a long time to get into your computer. Two examples are:

- FTP to `ftp.sura.net`, type **cd /pb/nic** and **get interest-groups.txt**

- World Wide Web: `http://www.ii.uib.no/~magnus/paml.html`

(To learn how to use the features of FTP and WWW, finish reading this chapter.)

Watch out! If you subscribe to too many list servers, you may receive hundreds of messages a day and not have time to read them all. Be selective, and if you get flooded with too much mail, unsubscribe. To unsubscribe, follow the directions for subscribing but replace the word "subscribe" in the message area with "unsubscribe."

Tip

Great Gopher Sites

MTV Gopher	gopher to `mtv.com`
Education Gopher at Florida Tech	gopher to `gaia.sci-ed.fit.edu`
Film Gopher with information about 6,500 movies made before 1986	gopher to `info.mcc.ac.uk` and look for `/Miscellaneous/Film Database`
Professional Sports Schedules	gopher to `gopher.bsu.edu` and look for `/Ball State University /Professional Sports Schedules`

Gopher

Computers on the Internet contain articles and files about all sorts of topics. To find these computers, you can use a computer program called Gopher, which was created at the University of Minnesota, home of the "Golden Gophers." Just like the real rodent that tunnels through the ground, the program tunnels through the Internet to point out articles that you can bring into your own computer. Gopher is easy to use because it has menus of choices at every step. You can select the item you want, which may take you to another list, and eventually the file you want. For an example, check out the MTV Gopher in Figure 1.3. Each computer that uses the Gopher software is called a "Gopher server," and all these Gophers together do their work in Gopherspace.

Figure 1.3

From the MTV Gopher, you can get the latest news and information from the world of popular music.

```
                        MTV Gopher

    --> 1.   I-quit.txt.
        2.   README.AOL.Users!.
        3.   README.FTP.
        4.   README.GOPHER.
        5.   aboutus/
        6.   brainwaves.txt.
        7.   charts/
        8.   concerts/
        9.   hotnews/
        10.  i-am-not-alone.txt.
        11.  images/
        12.  index.txt.
        13.  interviews/
        14.  kenscol/
        15.  misc/
        16.  mmwld/
        17.  mtv-censors.txt.
        18.  mtv-lawsuit-update.txt.

    Press ? for Help, q to Quit, u to go up a menu
```

To help people find what they need more easily, another program, called Veronica, was created. Veronica searches Gopherspace to find things that match your interests. Each Gopher can contain text files, searchable databases, or directories that will lead you to a new menu of files or databases. Veronica lets you use *keywords* (words that say what you're searching for) to express your interests—for example "soccer" or "Mexico"—and points you to a list of Gophers about that topic.

Telnet (Remote Log-In)

Telnet allows you to connect directly to another computer on the Internet and operate this computer remotely. Just as you log into a system to use e-mail or get information through a Gopher, you can telnet to a totally different computer and explore or even get an account there.

To use telnet, you will need to know the specific Internet address of a computer with information you would like to explore. The address will look just like the part of your own personal address that comes after

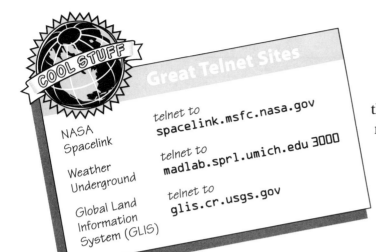

Great Telnet Sites

NASA
Spacelink

telnet to
`spacelink.msfc.nasa.gov`

Weather
Underground

telnet to
`madlab.sprl.umich.edu 3000`

Global Land
Information
System (GLIS)

telnet to
`glis.cr.usgs.gov`

the "@" symbol. For example, the telnet address for NASA Spacelink is `spacelink.msfc.nasa.gov`. This is a telnet site operated by the National Aeronautics and Space Administration (NASA); it has information about space travel and experiments.

Tip

When you telnet to a site and see a "login" prompt, try typing **guest** or **newuser**.

Once you know where you are going, you'll need to know how to launch the telnet program on the network you are using. On some systems you type **telnet** and then the address of a computer. On others, telnet is a menu choice or a button you click. Ask your parent or teacher how to launch telnet on your system.

Tip

Always read the welcome screen whenever telneting to a new site. Very often the system will tell you how to log in, how to become a member or regular user, and how to log off.

Now you are ready to go. Because each computer you will telnet to will be a little different, it is important to read the information that appears when you first connect to the other computer.

When you use telnet, the initial screen will usually have directions explaining the commands you will need to use to move around the computer, special policies or rules you must respect for continued use of the computer, and a description of what files and programs are available to you. This looks similar to what you see for NASA Spacelink in Figure 1.4.

Figure 1.4

NASA Spacelink welcomes new users.

```
                    W E L C O M E

                         to

                    NASA SPACELINK

        NASA's Computer Information Service for Educators
            Managed by the NASA Education Division
        In Cooperation with the Marshall Space Flight Center

                 ******IMPORTANT!******
    Do not press RETURN until you have read the following information.
      You are about to be asked to provide a Username and a Password.
             If this is your first call to NASA Spacelink,
      Enter NEWUSER as your Username and enter NEWUSER as your Password.
    If you have called before, enter your assigned Username and Password.
        You may send Carriage Returns or Line Feeds but NOT BOTH.

                 You may now press RETURN, or
            To redisplay this message press CONTROL-D.
```

Tip

In case you get stuck somewhere and want to get out, learn an emergency exit command (one that will get you back to your host network)! A common one is "ctrl-]". This means you press the control key and hold it while typing] (the right bracket). You may want to ask someone who answers technical questions on your network (your network *administrator*), to suggest an emergency exit command *before* you telnet to another computer.

Usenet Newsgroups

Usenet Category Abbreviations

comp	computer
news	news server software and networks
rec	hobbies and recreational activities
sci	scientific research
soc	social issues
talk	debate on controversial topics
misc	everything else
alt	alternative

Newsgroups are also called *conferences*. There are thousands of different newsgroups covering many topics, from television shows to politics to chess. In newsgroups, anyone can leave a message, read a message, or respond to a message. These newsgroups run on a network called Usenet, which is part of the Internet.

Usenet is made up of seven categories of newsgroups (see *Usenet Category Abbreviations* for a complete list). In most newsgroups (except those in the category alt),

someone makes sure the messages are current, that people are being reasonably polite to each other, and that the topic is still interesting.

Middle school students discuss what's on their minds in the Usenet newsgroup called **k12.chat.junior**. (See Figure 1.5 for a screen from this newsgroup.) People talk about college, campus life, and college activities in **soc.college**. These are just two groups chosen as examples from a list of more than 4,000 groups. (By the way, alternative newsgroups—those groups that end with **alt** —are not supervised, and people post all kinds of notes that sometimes are not appropriate or respectful. Because of this, not all of the **alt** newsgroups are available at every Usenet site. Even though the network where you have your account decides which Usenet groups to offer to users, you're sure to find something that interests you.)

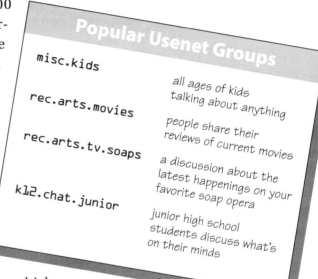

Popular Usenet Groups

misc.kids — all ages of kids talking about anything

rec.arts.movies — people share their reviews of current movies

rec.arts.tv.soaps — a discussion about the latest happenings on your favorite soap opera

k12.chat.junior — junior high school students discuss what's on their minds

Figure 1.5

This Usenet group offers opportunities for kids in middle school to talk to each other about a variety of topics.

```
                k12.chat.junior (73T 204A 0K 0H)              h=help

      1  +      New computer store open               Bryan Kaplan
      2  +      Re(2): Juniorchatowners PLEASE read!  Stephanie L. Hull
      3  + 1    I'm <sob> leaving                     SCOPE Class
      4  + 2    I know you think I'm insane.....      SCOPE Class
      5  + 4    Juniorchatowners PLEASE read!         Andy Jacob
      6  + 1    School Dances                         Bernie Gorski
      7  + 1    Girls, stupid?                        Bernie Gorski
      8  + 4    Hey all!!                             Bernie Gorski
      9  + 2    Juniorchatown Courthouse; MACEL PLEASE READ!  Andy Jacob
     10  + 45   Joey's Coffee House                   Timothy J Robinson
     11  + 1    short                                 H
     12  + 2    URGENT!                               Helen C. Estabrook
     13  +      UM ALEI&Patrick                       Macel L. Hubbard
     14  + 1    Juniorchatowners Please Read          Christopher B. Col
     15  + 1    Juniorchatown Mall                    Bernie Gorski
     16  +      Juniorchatown School                  SCOPE Class

  <n>=set current to n, TAB=next unread, /=search pattern, ^K)ill/select,
  a)uthor search, c)atchup, j=line down, k=line up, K=mark read, l)ist thread,
    !=pipe, m)ail, o=print, q)uit, r=toggle all/unread, s)ave, t)ag, w=post
```

FTP (File Transfer Protocol)

As the name suggests, FTP lets you transfer files from one computer to another. By learning a few commands, you can find a file that you would like to read and then make a copy of it on your own computer. You must know the directory path, the name of the file, where it is located, and the address of the computer that has it. It's as if there were many folders inside each other; you need to know how to get to the folder that contains the file you want.

Many times when notice of a file is posted on the Internet, the person who wrote the notice will include the directory path. For example, you can get the latest travel advisories from the U.S. State Department by directing your computer to `ftp.stolaf.edu`. First, log in as **anonymous**, and then you'll be asked to type in a password—use your e-mail address. The directory path to find files about countries all over the world is `pub/travel-advisories`. To get there, you would follow the directions in *Logging Into an Anonymous FTP Site* and go into the directory called `pub` and then into the directory called `travel-advisories`. When you ask for a list of files in that directory, you will see the names of many countries (without capital letters)—like *india*, *malaysia*, and *uruguay*—with other information; it will look like the screen in Figure 1.6.

Logging Into an Anonymous FTP Site

To log into an anonymous FTP site, follow these steps:

1. Start the FTP program on your network.

2. Type in the address of the computer you want to go to.

3. When the computer asks you to log in, type **anonymous**.

4. When the computer asks for your password, type in your e-mail address.

A common method of using FTP is called "anonymous FTP." This allows you to log into another computer without being a registered user. Most of the FTP sites listed in this book will accept an anonymous FTP log-in. Follow the directions in *Logging Into an Anonymous FTP Site*.

Although a directory of files from an FTP site can look very technical and confusing, FTP is fairly easy to use and understand. You tell the computer what to do by typing commands at the FTP prompt, which looks

Figure 1.6

This directory contains files of travel warnings from the State Department and can be found at `ftp.stolaf.edu` *in* pub/ travel-advisories.

```
-rw-r--r--   1 cdr      daemon      17710 Jun  3  1993 suriname
-rw-r--r--   1 cdr      daemon       8494 Oct 19  1993 swaziland
-rw-r--r--   1 cdr      staff       11542 Apr 29 16:28 sweden
-rw-r--r--   1 cdr      staff       13027 May 11 13:27 switzerland
-rw-r--r--   1 cdr      daemon      11195 Oct  6  1993 syria
-rw-r--r--   1 cdr      daemon       2666 Nov 19  1992 taiwan
-rw-r--r--   1 cdr      staff       37219 Jun  9 17:32 tajikistan
-rw-r--r--   1 cdr      staff       28996 May 11 14:28 tanzania
-rw-r--r--   1 cdr      daemon       8382 Jul 14  1993 thailand
-rw-r--r--   1 cdr      staff       36634 Mar 16 20:26 togo
-rw-r--r--   1 cdr      staff        8047 Jul 22 16:30 tonga
-rw-r--r--   1 cdr      daemon       8835 Jun  4  1993 trinidad-&-tobago
-rw-r--r--   1 cdr      daemon       7779 Sep  1  1993 tunisia
-rw-r--r--   1 cdr      staff       46343 Jun 17 13:31 turkey
-rw-r--r--   1 cdr      staff       13446 Aug  1 18:31 turkmenistan
-rw-r--r--   1 cdr      daemon      18594 Nov  9  1992 u.s.s.r.
-rw-r--r--   1 cdr      staff       23769 Jul 27 23:31 uganda
-rw-r--r--   1 cdr      wheel       23347 Feb  9 16:32 ukraine
-rw-r--r--   1 cdr      daemon       7057 Sep  1  1993 united-arab-emirates
-rw-r--r--   1 cdr      staff       24266 Mar 16 21:28 united-kingdom
-rw-r--r--   1 cdr      daemon        959 Nov  9  1992 united-states-of-america
-rw-r--r--   1 cdr      staff       11061 May  9 17:28 uruguay
-rw-r--r--   1 cdr      daemon       3460 Nov  9  1992 ussr
-rw-r--r--
                 Screen paused.  Press any key to continue...
```

like `ftp>`. The first thing to do is type **dir**, which will give you a list of other directories and actual file names. If there is one called `README`, you will want to read it first; it will tell you where to go. To go into another directory, type **cd**, which is short for "change directory," then type **dir**. You will see a list of the files that are in the new directory. When you find a file that you want to bring into your computer, type **get** and then the name of the file exactly as it appears in the directory. (By typing **get** and the file name, you are *downloading* that file into your computer.) The computer will tell you if the file has been transferred successfully from the FTP site to your own computer.

COOL STUFF

Great FTP Sites

Library of Congress Archives — anonymous FTP to `ftp.loc.gov`

Star Trek Archive — anonymous FTP to `ftp.uu.net`

University of Michigan's Software Archives — anonymous FTP to `archive.umich.edu`

When you download a file from an FTP site, write down (1) the size of the document, (2) the date it was put into the computer, and (3) the file name. All three of these can be found on the far right side of the screen. With this information, you'll be able to check to see whether you got the whole file, and you can check to see if the file has been updated when you're looking again for similar information.

Tip

There is a search tool, Archie, that will help you find files that you might find interesting. Archie is a great help. If you don't know the name or directory path for a file, you can use Archie to search many directories of files at one time to find something that matches your interests.

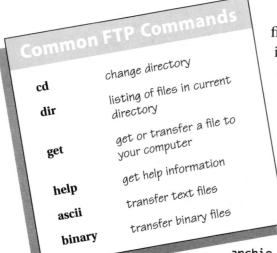

Common FTP Commands

cd	change directory
dir	listing of files in current directory
get	get or transfer a file to your computer
help	get help information
ascii	transfer text files
binary	transfer binary files

Check to see if your Internet host (the network your computer is connected to) has Archie installed on it. If not, you can telnet to one of the following public Archie sites to do your search:

Note

archie.internic.net   archie.ans.net
archie.rutgers.edu   archie.sura.net

Archie uses keywords (just like Veronica) to find the files you want. Your search will be more successful if you keep your keywords short and simple, like "music" or "earthquake."

When you search for a file, Archie tries to match your keyword to a file *name*. Archie does not search the actual files.

Tip

Wide Area Information Service (WAIS)

A WAIS (pronounced "ways" or "wase") database is indexed so you can search for articles containing groups of words. You will actually be searching within the text of the article, not just the title. To use WAIS you will need to have access to the WAIS client program on your host network.

The 500-plus WAIS computers on the Internet have databases with articles on a limitless number of topics, everything from science to business to cooking. To get to these databases, you can telnet to `wais.com`. (First check to see if WAIS is already a choice on your network's Gopher.) See Figure 1.7 for an example.

```
SWAIS                              Source Selection              Sources: 505
  #             Server                     Source                      Cost
109: [fragrans.riken.go.jp]  CCINFO                                   Free
110: [          cs.uwp.edu]  cdbase                                   Free
111: [    istge.ist.unige.it]  Cell_Lines                             Free
112: [    wais.wu-wien.ac.at]  cerro-1                                Free
113: [      wais.concert.net]  cert-advisories                        Free
114: [      wais.concert.net]  cert-clippings                         Free
115: [cicg-communication.g]  cicg.bibliotheque                        Free
116: [    cirm5.univ-mrs.fr]  cirm-papers                             Free
117: [      sunsite.unc.edu]  cisco-packet                            Free
118: [      sunsite.unc.edu]  clinton-speechess                       Free
119: [ cmns-moon.think.com]  CM-fortran-manual                        Free
120: [ cmns-moon.think.com]  CM-paris-manual                          Free
121: [ cmns-moon.think.com]  CM-star-lisp-docs                        Free
122: [ cmns-moon.think.com]  CM-tech-summary                          Free
123: [      zenon.inria.fr]  cm-zenon-inria-fr                        Free
124: [ cmns-moon.think.com]  CMFS-documentation                       Free
125: [          cnidr.org]  cnidr-directory-of-servers                Free
126: [      biome.bio.ns.ca]  coastal                                 Free

Keywords:

<space> selects, w for keywords, arrows move, <return> searches, q quits, or ?
```

Figure 1.7

This sample from wais·com *shows a few places you can go.*

Once you have highlighted the database you want to search, a tap of the spacebar will take you there. (You can search many databases at once by marking each one you choose with an asterisk, *.) (If you want to search for keywords, press the "w" key; it will give you a space to type in the word(s) that you think might show up in the text of an interesting article. Then let WAIS do the rest. There will be a list of other commands you can use at the bottom of the screen. When the search is completed, you should receive a list of all the articles found, like the list in Figure 1.8. Select an article by using your arrow key to highlight it, press Enter, and the computer will bring you the complete text. You can then download the text (bring the Internet file into your computer).

Figure 1.8

These are the top 18 articles the WAIS server found by searching for "smoking." If a headline looks interesting, you can bring up the complete article.

```
SWAIS                              Search Results                          Ite
  #    Score    Source              Title                               Lines
001: [1000] (      dowvision)  AFTER A DECADE OF GRIM SMOKING TESTS RES   -1
002: [ 783] (      dowvision)  40 YEARS OF THE POLITICS OF SMOKING        -1
003: [ 518] (      dowvision)  DANNY GLOVER APPLAUDS U.S. JUNIOR CHAMBE   -1
004: [ 489] (      dowvision)  TWIN PROTESTS AGAINST AIRLINE SMOKING      -1
005: [ 467] (      dowvision)  DynaGen initiates phase 2b NicErase-SL s   -1
006: [ 421] (      dowvision)  DynaGen Begins Phase 2b Trial Of Smoking   -1
007: [ 336] (      dowvision)  NEW YORK TIMES EDITORIAL: CHILDREN AND S   -1
008: [ 314] (      dowvision)  Insider Who Turned On Tobacco Industry C   -1
009: [ 312] (      dowvision)  NICOTINE PATCHES HELP ONE FOURTH OF SMOK   -1
010: [ 281] (      dowvision)  Who's News: The Insider Who Copied Tobac   -1
011: [ 274] (      dowvision)  JAMA Article Recommends Shorter-Duration   -1
012: [ 242] (      dowvision)  Letters to the Editor: I (deleted) in Pu   -1
013: [ 235] (      dowvision)  Cdn Committee - Tobacco -2-: Opposed By    -1
014: [ 230] (      dowvision)  British Tobacco/Newspaper-2: Suggests BA   -1
015: [ 222] (      dowvision)  NEW MANAGEMENT TEAM AT PHILIP MORRIS AGG   -1
016: [ 202] (      dowvision)  Canadian Committee To Report On Cigarett   -1
017: [ 200] (      dowvision)  Cdn Committee Urges Delay In Plain Pack    -1
018: [ 196] (      dowvision)  U.S. COMPANY DEVELOPED HIGHER NICOTINE T   -1
```

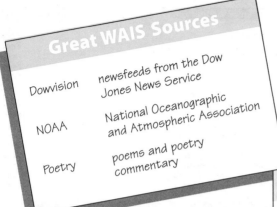

Great WAIS Sources

Dowvision	newsfeeds from the Dow Jones News Service
NOAA	National Oceanographic and Atmospheric Association
Poetry	poems and poetry commentary

If you don't have a WAIS client on your host network, you can telnet to `wais.com` or `quake.think.com` (log-in: **wais**) to search the WAIS databases. You will find the commands that let you search the databases at the bottom of the screen. These are the most important:

<space bar>	selects the WAIS database you want to search
"w"	lets you type in a keyword to use in the search process
"s"	takes you back to the list of WAIS databases (or sources)
"?"	gives you some help

You may have to practice with WAIS a few times before you are able to find information that matches your intended search. It can be a bit difficult to use, but once you get used to it, you will find a great deal of useful information.

World Wide Web (WWW)

The World Wide Web (WWW) uses *hypertext* (text that is highlighted or underlined). When you click on hypertext, you are directly connected to resources previously found for you through FTP, Gopher, or WAIS. Hypertext lets you connect to the information you want in an order that makes sense to you. Just like a spiderweb, the World Wide Web connects to all kinds of sources—text, illustration, audio, or video.

You will need to have a WWW "browser" on your host network that lets you follow links between sources of information. Depending on your system, you'll follow links by clicking a mouse, pressing a key, or entering a number. Some common browsers are *Lynx* and *Mosaic*. Each browser works and looks a different way, so you will need to review the instructions for commands and functions.

Just like telnet and FTP, WWW sites have specific addresses. The Web is designed so you don't *have* to know addresses, you can just point and click to get around. But your computer needs the addresses, and sometimes

you'll want to go straight to a specific address instead of pointing and clicking your way to it. An example of a WWW address is `http://curry.edschool.virginia.edu/murray`, which happens to be the Murray Elementary School in Ivy, Virginia. Take a look at what the main screen, or *home page*, of this site looks like—in Figure 1.9—when using a Lynx browser. Figure 1.10 shows the home page that you see when using a Mosaic browser.

Figure 1.9

This is the home page for the Murray Elementary School.

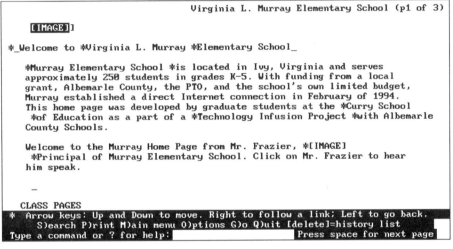

```
                              Virginia L. Murray Elementary School (p1 of 3)

       [IMAGE]]

  *_Welcome to *Virginia L. Murray *Elementary School_

     *Murray Elementary School *is located in Ivy, Virginia and serves
     approximately 250 students in grades K-5. With funding from a local
     grant, Albemarle County, the PTO, and the school's own limited budget,
     Murray established a direct Internet connection in February of 1994.
     This home page was developed by graduate students at the *Curry School
      *of Education as a part of a *Technology Infusion Project *with Albemarle
     County Schools.

     Welcome to the Murray Home Page from Mr. Frazier, *[IMAGE]
       *Principal of Murray Elementary School. Click on Mr. Frazier to hear
     him speak.

       —

     CLASS PAGES
  * Arrow keys: Up and Down to move. Right to follow a link; Left to go back.
       S)earch P)rint M)ain menu O)ptions G)o Q)uit [delete]=history list
  Type a command or ? for help:                        Press space for next page
```

Figure 1.10

The Murray Elementary School home page as seen through the Mosaic browser.

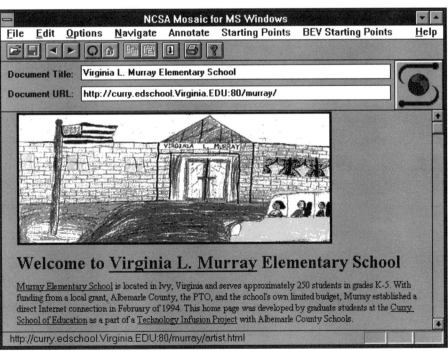

Great WWW Sites

Seattle Metro Washington Park Zoo
`http://davinci.vancouver.wsu.edu/zoo/zoo.html`

Murray Elementary School, Ivy, Virginia
`http://curry.edschool.virginia.edu/murray`

Janice's K-12 Cyberspace Outpost
`http://k12.cnidr.org/janice_k12/k12menu.html`

The Exploratorium, San Francisco, California
`http://www.exploratorium.edu`

Internet Relay Chat (IRC)

IRC offers a new way to use the Internet. People who are online at the same time can send messages to each other and read them instantly, as if they were "chatting" on the telephone.

Telnet Site with IRC

IRC Client   telnet to
`exuokmax.ecn.uoknor.edu 6677`

IRC is called a *multiuser* system, which means that several people come online to groups (called *channels*), which are usually devoted to a specific topic of conversation. It's a kind of online party with different rooms for different topics of conversation.

You can get to IRC in two ways. Using telnet, you can connect with another computer that is running a public IRC client, or you can have your own client on your computer. To find out how to get your own client —which is a more reliable method of using IRC—read the Usenet newsgroup `alt.irc`, where you can learn more about IRC. There are also IRC tutorials you can find via anonymous FTP at `cs.bu.edu` in the directory `/irc/support`. The file name of a good beginning tutorial is `IRCprimer1.1.txt`.

Once you get into IRC, you will need to join a channel to chat with other people. Here are three IRC commands that will help you get started:

/list<enter>	gives you a list of all of the active channels
/channel #<channel name>	gives you access to a particular channel
/quit<enter>	gets you out of IRC

IRC tutorials provide many more commands that you can learn to move around the system and talk to more people.

Multi-User Dungeon (MUD)

In a MUD you participate in a game where you become another character and play that character's role in the environment you find yourself in. MUDs are similar to IRCs in that you will be interacting with people immediately rather than just leaving messages. Similar to the game "Dungeons and Dragons," people log in and out of a MUD where they are participants in a game or simulation. Some MUDs are modeled after fantastical stories where the characters live in a world described in a book. Others are focused on interaction between the users in a chat mode, rather than playing parts in a story.

Each MUD has a set of commands all its own, which makes learning how to move around and interact in a MUD a challenge. Fortunately, there is a MUD for beginners where you can start your adventure. As you become a more experienced player, you can explore other MUDs that you find interesting.

There are many different names for multiuser environments on the Internet. In addition to MUDs, there are MOOs, MUSHes, MUSE-MUDs, and others. Each of these usually has a particular personality. For instance, DIKU-MUD usually involves a combat game. MUSE-MUDs are focused on social interaction.

COOL STUFF — Great MUDs

Worlds of Conquest
telnet to 28.174.31.163 4000. This MUD is for novice (beginning) players.

The NeverEnding Story
telnet to snowhite.ee.pdx.edu 9999. This is a place where you are a character in a never-ending story.

Wisney World
telnet to levant.cs.ohiou.edu 5000 or 132.235.1.100 5000. This is a wacky online world with many different areas to explore.

Note
Don't forget to type in the port number, the last four numbers separated by a space, after the telnet address. Without the port number, your computer won't be able to find the MUD.

The World of Communications Software

There are several activities that you will probably want to do that are entirely separate from the Internet. These actions, like printing, are done with your communications software. There are many different commercial or *shareware* programs you can use, each of which will have its own ways of doing things. Be sure to read the instruction manual that comes with the software to learn about all of the commands. (Shareware programs are made available to you so you can try them out before you buy them. If you like them, follow the instructions in the program, and send the developer what he or she asks for: a postcard, money, etc.)

Are You on the Internet?

When you are just learning to use telecommunications and the Internet, it is difficult to figure out where the worlds of the Internet and your own computer begin and end. There are times when you may ask yourself, "Am I on the Internet right now?" If your modem is in use, and you are moving from your network to another computer by using telnet, FTP, Gopher, WWW, WAIS, or IRC, you are on the Internet.

Communications software will let you:

 set up your computer for telecommunications

 make a log of your online session

 upload and download files

 print files

Communication Setup

In order to use your software, you will need to get it set up, or *configured*, correctly. For example, a typical configuration might be *8 databits, 1 stopbit, no parity*. (You don't have to know what everything here means, you just have to enter the correct information.) Your host network should give you a list of the information you will need to enter into your computer. Ask your teacher, parent, or an Internet expert for help if you need it.

Session Log

As you tunnel through the Internet, you will probably lose track of where you are, what computer you are connected to, and how to get back to something wonderful you found. One way to make a record of where you go on the Internet is to make a *log* (like a ship's log or the captain's log on "Star Trek") of your session. Many communications software programs have a command that will make a record of everything you do in a particular session. When you are finished with your session, you can review the session log on screen or print it out to see exactly where you went. Then you can make notes about where you would like to go again.

Tip

Keep a folder or three-ring binder with copies of all your session logs. Use a highlighter pen to mark those places you liked and want to visit again.

Uploading and Downloading

When you want to take a file from your computer and put it up on the Internet, that's called *uploading*. When you want to get a file from the Internet and bring it into your computer, that's called *downloading*. Both are done with your communications software. You can find out how to upload and download by reading your instruction manual or asking someone who already knows how to do these procedures.

Printing

Printing is one of several things you do on the computer that is controlled by your software. There are many different word processing and communications software packages, and the directions for printing and other commands are different for each. (This is also true for uploading, downloading, and logging on and off.) There are a lot of places to get help with all of these procedures. Check with your parents or teacher to find out where to go for help.

You're on Your Way!

The best way to learn is to try. As the saying goes, "If at first you don't succeed, try, try again!" If you run into problems, don't worry. People on the Internet are usually very helpful if you don't know what to do and very forgiving if you make a mistake. The most important thing you can do is learn from your mistakes and keep going. That will make you a better explorer on the Internet.

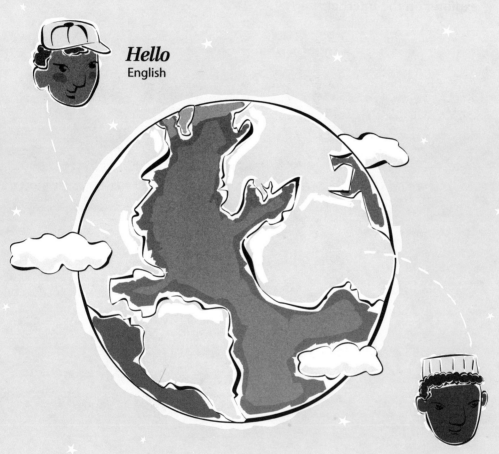

Hello
English

Jambo
Swahili

Crisscrossing the Globe

Many people dream about traveling around the world, but few get the chance to do it. On the Internet, you can be a lucky traveler in a unique way. You won't be taking a plane or car or ship to faraway destinations. Instead, you'll use your computer and modem to meet people in foreign countries, ask questions, and experience other cultures without even leaving home.

Your journey across the globe can happen in many different ways. You can share your ideas for the future with other kids in *F³: Finding Foreign Friends*. You can learn about historical events by talking to someone who was alive when the events happened in *Exploring the Past*. And you'll make your own map of different geographical formations, regions, and population levels with *Map Mania*. Finally, you will be able to interview people from all over the world and ask questions about any topic you want in the *International Surveys*. Cross the globe and have fun along the way!

Note

While in this book we've described how to participate in these activities using the most generally available Internet tools, you can also do the activities using NetCruiser, the software that came with this book. Turn to Appendix C to find out more about NetCruiser.

F³: Finding Foreign Friends

Note

Making friends and learning about their interests and hobbies is something we all like to do, but where can you easily find opportunities to make friends who have different cultures, languages, and customs? The *F³: Finding Foreign Friends* project is your around-the-world plane ticket.

Tracy wants to be an explorer and world traveler when she grows up, and she wants to get started now. In two months' time on the Internet, Tracy has visited at least fifteen countries and made dozens of new friends all over the world.

Tracy is not the only lucky traveler; our reservation book tells us that you also have a free unlimited-mileage ticket to travel anywhere you'd like to go. Hurry up! Your trip is about to begin, and there are many people eager to meet you.

Note

The Internet features you will use in this project are e-mail and list servers.

COOL STUFF
Places to Find a Net Pal

Penpal-L	subscribe to listserv@unccvm.bitnet
k12-euro-teachers	subscribe to majordomo@lists.eunet.fi
Kidlink Project	send an e-mail message to listserv@vm1.nodak.edu and in the text of the message, type **get kidlink general**
e.Club	telnet to freenet-in-a.cwru.edu and register for an account on the Cleveland Freenet, which will allow you to go to Academy One's e.Club
Educational Native American Network (ENAN)	call to get a password and log-in directions: (505) 277-7310

1. **Subscribe to a list server to meet people who live in other countries.**

As you can see from the list in *Places to Find a Net Pal*, there are many different projects and list servers that help bring people together who have similar interests. Follow the directions for subscribing to a list server, found in Chapter 1, to begin your search for fun and interesting people to talk to.

2. Post a message on at least one list server.

Using your e-mail program, compose a message to send out to the people who subscribe to the mailing list you have selected. In your message, include questions that you want people to answer. Ask for their opinion, whether or not they agree with your opinion, or for descriptions of specific experiences. For instance, to learn more about different cultures, you could ask a question about traditional food: "What kinds of food does your family cook for special holidays?" To get more responses, post your messages to several list servers and be patient—it may take a little time for everyone who is interested to read your message and compose a response. You could also find a pen pal through an online service like the e.Club, as shown in Figure 2.1.

Figure 2.1

The e.Club is a bulletin board where you can find an electronic pen pal.

```
THE e.CLUB (Electronic Pen Pals)

     One project that anyone with any kind of network connection
can participate in is the e.Club.

     Essentially the e.Club is a place where electronic addresses
can be exchanged between students (and teachers) who would like to
engage in an electronic mail project.  This correspondence can
occur completely within the Cleveland Free-Net (via direct
telephone or Internet access), or e.mail can be sent back and
forth between Free-Net users and users with remote BITNET,
CompuServe or other network addresses.
End of File, Press RETURN to quit
```

You may begin to communicate regularly over the network with an Internet "net pal." A net pal is like a pen pal, except you are using the Internet to share your thoughts and ideas instead of a pen.

3. Communicate regularly with your new net pal.

Once you have a net pal, you can talk about anything you want. You can ask questions, share your writing, plan a project, play a game, and maybe even plan to meet each other.

When your net pal sends a message, answer right away. You know how much you like getting a quick response!

Tip

Learning a New Language

If you are learning another language, try to find a net pal who is a native speaker of the language you are studying and write your messages in that language. Don't forget to ask your net pal to answer your questions in his or her language. You'll be amazed at how quickly you can learn a language when you are sent a personal message that you have to translate.

Maybe you will want to become an exchange student and go to school in a foreign country. It certainly would be fun to visit your net pal's country.

Share what else you have done on the Internet with your net pal. Sharing adventures and journeys over the Internet makes them even more enjoyable and memorable.

Exploring the Past

Note

Exploring the Past is a project that lets you design your own journey through time. By using the Internet and list servers, you conduct personal interviews with people who lived through different historical periods such as the Depression, World War II, the rock'n'roll fifties, or the hippie sixties and the Vietnam War. Now you will have a chance to learn about everyday life in the past.

Wouldn't it be great if you owned a machine that allowed you to travel back in time? Imagine that you could see what your mother was like as a kid. Or imagine that you could travel back to a place where a recent historical or social event took place, for example the Woodstock concert in 1969. Can you imagine what life was like 20 years ago? 30? 50? Many people can't even remember what life was like without TVs, VCRs, or computers. Can you imagine going to school in a one-room schoolhouse and doing all your math calculations on a small slate chalkboard?

> It's fun. It's kind of like a pen pal. They [Seniors] know more about history and you can learn from them.
>
> *Jillian, Fifth Grade*

Unless you're Michael J. Fox in *Back to The Future*, you probably don't have access to a time machine. Until now.

On the Internet, you can compare different peoples' experiences of a historical event. For example, you might want to compare what people were doing when Neil Armstrong became the first person to walk on the moon. Not only will you find out what everyday life was like in the past and what was happening in history, but you will have a chance to share the experiences of your own life today.

Note

The Internet features you will use in this project are telnet, list servers, and WAIS.

Planning Your Trip

Where you go on your journey into the past is entirely up to you. You might already be interested in a particular historical event, like the gold rush of 1850, or maybe you're just curious about what it was like to be your age at the turn of the century in the year 1900. To find people who have lived in generations other than your own, you can access a variety of Internet list servers and other resources.

1. Find an event or period in recent history that interests you.

To get some historical facts about a recent historical event, you can access several different services. One resource is a history database called *HNSource* that lets you search for historical events. You will be able to find historical information to help you learn about events in the past. Figure 2.2 shows some of the things you can explore through HNSource.

History Resources on the Internet

HNSource	telnet to **ukanaix.cc.ukans.edu** or **129.237.33.1** and type: **history**. It offers access to historical events and documents.
Omni-Cultural-Academic-Resource	A WAIS source that includes historical information about different cultures around the world.

Figure 2.2

HNSource has a number of different resources, indexed by historical era, for you to explore.

```
                                              HNSource Main Menu

              *************** HNSOURCE ***************

              *** THE CENTRAL INFORMATION SERVER ***

              *********** FOR HISTORIANS ***********

    * How to use this system
    * Index of Resources
    * Resources: Historical Data Bases
    * HNSource News Center
    * Kansas On-Line
    * Internet Search Utilities
```

```
                                    Resources: Historical Data Bases

              RESOURCES: HISTORICAL DATA BASES

    * Bibliographies of historical works and access to library services.
    * Internet Guides Guides for using the resources found on Internet,
      KARENET, BITNET and others.
    * Scholarly Exchange News groups and discussion lists for
      historians.
```

```
                                                      Subject Tree

              RESOURCES INDEXED BY ERA

    The following is an index of resources categorized by historical era.

    * Prehistory and Archaeology
    * Ancient: ca. 4000 BC - AD 500
    * Medieval: 500-1500
    * Modern: 1500-present
    * Recent: current materials
```

Questions to Ask

- When and where were you born?
- What kinds of games did you play as a kid?
- What was a typical day like for you at school?
- What jobs did you have?
- What is the most important thing that has happened in your lifetime?

2. **Gather information about a specific historical event or the first-hand experiences of a person from a different generation.**

You can decide what you want to do first: do your historical research or find a friend from an older generation. For sample questions that you might want to pose, see *Questions to Ask.*

3. **Find a net pal who was living at the time of the historical event you are researching.**

If you want to have an eye-witness account of events, you'll have to limit the periods you research to the 20th century. If you go back further, you'll need to check newspapers or diaries for firsthand accounts. For suggestions on historical events to investigate, check the list of *Historical Events & Eras.* You may get several responses from different people who all lived through the same event.

Historical Events and Eras

- The Roaring '20s
- The Depression
- World War II and the Holocaust
- The Rock'n'Roll '50s
- The Civil Rights Movement
- The Beginning of the Computer Age
- The First Walk on the Moon

Internet List Servers

Send an e-mail message to eldersⓐsjuvm.stjohns.edu to find a senior pen pal.

Gerinet: subscribe to listserv@ubvm.bitnet

Post your message on one of the list servers listed in *Internet List Servers.* Once you start getting responses, you'll want to organize and record the data in a creative and exciting way. Eventually you will want to share this information with friends in your hometown or other friends you've made through this project.

Telling Others about Your Exploration of the Past

You will probably have great ideas on your own about how to record the findings of your journey, but if you're stumped, take a look at some of these projects:

- *Make a newspaper of different people's accounts of a day in history. For example, you might want to write several short articles about what people were doing when Neil Armstrong walked on the moon, or where they were the day Charles Lindbergh made the first transatlantic flight.*

- *With the help of your friend who lived back then, create journal or diary entries that describe what life was like in the past. You could also do a mirror diary of your own that shows what life is like for you today. This might be fun for the two of you to compare.*

- *Once you find out your new friend's birthdate, investigate everything that was happening on that day on the HNSource. Make your friend a birthday card that includes this information and send it to him or her.*

- *Imagine what everyday life will be like in the 21st century. Write a story about what peoples' everyday lives might be like.*

Once you have created your final product, share it on the Internet with others. Post it on a list server and let others read about your explorations of the past. To post a document you've already written, ask your network administrator how to upload a file into an e-mail message. Once you do that, just send the message to the list server address.

Map Mania

Note

Map Mania is a project that lets you have fun collecting and putting information together on creative maps. By exploring different Internet sources, you will have a chance to find geographical and cultural facts that you can use on your map. No longer do maps have to include only dull route numbers. Join the *Map Mania* craze by including some fun facts on maps that you can give to friends and family!

When was the last time you really looked at a map of the United States? Most people use maps only for directions while traveling. But maps can contain much more information, such as showing where recent earthquakes occurred, land elevations, and populations. Suppose you are the president of an outdoor sporting equipment company and you are looking to start a business in a new city. Wouldn't it be helpful to know the city's geography—what its terrain is like? After all, your business wouldn't do very well if you sold rock-climbing gear in Florida where the land is flat. Even if you don't own your own business, you might be interested in learning just how the forces of nature and geography shape the lives of people who live in different regions of the United States.

> [This project] helps you draw maps. It gives you all kinds of information about earthquakes and other details including latitude and longitude. It also gives you information about the population of different cities. This is a great computer program.
>
> *Scott, Fifth Grade*

Once you select a particular city and state, you can discover what geographical forces are at work in that area by logging into the various telnet sites listed in this project. Here you will find a lot of information that will help you design an artistic and scientific map of just about any place in the USA.

After you have accessed information from these geographical resources, you'll need to figure out how to organize the information and put it together into a map. This is how you become an expert cartographer—a person who makes maps—and share your knowledge with people everywhere.

....

The Internet features you will use in this project are telnet and WAIS.

Note ....

Getting the Information

1. Choose an area or city to explore and research.

Obviously you have to choose a place to explore before you can log onto the Internet and search for information. If you don't already have a place in mind, use the suggestions in *Pick a Place Where*.

Pick a Place Where:

- you or a relative was born
- there is a unique geological land formation, such as Niagara Falls, Grand Canyon, Alaskan glaciers, Hawaiian volcanoes
- your favorite story is set
- your favorite famous person was born

2. **Gather information about your selected location.**

Now take a look at *Map Mania Hits the Internet*. Each of these telnet sites has a different log-in procedure, so follow the directions carefully. One of the sites, the Geographic Server, has actual map images that can be downloaded and shown on a personal computer. GLIS has all sorts of information about land worldwide; Figure 2.3 shows some examples. It may take some time to become familiar with the services, but once you are, you can quickly find the information you need. How to download and print the information you get is different for every computer and software combination. (Look in Chapter 1 for tips on downloading.)

Map Mania Hits the Internet

COOL STUFF

Earthquake Information
: telnet to **geophys.washington.edu** and use the log-in/password: **quake**

Geographic Server
: telnet to **martini.eecs.umich.edu 3000** (no log-in required) and type **?** for directions

Global Land Information System
: telnet to **glis.cr.usgs.gov** and log in as **guest**

Xerox PARC Map Viewer
: **http://pubweb.parc.xerox.com/map** This is a map program where you enter information, and then it creates a map.

world-factbook93
: telnet to **wais.com**, log in as **wais**, and select "world-factbook 93" This WAIS source is maintained by the CIA and includes detailed information about locations around the world.

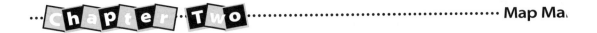

Figure 2.3

GLIS is jam-packed full of geographic data from all around the world.

```
MAINMENU                    GLIS MAIN MENU              Page 1 of 1

                  Global Land Information System - Ver. 1.2

                  PRIMARY Options
      1. OVERVIEW     System Overview
      2. DIRECTORY    Summary Information of Data Sets
      3. GUIDE        Detailed Information of Data Sets
      4. INVENTORY    Individual Items within Data Sets
      5. ORDER        Order Verification

                  ANCILLARY Options
      6. NEWS         General News
      7. REMOTE       Access to Remote Systems
      8. USERINFO     User Specific Information

      9. EXIT_GLIS    Exit the GLIS System
```

```
GLIS NEWS               NEWS AND INFORMATION             1 of 1
                                              DOC
                         GENERAL TOPICS
GLIS            What Is GLIS?
PC-GLIS         What is It, How Do I Get It?
FTP PC-GLIS     PC GLIS software available via Anonymous FTP (posted 12/16/93)
XGLIS           Limited Graphical User Interface Capabilities (posted 04/09/93)
BROWSE          Online Image Browse in GLIS
PRICES          GLIS Product Estimates (posted 2/1/93)
GCH             Global Change and Climate History Program Data (posted 10/21/93)
WWW             GLIS Guides on World Wide Web (posted 12/16/93)
AVHRR UPDATE    AVHRR archive exceeds 70,000 scenes (posted 12/16/93)

                       NEW RELEASE TOPICS
LGSOWG          Landsat Ground Station Operators Working Group Data (6/1/94)
NALC            North American Landscape Characterization Data Set posted 3/15/94
NASAPHOTOS      NASA Aerial Photography (posted 3/15/94)

       Use arrow keys to highlight subject and press return.
```

```
EROS_DS                 EROS DATA SETS                  1 of 3
                         VALIDS LIST

        NAME    :          DESCRIPTION
      ==========!=======================================!
  1.  100KDLG  :1:100,000-Scale Digital Line Graphs    :
  2.  1_250_LULC:USGS Land Use and Land Cover Data      :
  3.  1_DGR_DEM :1-degree USGS Digital Elevation Models  :
  4.  2MIL      :1:2,000,000-Scale Digital Line Graph    :
  5.  2MILHUC   :1:2,000,000-Scale Hydrologic Unit Maps  :
  6.  30ASDCWDEM:30 Arc-Sec. DCW Digital Elevation Model :
  7.  30ASDEM   :30 Arc-Sec. Digital Elevation Model Data:
  8.  AKAVHRR   :Alaska AVHRR Twice-Monthly Composites   :
  9.  AVHRR     :Advanced Very High Resolution Radiometer:
 10.  BLKHLS    :Black Hills GIS Data                    :
 11.  DCW       :Digital Chart of the World - DOS        :
 12.  ECOREGIONS:Omernik Ecoregions Data                 :
 13.  ETOPO5    :5 Minute Gridded Earth Topography Data  :
 14.  GGHYDRO   :Global Hydrographic Data                :
```

You'll also want to learn about the kinds of people who live in the regions you have selected and how the area's geography affects them. For example, how do the Inuits in Alaska manage to survive extremely cold conditions? What tribes of Native Americans live in the Grand Canyon? Take the time to explore your area completely; as a thorough cartographer you don't want to leave anything out of your map.

3. Organize and summarize your information to share with others.

Congratulations! You now have a large amount of information with which to create your map. As you continue to explore the Internet, you may come across other resources that have additional information about the area you are studying.

4. Create a map that includes all the information you researched.

Now comes the creative part. You have to figure out a way to show others what you have learned. You might want to use your computer graphics tools to create a map of the city or state you are studying. For example, if the state has a variety of elevations, you could show this on the map by using a different color for each elevation.

Or you might want to make a map that shows where different ethnic groups tend to cluster in a certain state or city.

Making Your Map

You should include all the facts you found on your map in some way. The job of a cartographer is to include as much information as possible on the map without cluttering it up with too much stuff.

Sharing Your Map around the World

Once you have finished your map mania adventure, you will want to share it with people around the country or even around the world. Send your map by postal service to someone you may know who lives in the state or city you studied to see what they think of it. As you continue your explorations with map making, you could even create a personal atlas with all of your maps. Maybe you'll get lucky one day and travel to a place you studied or actually meet someone from that area. People will be surprised when they find out how much you know about lands far away from your own!

International Survey

Note

You have probably taken part in at least one survey at some point in your life, but have you ever conducted a survey? The *International Survey* project is your chance to create a survey for kids all over the world to respond to. After you learn about differences in sports, schools, hobbies, games, foods, or religions all over the world, you can circulate a newsletter or creative *compilation* (a collection) of your findings to share with others.

Surveys Then and Now

As far back as 2000 B.C., during Ancient Egyptian times, governments have been taking surveys to determine how much money citizens owed in taxes. Now the U.S. government takes a survey every ten years to get an official count of the number of people who live in this country. This survey is called a census, and from it the government learns about what kinds of jobs people have, what their backgrounds are, and other information.

Every day people learn about other people's lives through storytelling, letter writing, poetry, and conversation. You are probably already familiar with these ways of communicating, but did you ever think of using interviews and surveys to learn about other countries and cultures?

You can use surveys to learn more about kids in other countries or to make friends with people from other cultures. In this project you will create your own survey with questions for kids all over the world. The questions on your survey can be about anything you want. Once people write back to you, you will have their electronic mail addresses so you can continue to communicate with them.

> The Internet feature you will use in this project is list server.

Note

Creating and Distributing Your Survey

1. **Create a survey that is as fun to give as it is to take.**

Creating a survey is fun and easy to do. The first thing to do is to choose a topic that interests you—music, sports, movies, science, or anything else you want to learn more about. If you are stumped for ideas, talk to your friends or ask yourself what you would want to know if you were moving to a new city or country. Look at *Survey Topic Ideas* for more ideas.

Survey Topic Ideas

- Traditional foods
- Holiday celebrations around the world
- Sports around the world
- Popular musical groups

2. **Write survey questions that will give you the most interesting responses possible.**

Once you decide what topic you want to investigate, it's time to write the questions you want people to answer. Try to write a variety of questions—some that can be answered with a simple "yes" or "no," some that can be answered with interesting descriptions, and some that can be answered by selecting a number on a scale of one to ten. The sample questions in *Survey Question Examples* might give you some ideas for how to write your own. When you are done creating your questions, ask a friend to read them to make sure they can be clearly understood.

3. **Find a list server in *Internet List Servers* that you think would be an appropriate place to post your survey.**

Survey Question Examples

- What sport is most popular in your country?
- On a scale from 1 to 10, how much do you like your country's most popular sport (10 means it's your favorite)?
- What are other sports that kids play in your country?
- Who is the most popular athlete in your country?
- Which athlete do you like best?
- If you could be the best athlete in the world in one sport, what sport would it be?

To learn about other countries from a survey, you have to be able to send the survey to people all over the world. When the ancient Romans conducted a census, they had to travel all over the country on horseback to ask people questions. Fortunately the Internet lets you conduct your survey without even leaving your house.

There are a number of list servers specifically designed to bring together kids from around the world. No matter where you send your survey, you will be able to get responses from all sorts of people from many different countries.

Tip

Because people check their e-mail at different times, you may need to wait at least a day before you receive any responses to your survey. Check your messages regularly for at least a week; this gives people some time to think about the questions you are asking.

Because you are the only one who reads all of the responses to the survey, you instantly become a research expert on your topic. As an expert, you can get your information about cultures and countries to people on the Internet as well as your hometown friends.

Internet List Servers

Kidlink	subscribe to `listserv@ndsuvml.bitnet`
Kidsphere	subscribe to `kidsphere-request @vms.cis.pitt.edu`
KIDZMAIL	subscribe to `listserv@asuacad.bitnet`
Penpal-L	subscribe to `listserv@unccvm.bitnet`

Sharing Your Results with Everyone

Once people send you answers to your questions, they will be very curious to know what other answers you received. Even those people who didn't respond but who may have seen your survey will want to learn about your findings. Think of a creative way to summarize the answers to share your research with everyone. In addition to writing a brief summary that you can post on the same list server you used for your survey, you may also want to create something to share with your hometown friends.

What you create is up to you; it may depend on the kinds of questions you asked. For example, if you asked people about traditional food, you may be able to make a cookbook full of recipes. Or you could create a poster of magazine pictures that show all of the sports people said they play. You can also look for similarities between answers from people in countries on the same continent, or from people in countries whose language is the same. If you include a rating question, you can make a graph or chart to illustrate what you found out. At any rate, however you choose to share what you've learned, your findings will be of interest to your audience.

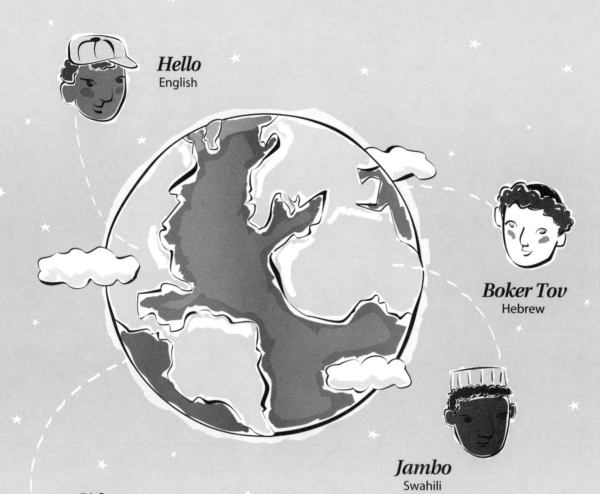

Hello
English

Boker Tov
Hebrew

Jambo
Swahili

G'day
Australian

Chapter Three

Challenged by the Best

When you conquer a challenge, you feel like you are on the top of the world and can accomplish anything you set your mind to. Whether your interests are in math, writing, science, or games, the projects in this chapter will connect you to experts through the Internet.

Awesome Authors is a perfect project for aspiring writers like yourself because you'll communicate with and learn writing techniques from published authors. Mathematicians prepare challenging problems for you to solve in *Mission: Mathematics*. If your curiosity in science goes beyond what your textbook covers, write to an expert scientist about your questions in *Scientific Explorations*. If you are a talented game player without any opponents, then *Game Gurus* is the challenge for you. Whatever project you choose, you will definitely be challenged by the best.

You can also participate in these activities using the NetCruiser software that came with this book. Turn to Appendix C to find out more about NetCruiser.

Note

Awesome Authors

Note

With the *Awesome Authors* project, you can explore the world of writers before you start writing on your own. You will get an idea of how to go about writing and publishing, and you'll also find ideas about what to write. After you learn more about how famous authors got started and what they think makes a good story, you can share your ideas with other young authors through discussions and your own stories. You might even have your stories published, in which case you too will be an Awesome Author.

Did you ever stop to think that the games you plan and play, funny experiences you have, or stories that you imagine can be the subject of great books? All you have to do is recreate those stories on paper so other people can read them. You probably already share these stories with your friends through storytelling. Now you can expand your audience by sharing your stories, games, or experiences with readers on the Internet.

> This is a great program. You can talk to people in other states or here. You can also learn about many backgrounds of authors. I think you should try this.
>
> *Scott, Fifth Grade*

Begin your journey as an author by seeing how other people have transferred stories from their heads onto paper. Why not take a peek into the writing experiences that famous authors of children's books have had? Or you can read classic works by famous historical authors.

The Internet features you will use in this project are telnet, FTP, and e-mail.

Note

Exploring the Writer's World

1. **Write a few questions you would like to ask writers about their work.**

Sample Questions for an Author

- What first made you want to become a writer?
- How do you think of good ideas for stories?
- Did you join writing contests when you were younger?
- How do you create your characters?

At some point famous authors have asked themselves, and others, the question, "What makes a good story?" As an aspiring writer, you probably have some ideas of your own, but it is interesting to find out what other writers think. What made them want to write children's books? What were some of their favorite childhood experiences? *Sample Questions for an Author* has some other questions you may want to ask.

2. **Use the Internet to ask a writer your questions.**

Find out who is the currently featured author in "Spotlight on Authors"—find your way to it with the directions in *How to Get to the Spotlight on Authors Project.* This resource, shown in Figure 3.1, regularly provides an author's work as well as related biographies, interviews, and discussions about the work. To help you become familiar with the author's writing, read some of the featured author's books, then post specific questions you have about what you've read.

How to Get to the Spotlight on Authors Project

Spotlight on Authors (and a similar project called Spotlight on People) can be reached through Academy One on the Youngstown Freenet: telnet to `yfn2.ysu.edu` and log in as **visitor**. Once you establish an account with the Freenet (there is no charge) you can have full access to all of the projects on Academy One.

Figure 3.1

Spotlight on Authors puts you in touch with published writers.

```
           The National Capital Area Public Access Network

                     <<< SPOTLIGHT ON AUTHORS >>>

                                            (go author)
        1 Featured Author: Carolyn Reeder
        2 Talking About Writing . . .
        3 Resources for Writing
        4 Previously Featured Authors
       ------------------------------------------------------------
       h = Help, x = Exit CapAccess, m = Main Menu, p = Previous Menu
```

3. **Read stories and other writing to get ideas for your own writing.**

You can also read classic literature and myths to get some ideas of how to write or what to write about. It could be an exciting challenge to rewrite a famous historic classic so it takes place in modern times. For example, you could modernize the heroes and journey in either *The Iliad* or *The Odyssey* so they relate to famous events or heroes of today. Look in *Where to Get Books on the Internet* to find out how you can retrieve different books that you may not be able to find in your local library or bookstore. You also might get some ideas from subscribing to a few list servers devoted to writing discussions.

Where to Get Books on the Internet	
Project Gutenberg	anonymous FTP to `mrcnext.cso.uiuc.edu` or `128.174.201.12` and at the first FTP prompt, type **cd gutenberg**. In this directory there are several new user and index files that list all available texts.
Wiretap	anonymous FTP to `wiretap.spies.com` or `130.43.43.43` and at the first FTP prompt, type **cd Library**. In this directory there is a list of directories of electronic texts separated into categories like classic, humor, and others.
crert-l	subscribe to `listserv@uvmcvmb.missouri.edu`. This is a list server of authors who discuss the process of writing.
Fiction	subscribe to `listserv@psuvm.psu.edu`. This list server is about fictional writing.

Putting Your Imagination to Work

Now that you have explored the world of another author's writing, you can put your own imagination to work. Write your own story, poem, or other creative work to share with others. If you're unsure about what to write, take a look at *Possible Story Ideas*. Your best tool is your imagination, so go ahead and set it free.

Many writers start their writing careers by submitting their work to creative writing contests. Once you win, the writing community will start to recognize your name, and the possibility of getting your work published begins to become real. To find out more about online contests, check out the project *Adventures in Cyberspace* in Chapter 6.

Possible Story Ideas

The Great Scare	a story about the scariest moment in your life
Kitchen Chaos	a story about kids taking over the kitchen and making crazy concoctions
A Day in the Life of a Dog	a story about a day in a dog's life written from the dog's perspective

Mission: Mathematics

Note

The *Mission: Mathematics* project is a great way for you to challenge your math skills and explore what other mathematicians are doing around the world. This project provides all sorts of complex math problems that you can solve by communicating with expert mathematicians. Not only will you solve problems on your own, but you will also communicate with experts and other mathematical minds to talk about your interest in math. Good Luck! You are now part of the Mission: Mathematics team!

The first part of your mission is to find the places on the Internet with difficult math problems of all types—geometry, algebra, elementary mathematics, and even calculus. You will find a variety of challenges and specific directions about how to submit your solutions.

The second part of your mission is to show your friends and others how math can be creative and fun. Show them ways to think creatively so they can also solve difficult problems. They will see how much fun it is to discover the correct solution.

Note

The Internet features you will use in this project include e-mail and Gopher.

Your Mission

1. Find the challenges.

You will find challenges in *Places to Go*. Some places present math problems to solve, others provide information about math software and mathematics organizations.

As you explore the Internet in other projects, you may come across new places to find math challenges or to work with mathematicians on math projects, such as the Math Archives Gopher, which you can see in Figure 3.2. You can learn many things from the experts who use math every day in their jobs to solve real problems worldwide.

Places to Go

Problem of the Week Club	send an e-mail message to **mspanswick@rmecco.cerf.fred.org**. Participants will solve problems, evaluate others' solutions, and communicate solutions to other groups in the project using mathematical formulas and rules.
Math Archives Gopher	gopher to **archives.math.utk.edu**. This Gopher provides math software and access to other Gophers.
Mathematical Association of America	gopher to **maa.org**. This Gopher includes information about the Association, mathematical news, and a monthly profile of a mathematician.
MathMagic	send an e-mail message to **cshooper@tenet.edu**. This is a project that supplies new math challenges every three or four weeks to MathMagic teams. There is a $10 fee to establish a MathMagic team. Once your registration is approved, you will receive instructions for establishing a team and participating in solving problems.
Geometry Forum	send an e-mail messge to Annie Fetter at **annie@forum.swarthmore.edu** or Gene Klotz at **Klotz@forum.swarthmore.edu**. You will receive a response explaining how to join the forum.

Figure 3.2

The main menu of the Math Archives Gopher

```
 Internet Gopher Information Client v1.12S

        Root gopher server: archives.math.utk.edu

 --> 1.  About the Mathematics Archives Gopher.
     2.  Organization of the Mathematics Archives Gopher.
     3.  Software (Packages, Abstracts and Reviews)/
     4.  Teaching Materials and Other Information/
     5.  Other Mathematics Gophers and Anonymous FTP Sites/
     6.  Submitting Materials to the Mathematics Archives.
     7.  Other Ways of Accessing the Mathematics Archives.
     8.  What is Gopher? (adapted from Texas A & M's Gopher).
     9.  Information About Gopher (from Univ. Minnesota)/
```

2. Submit your solutions.

When submitting your solutions to a math site on the Internet, be sure you check to see whether there are any specifications *unique* (specific) to that site. For example, a site may use mathematical symbols different from those you are using. *Try This One!* is an example of how you might write up a solution to a math challenge for submission.

Try This One!

Problem:

What is the smallest positive number divisible by 1, 2, 3, 4, 5, and 6?

Solution:

I decided to use a "trial-and-error" method. I knew that the numbers that would give me the most difficulty were the larger ones (4, 5, and 6) because they divide evenly into fewer numbers. So I started with 5 x 6 = 30. I tested 30 to see if all the numbers would divide into it:

$$30 \div 1 = 30 \quad \text{yes}$$
$$30 \div 2 = 15 \quad \text{yes}$$
$$30 \div 3 = 10 \quad \text{yes}$$
$$30 \div 4 = 7.5 \quad \text{no}$$
$$30 \div 5 = 6 \quad \text{yes}$$
$$30 \div 6 = 5 \quad \text{yes}$$

4 did not divide into 30 evenly, so I knew 30 was not the answer. I also knew that the only number that didn't divide into 30 was 4. I needed to deal with 4. Then I tried 4 x 5 x 6 = 120. I knew that this would work because 120 is a product of the three numbers I was trying to divide into it...but is it the smallest number that would work? I decided to divide 120 in half and try 60, just to see.

$$60 \div 1 = 60 \quad \text{yes}$$
$$60 \div 2 = 30 \quad \text{yes}$$
$$60 \div 3 = 20 \quad \text{yes}$$
$$60 \div 4 = 15 \quad \text{yes}$$
$$60 \div 5 = 12 \quad \text{yes}$$
$$60 \div 6 = 10 \quad \text{yes}$$

Ah-ha! 60 does work! The solution is 60.

3. Recruit your friends to make a math team.

Do you have some friends who might want to join you in your mission? Challenge them to accept the mission and make a team of problem solvers. You can all work together to solve some of the most difficult problems, or you can race each other to see who can solve them first! You might want to start a competition to see who can solve the most problems correctly and be crowned "Math Master."

Tracking Your Successful Missions

Keep a copy of all the challenges you and your friends solve—maybe in a spiral or three-ring notebook. *Tips for Solving Math Problems* gives you a list to check as you solve problems and prepare to submit them online.

Tips for Solving Math Problems

1. First find out how to type mathematical symbols and Greek letters.

2. Then restate the problem.

3. List the knowns and unknowns.

4. Explain the strategy you used (looking for patterns, making a chart, etc.).

5. State the solution.

6. Check your solution for accuracy.

Sometimes the way you solved a challenging problem in the past will give you ideas for solving another one in the future. You can also use the problems and solutions in your notebook to teach others new mathematical skills.

Because you may be communicating with kids from other cities and countries, you can exchange information about yourselves. Ask each other questions.

> ➤ Are there any famous mathematicians from your city or country?
>
> ➤ What geometric shapes (squares, triangles, angles, octagons, etc.) do you see in your city?
>
> ➤ What is your math class like?

Try creating your own math challenges to send to the friends you make on the Internet. See how fast or how thoroughly they can solve the math problem you create. Maybe you can even think of a prize to send to the person with the most creative answer—such as a souvenir from where you live.

Now that you have had some fun with your mathematical challenges, you can share your expertise with friends and have even more fun with math.

Scientific Explorations

Note

Sometimes a question about how things work or why certain things exist in nature might pop into your mind. How do you find the answer? *Scientific Explorations* is the place for you to ask science experts these questions and get their answers. But getting the answers is only half the fun; once you get responses, you can compare what the different scientists said. Join the world of science explorers in their quest to answer questions about why things are the way they are.

Do you know why a rainbow appears after a rainstorm? Or how long a rainbow lasts? You may be able to find the answers to these and other scientific questions by asking expert scientists. Once you come up with a scientific question, you can submit it to a scientist, who will send you an answer on the Internet. You, or a group of your friends, can ask questions on topics like astronomy, biology, chemistry, geology, physics, or any other interesting scientific topic.

👆

The Internet features you will use in this project are telnet, list server, and e-mail.

Note ....

Beginning Your Scientific Quest

1. **Think of a question to ask the expert scientists.**

> ❝
>
> It was neat getting information from another computer far away. Reading the answers was pretty cool. It's cool that they can also send information to my house.
>
> *Ben, First Grade*
>
> ❞

Think about those areas of science that spark your curiosity. If you are stumped for a good question, just look around you in nature or even in your science text-book—there are questions everywhere! Once you have written out your question, you will use the Internet to send it in an e-mail message to a scientist. After giving the scientist enough time to research and answer your question, you can check your electronic mail for a response. It's that easy!

If you are having a hard time coming up with a good question, check *Sample Science Questions*. Each sample question reflects a different scientific area: chemistry, biology, and others. What kind of science do you like best?

2. **Post your question to a scientist on the Internet.**

There are several places on the Internet where scientists are ready to answer questions—see *Where to Post Your Question.* You decide where on the Internet to post your question. Try posting a question in several different places and then compare the answers you receive.

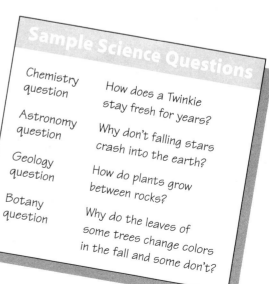

Sample Science Questions

Chemistry question	How does a Twinkie stay fresh for years?
Astronomy question	Why don't falling stars crash into the earth?
Geology question	How do plants grow between rocks?
Botany question	Why do the leaves of some trees change colors in the fall and some don't?

While questions are answered as quickly as possible, the solutions and explanations may take a few days to receive. Be sure to allow the scientists enough time to research and answer your question before sending them a note reminding them of your request. It is usually a good idea to wait at least one week before expecting any response. Also, if you send your question on a Friday night, the scientist might not look at it until the next week.

3. Do your own research while you wait for a response from the scientist.

While you are waiting for a response to your question, you can do a little research on your own, like reading about other scientists, as in Figure 3.4. You might want to see if you can stump the scientist next time with an extra hard question.

Where to Post Your Question

NASA Spacelink	telnet to **spacelink.msfc.nasa.gov** or **192.149.89.61**. Explore this site, and when you are done, the computer will ask you if you want to send a question to a scientist. This is a very popular telnet site, so you might want to try it late at night or early in the morning. You can see the main menu in Figure 3.3.
Ask a Young Scientist	e-mail your question to **apscichs@radford.vak12ed.edu**. It may take up to 48 hours to receive a response. This service is only available October through March.
rocks-and-fossils (list server)	subscribe to **majordomo@world.std.com**. Send questions to **sshea@world.std.com**.

Figure 3.3

The main menu of NASA Spacelink

```
NASA/SPACELINK     MENU SYSTEM      Revision:1.68.00.00  [@TCON3 NETWORK]

NASA Spacelink Main Menu

   1.   Log Off NASA Spacelink
   2.   NASA Spacelink Overview
   3.   Current NASA News
   4.   Aeronautics
   5.   Space Exploration: Before the Shuttle
   6.   Space Exploration: The Shuttle and Beyond
   7.   NASA and its Centers
   8.   NASA Education Programs
   9.   Instructional Materials
  10.   Space Program Spinoffs/Technology Transfer
  11.   Frequently Asked Questions (FAQ)
  12.   NASA FOSTER On-line Project


Enter an option number, 'G' for GO TO, ? for HELP, or
   press RETURN to redisplay menu...
```

Or you may want to learn more about the scientist by writing personal messages to find out what kind of science he or she is interested in or what questions he or she is currently researching.

Figure 3.4

Learn about the great ideas of a master scientist, Isaac Asimov.

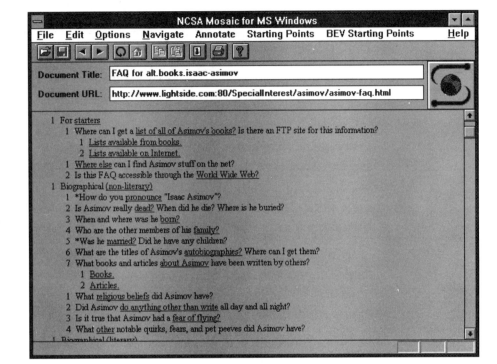

Becoming a Young Scientist

Look around your community. Is your drinking water being tested for toxic chemicals? What is the recycling plan? How much acid is in your rainfall? If you tackle local problems with scientific research, the people who make the decisions will take you more seriously and may listen to your concerns.

Start a Club

With some friends, start a scientific explorers club. Brainstorm to come up with tough questions. Have each person think of a question on a different topic to post online and then use the answers to learn with each other about different types of science.

Game Gurus

Note

Playing games and competing against a computer is something just about everyone likes to do. Wouldn't it be even better if you could compete against a real person on the computer? *Game Gurus* is a project where you can find your favorite games on the Internet and then play with people from all over the world. Whether you are a beginner or an expert, you can find a worthy challenger.

Everyone has had the experience at some point in life of wanting to play a game like chess, checkers, Scrabble, or Dungeons and Dragons and not being able to find anyone who was a strong-enough challenge. All over the country there are kids and adults who are also looking for the ultimate challenger for their favorite games.

It's not very convenient for most people to travel or participate in professional matches, but you have two other options. You can either give up your game, or you can meet and compete with new opponents in one of the world's most exciting arenas—the Internet game servers.

This is your chance to become a guru at your favorite game. (A *guru* is a wise and talented person who is an expert on a specific subject.) Your talent is game playing, which will be challenged by other players on the Internet who, like you, want to improve their game-playing skills.

There are many different servers on the Internet that offer game challenges. Now you can find people who will not only play with you but will also give you an awesome challenge!

Note

The Internet feature you will need for this project is telnet.

Playing the Games

1. Access the game servers of your choice and learn the game rules and terminology.

Once you reach a server listed in *Internet Game Servers* and learn how matches are played, you'll probably find a whole new set of rules and terms for playing your game online. For example, if you decide to compete on the Internet in chess, you'll have to learn the computer code names for king, queen, rooks, and knights as well as the codes for making moves. Playing a game online adds new dimensions to old strategies!

Internet Game Servers

Chinese Chess	telnet to **coolidge.harvard.edu 5555** or **128.103.28.155555**. On connection, you will be guided through an automatic registration. Once registered, you can play games in real time.
WISDOoM crossword server	telnet to **next7.cas.muohio.edu 8888**, no log-in is required. On the first line type **help**. Offers a variety of crossword challenges, including Scrabble. See Figure 3.5 to see what it looks like.
MarlDOoM crossword server	telnet to **seabass.st.usm.edu 7777**, no log-in is required. Use if WISDOoM is busy.
Game servers	telnet to **herx1.tat.physik.uni-tuebingen.de** or **pavax3.iap.physik.uni-tuebingen.de**, user name: **games**. This server, maintained by the University of Tuebingen in Germany, offers a variety of adventure games, thinking games, and board games.
Go server	telnet to **hellspark.wharton.upenn.edu 6969** and log in as **guest**. Once connected, type **help go**. This very active server offers a two-player strategy board game called Go.

2. Play your game.

Each server is going to have a different set of instructions. The nice thing about playing a game on the Internet is that you can take your time and strategize about the best move to make. This way the fun of the game is stretched out over days or maybe even weeks.

Figure 3.5

This is WisDOoM, an Internet game server. You can move from room to room and try out different games, such as crossword puzzles, Scrabble, and other board games.

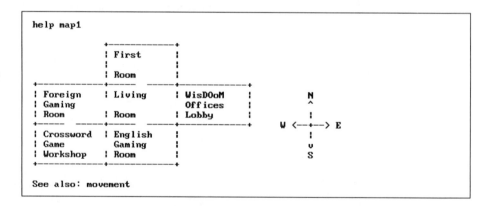

```
help intro

Welcome to DOoM.  If you know the buzzwords, DOoM is a networked textual
virtual reality and you can skip the rest of this paragraph.  This means that
you, a `player' move through and interact with an imaginary world of objects
and rooms by typing commands (e.g. `north' to go north, `take box' to pick up
a box) and reading responses to your commands (e.g. `The box is too heavy.').

You're probably not here for the virtual reality experience, but rather
because you've heard that you can play games here.  To get started, you'll
need to read several other help screens to learn the commands you can use.
`help player1', `help player2' etc. list generally available commands; `help
play1' etc. tell how to play games here; `help map1' etc. contain a map of the
DOoM; and `help index' lists available help screens.  If you forget what the
appropriate command is in a situation, `help here' lists commands specific to
your location or game state.

See also: index map1 play1 player1
```

```
help map1
                 +---------------+
                 : First         :
                 :               :
                 : Room          :
+---------------+-------   -------+---------------+
: Foreign       : Living         : WisDOoM       :           N
: Gaming        :                : Offices       :           ^
: Room          : Room           : Lobby         :           :
+---------------+-------   -------+---------------+     W <---+---> E
: Crossword     : English        :               :           :
: Game          : Gaming         :               :           v
: Workshop      : Room           :               :           S
+---------------+---------------+---------------+

See also: movement
```

Who Is the Ultimate Game Guru?

Because most of the games on the Internet are organized as matches, the winners of individual games will go on to compete to see who is the best. Each server has a different way of calculating scores. See how long it takes you to make your journey to the top of the mountain. Within a short period of time, you could become the Game Guru that everyone wants to beat!

Guten Tag
German

Bonjour
French

Hello
English

Boker Tov
Hebrew

Jambo
Swahili

G'day
Australian

There's Power in Numbers

Everyone has opinions about how to make the world a better place to live. Sometimes you have such strong opinions that you want to share them with others or take some kind of action to let people know how you feel. In this chapter you will find projects that will give you a variety of opportunities to express your opinions to others as well as communicate with people who can make the changes you want. The more people there are expressing their ideas, the greater the chance there is for change.

A Capitol Idea is a great opportunity for you to explore current issues being debated in government and to communicate your opinions to the politicians in Washington, D.C. You can *Contribute to Finding a Cure* for AIDS by informing yourself and others about this disease. If you also express your opinions through art or music, then *Artistic Reflections* is the project for you. If you see yourself as a dreamer about what is to come, then *Visions of the Future* is a great way to contribute your opinions on using the Internet for learning. Choose any or all of these projects and be part of a powerful network of people!

The NetCruiser software that came with this book offers an alternative way to do these activities. See Appendix C for more about this software.

Note

A Capitol Idea

Note

You can use the Internet to voice your opinion. Is there something going on in your city or country that you don't like? Do you think something should be done differently? With *A Capitol Idea*, you can speak your opinions, make suggestions, and get to know other people who may agree or disagree with you. You can even work with other people to solve a problem.

What would you do if the U.S. government decided that kids under the age of sixteen were required to observe an 8 P.M. curfew? Everyone caught disobeying the curfew would lose their right to get a driver's license when they turned sixteen. Chances are you would be pretty upset about this law. But what could *you* do about it?

The Internet gives you a way to do something: say what you think to people who can make changes. If you don't like what congress is doing, you can try to convince your congressional representatives to change their minds. If you like something politicians are doing, you can let them know. They need to hear directly from you to convince other politicians to vote with them. Make a difference today—voice your opinion now!

The Internet features you will use for this project are Gopher, FTP, list servers, telnet, and WAIS.

Note ....

Using the Internet to Become an Informed Voter

If you want to make your point and be effective, you need to be well informed. Here's a way of using the Internet to inform yourself about social or political issues.

1. Choose a topic you feel strongly about.

The "hot topics" on Capitol Hill are changing every year. The best way to find out what's hot is to look in the newspaper or a weekly news magazine.

An example of a hot topic in 1993 was a bill known as "motor voter." The voter turnout in the 1992 presidential election was very low because many people had not registered to vote. One solution proposed by the bill would allow people to register to vote when they apply for or renew their driver's licenses. The supporters argued that more young people would register this way. The opposition argued that this bill did not address the needs of underrepresented groups, such as the elderly and the poor, many of whom do not drive. This bill was debated for many months, and finally it was passed and signed into law in May 1993.

2. Get the latest information about your topic.

Use the listings in *Political Resources on the Internet* to get the most up-to-date information about a particular bill being debated in congress.

Ask yourself some questions about your topic: Why did people want to pass this bill? Who wanted it? Who is opposed to this bill?

Tip

When you are researching an issue, it is very helpful to begin with a few questions. If you are reading articles to locate answers to specific questions, the information you find will make more sense.

You can search the Internet for files on any topic you want. There are two programs that will help you with this: Veronica and Archie. Veronica searches Gophers, and Archie searches files in FTP sites. Check out the Resources appendix in the back of the book to find out where you can go on the Internet to use Veronica and Archie.

To start your search, the computer will ask you for a word to use in the search. Try typing "motor voter" and see what information you get. As you can see from Figure 4.1, there were six files found on the particular day of the search. Which titles catch your interest? Maybe you are curious about the one that describes how a compromise is sputtering or about the transcript of the President's remarks about the bill.

Figure 4.1

This is the result of using Veronica to find files about the motor voter bill.

```
Internet Gopher Information Client v1.11.I

Search GopherSpace by Title word(s) (via UNINETT/U. of Bergen): motor voter

    1.  Compromise sputters for motor voter issue.  News story by Ann.
    2.  TRanscript-of-Presidents-Remarks-at-Motor-Voter-Signing.
    3.  Two Columbians Help Drive Home 'Motor Voter' Bill.
    4.  motor-voter.
    5.  motor-voter.
--> 6.  Motor Voter/
```

3. Identify the people who support your position and those who oppose it.

You can use the *Legi-Slate Gopher Service* to find out which politicians support and which oppose your position. For example, if you want to find the information about the "motor voter" bill, choose "Legislation" from the main menu and then look at the "103rd Congress." Under a "Hot Topics" list like the one you see in Figure 4.2, you will find "Motor Voter." If you select this topic, you will see the names of the congresspeople

that sponsored the bill. You can also get a description of the bill so you can understand exactly what changes the bill calls for.

Legi-Slate Gopher Service

Gopher to `gopher.legislate.com`. Choose "Legislation" and then "Current Congress" for the latest legislative information. You will get directions for searching either by the congressperson's name, the name of the bill, or a keyword like "crime." Another way you can reach this service is to telnet to `consultant.micro.umn.edu` and log in as **gopher**. Once the main menu appears, choose "search gopher titles at UMN gopher" and type **legi-slate** for the search word.

Figure 4.2

Here is the "hot" topics list from the Legi-Slate Gopher Service.

```
        Internet Gopher Information Client v2.0.16

                        "Hot" Bills

  -->   19. Motor Voter/
        20. National Competitiveness/
        21. National Service/
        22. OSHA Reform/
        23. Paperwork Reduction/
        24. Public Debt Limit/
        25. RTC Funding/
        26. Striker Replacement/
        27. Student Loan Reform/
        28. Tax Bill/
```

Knowledge Is Power

Whatever your topic—prison reform, year-round education, gun control, or something else—there is plenty you can do with your new knowledge:

✳ *Exchange opinions with people interested in the same topic*

✳ *Write a letter to someone in power*

✳ *Organize a group of people to visit a congressional office*

Legislative Resources

Congressional Quarterly
gopher to **gopher.cqalert.com**. This is a magazine that has comprehensive information about current legislation.

Y-Rights
subscribe to **listerv@sjuvm.bitnet**. This is a list server about the rights of youths.

USHOUSE_house_bill_text_103rd
telnet to **wais.com** and log in as **wais**. This WAIS source includes the full texts of all bills under consideration by the 103rd session of the House of Representatives.

Talk to People

Usually you can find at least one other person who is concerned about a topic you really care about by trying one of the list servers in *Legislative Resources*. As more and more people learn about a topic, there is more discussion about it. You can stir up discussions with many different people on the Internet through list servers. Through your discussions you can develop your own position on an issue by asking yourself: "Do I support or oppose this new bill on congress?" With the information you have gathered online, you can support your opinion in discussions with friends.

Go to the Top

If you are interested in a topic that concerns the whole country, you could try sending an electronic message to the president that describes your concerns and suggestions. Send your e-mail message to one of the addresses listed in *Internet Addresses for Congress and the White House*.

There is also a listing of congressional addresses you can have sent to you by e-mail. Figure 4.3 shows the home map for the White House Citizens Interactive service, another way you can voice your opinion.

Internet Addresses for Congress and the White House

The President
president@whitehouse.gov

The Vice President
vice.president@whitehouse.gov

Congressional addresses
send an e-mail to **comments@hr.house.gov** for a list of congressional addresses

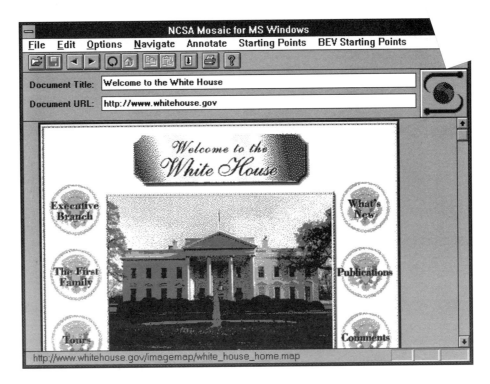

Figure 4.3

Become an informed citizen by using the White House Citizens Interactive service.

Speak Up

Researching issues is a tough job; people, called lobbyists, actually do this for a living. They research an issue, and they try to convince members of congress to vote a certain way. For example, a lobbyist for the American Association of Retired Persons (AARP) may have opposed the "motor voter" bill because it did not provide elderly people—many of whom do not drive and have physical limitations—with an easier way to register to vote. That lobbyist would then meet with members of congress to encourage them to oppose the bill.

> I want to talk to Hillary Clinton about the health program. My letter won't get lost and it will get there so they can read it.
>
> *Robbie, Fifth Grade*

Once you have completed this project, you should have a very good idea of what kind of legislation is or is not being passed concerning a topic you care about. So speak up! Become a volunteer lobbyist for your own issue. Let the politicians—and even the President— know exactly how you feel about what they're doing. The important thing is to write them and let them know what you think. Your opinions do make a difference.

Contribute to Finding a Cure

Note

Information is power. You can *Contribute to Finding a Cure* for AIDS by learning the facts and educating your community about the disease. You can educate yourself by exploring the wealth of information provided on the Internet by several organizations committed to wiping out this disease. You can also talk with people who have the AIDS virus, as well as medical professionals, to learn about their personal experiences. On the Internet you have access to the organizations and people that are all working together to find a cure for AIDS.

AIDS stands for Acquired Immune Deficiency Syndrome. It is a disease for which we do not yet have a cure. When a person is infected with the AIDS virus, the body actually destroys itself; the body's natural antibodies that usually protect it from disease begin to attack its own tissue.

There have been other diseases in history that have killed many people, but for most, cures have been found. To develop these cures, scientists, doctors, and many other people shared their knowledge and creativity. People learned about the disease so that they could help prevent its spread. The people who are working towards a cure for the AIDS virus are confident that one can be found if people work together, share ideas, and help others.

You can contribute to finding a cure for AIDS by educating yourself and others about the disease. In this activity, you will talk through the Internet with people who have AIDS and with the medical staff that is working on a cure for the disease.

The Internet features you will use are Gopher, telnet, and anonymous FTP.

Note

Educating Yourself and Others

Before you can educate others about AIDS, you need to know the facts yourself. When there is a disease as widespread and deadly as AIDS, there also tend to be rumors and myths about how you can get the disease. You can separate rumors from truth by following these steps.

1. Get updated information and statistics.

Things change quickly for people living with AIDS as well as in the scientific and medical community working on a cure for the disease. New treatments that scientists think might slow the virus or even stop it are approved for experimentation. Scientists learn more all the time about how the disease is contracted. Possible cures are being tested in laboratories all over the world.

To keep up with these changes, read the online AIDS resources listed in *Aids Resources on the Internet*. Here is a list of three organizations that maintain resources for the public:

* National Institute for Allergies and Infectious Diseases (NIAID)
* Centers for Disease Control (CDC)
* Federal Drug Administration (FDA)

These organizations are all agencies of the U.S. government that are committed to providing up-to-date and reliable information on different diseases, including AIDS. Figure 4.4 shows the main menu for NIAID's Gopher.

2. Create a brochure for people your age that includes the information you found.

AIDS is such a complex disease that it may seem difficult to put all the facts into a short brochure. If you focus on including the most important facts, you will be teaching people something they probably don't already know. Figure 4.5 shows some of the information you might find as you gopher around.

Figure 4.4

The main menu of the Gopher at the National Institute of Allergies and Infectious Diseases (NIAID)

```
┌─────────────────────────────────────────────────────────────┐
│        Internet Gopher Information Client v1.12S              │
│                                                               │
│             AIDS Related Information                          │
│                                                               │
│   -->  1.  Study Recruitment Information/                     │
│        2.  NIAID Press Releases/                              │
│        3.  Nursing HIV/AIDS/                                  │
│        4.  CDC Daily Summaries/                               │
│        5.  CDC Statistics/                                    │
│        6.  CDC National AIDS Clearinghouse/                   │
│        7.  Morbidity and Mortality Weekly Report/             │
│        8.  National Commission on AIDS/                       │
│        9.  VA AIDS Information Newsletter/                     │
│       10.  U.S. Community AIDS Resources/                     │
│       11.  International AIDS Resources/                      │
│                                                               │
└─────────────────────────────────────────────────────────────┘
```

AIDS Resources on the Internet

The National Institute of Allergy and Infectious Diseases (NIAID)	gopher to **odie.niaid.nih.gov** *and choose "AIDS Related Information" from the menu. It includes the National AIDS Clearinghouse from the Centers for Disease Control.*
National Library of Medicine	anonymous FTP to **nlmpubs.nlm.nih.gov** *and choose "AIDS" from the menu.*
AIDS Database	telnet to **debra.dgbt.doc.ca 3000** *and log in as* **chat**.
Federal Drug Administration	telnet to **FDABBS.FDA.GOV** *and log in as* **BBS**.
AIDS Hypercard Stacks	anonymous FTP to **ftp.sunset.se** *and follow the directory path* **pub/mac/misc/medical/hypercard**.

Figure 4.5

Current article from the NIAID Gopher

```
***** Research Strategy Proposal: High-Tech Exploitation of
      the Unexpected

by John S. James

What do we believe should be done differently in AIDS
research?

In the history of medical advances against other infectious
diseases, but our impression is that the key discoveries have
usually been unexpected -- not the result of institutional
programs based on the theories of the day. Therefore, we
propose a research strategy of being prepared to make the
+------------------------------------------------------------+
```

3. **Get your brochure printed and distributed.**

Ask a printing company in your city to make copies of your brochure for free because it is for public education. (Many companies donate services and materials for public-education projects.) Leave copies of your brochure at the library, school, recreation center, and anywhere else kids your age hang out. Update your brochure periodically to keep up with new breakthroughs in research.

Create a Wall

Now that you know the facts about the AIDS virus, use the Internet to talk to people who have the AIDS virus or to the medical professionals who work with them. Follow these steps:

1. **Subscribe to a list server about AIDS.**

Try one of the list servers in *AIDS List Servers*. If you need help, check out the section in Chapter 1 about list servers.

2. **Print copies of the questions and messages you post as well as the ones sent to you from others on the list.**

Sample Questions You Can Ask on a List Server might give you some ideas for questions to ask.

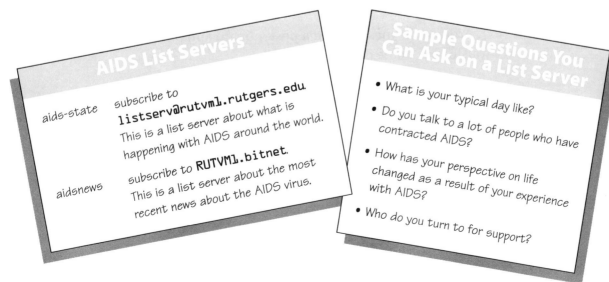

AIDS List Servers

aids-state   subscribe to `listserv@rutvm1.rutgers.edu`. This is a list server about what is happening with AIDS around the world.

aidsnews   subscribe to `RUTVM1.bitnet`. This is a list server about the most recent news about the AIDS virus.

Sample Questions You Can Ask on a List Server

- What is your typical day like?
- Do you talk to a lot of people who have contracted AIDS?
- How has your perspective on life changed as a result of your experience with AIDS?
- Who do you turn to for support?

With LOVE from your Friends on the Internet

3. Create an AIDS wall.

Arrange the messages on a poster board and put the poster up on a wall in your home or school.

4. Continue to update the AIDS wall with new messages and personal stories. For many people, it is the individual stories that make the strongest impact.

The idea for an AIDS wall comes from the AIDS quilt. This huge quilt (the size of several football fields) is made up of smaller cloth panels sewn by friends of people who have died from AIDS. With your wall of messages, you will be sharing stories from the courageous people you've met on the Internet with your family, friends, and community.

There's Power in Education

Contribute to Finding a Cure for AIDS is your chance to make a change. The best way to prevent people from getting a disease is to tell them about the disease, how people get it, and what people can do to prevent *contracting* (getting) it. By researching AIDS issues on the Internet and then designing your AIDS-awareness brochure, you will be helping people prevent the spread of AIDS.

You now have the skills to make a contribution to discovering a cure for *any* disease. If you can educate just one person, you may save a life.

Artistic Reflections

Note

People see many different things when they look at a piece of art. What people feel when they see a piece of art and what the artist felt while creating it are sometimes completely opposite. What is certain is that art evokes feelings in everyone. *Artistic Reflections* will help you find places on the Internet where you can see and learn about different types and styles of art. This may help you create your own style of artistic expression. And as you explore, you might notice that art often reflects the society in which it was created.

> Sculptors of the world unite!
> Painters of the world unite!
> Musicians of the world unite!

What do all of these groups of people have in common? ART! They use all kinds of media—such as words, paint, music, or clay—to create artistic pieces that express their feelings and opinions. No matter how unique your ideas, no matter what medium you use to create art, there are other people on the Internet who share your interest in expressing themselves through art.

How can you use art to express your feelings? How can you make a statement and voice an opinion about life? To answer questions like these, it will be helpful to learn about other artists and their work through the Internet. You can get ideas about creating art and gain an appreciation for the contributions of other artists.

> The Internet features you will use in this project are Gopher, FTP, WWW, and list servers.
>
> **Note**

Finding Art on the Internet

1. Choose one form of art you want to explore on the Internet.

There are so many different types of art that you will want to begin with your favorite. For instance, you might want to explore sculptures, paintings, or music by searching for files, pictures, or sounds on the Internet. You can also look at the musical side of art by searching for types of music like jazz, rock, blues, or classical.

2. Get examples of art from various sources on the Internet.

You will be amazed at the many sources on the Internet where you can find pictures of works of art, text files of lyrics, critical reviews of artists, and other information related to art. The information is available in different formats—graphic, text, and sound.

> You may need special software on your home computer to view images or listen to sounds. If this is the case, most sites will post a note about it and either include the software at the site's Internet address or tell you where to go to get the software. If you have any problems, ask your network administrator or your parents.
>
> **Tip**

In *Art Resources on the Internet* there are several different resources that contain thousands of images of works of art. One may be more useful than another depending on what type of art you are looking for. For

example, the art found in the Vatican Library may be religious in nature because this library is maintained by the Catholic Church. The Louvre, a huge museum in Paris, includes works by many European artists (see Figure 4.6 for a page from the WebLouvre). To get ready for your search:

1. *Pick your field of art.*

2. *Look at the resource list and decide which place might have the type of art you're looking for.*

3. *Select several keywords, like the name of an artist, to narrow your search.*

4. *Go online.*

Tip

Graphic files can be huge, which means they might take a long time to download. If you are going to try it, you should probably have a 14.4-kilobaud modem (that's the speed at which the modem sends and receives data).

Art Resources on the Internet

Smithsonian Online	anonymous FTP to **sunsite.unc.edu**.
Smithsonian Institution's Office of Printing and Photographic Services	anonymous FTP to **photo1.si.edu**. There are two files that will help you find your way around: **smithsonian.photo.info.txt** and **photo1.catalog**.
The Louvre Exhibits	WWW **http://mistral.enst.fr/~pioch/louvre/**.
The OTIS Project	anonymous FTP to **sunsite.unc.edu** and go to **pub/multimedia/pictures/OTIS** or anonymous FTP to **aql.gatech.edu** and go to **pub/OTIS**. This is an online gallery that offers original artwork.
Online History of Art	WWW to **http://life.anu.edu.au/**.
Vatican Library	WWW to **http://sunsite.unc.edu/expo/vatican.exhibit/Vatican.exhibit.html**.
Artcrit	subscribe to **listserv@yorkvm1.bitnet**. This is a list server about art criticism and analysis.
Artserve	WWW to **http://rubens.anu.edu.au/**. This is an art history database.

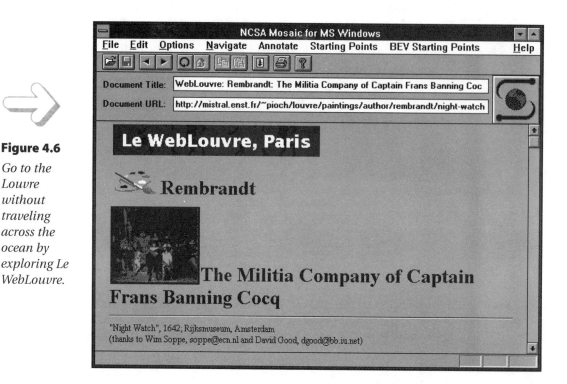

Figure 4.6

Go to the Louvre without traveling across the ocean by exploring Le WebLouvre.

Music is a popular form of art because you can experience it in so many different ways. You can sing, play an instrument, write lyrics, choreograph a dance, or just listen to the music. Use the listings in *Music Resources on the Internet* to research a type of music you don't know about or one that you don't listen to very often. (See Figure 4.7 for an introduction to the world of underground music.) You may develop a whole new perspective on classical, rap, country, or even operatic music!

Tip

All of the art and music resources are very popular, so try to use them at times when fewer people may be trying: maybe in the early morning or late at night.

3. Choose one artist or one style of art and find as much information as you can.

If you have a favorite artist—such as a painter, sculptor, or musician—or one style of art—such as pencil drawings, watercolors, or country music—search the Internet resources for information to expand your knowledge of the person or style. Learning about another person's experiences

Music Resources on the Internet

Allmusic	subscribe to `listserv@auvm.american.edu`. This is a list server about all types of music.
Music List of Lists	send an e-mail message to `mlol-request@wariat.org` or anonymous FTP to `cs.uwp.edu` and go to `music/info`.
University of Wisconsin Music Archive	anonymous FTP to `ftp.uwp.edu` and go to `pub/music`.
WNUR-FM Jazz Information Server	WWW to `http://www.acns.nwu.edu/jazz/`.
MTV Gopher	gopher to `mtv.com`.
Underground Music Archives	WWW to `http://sunsite.unc.edu/ianc`. This is from the University of California at Santa Cruz and has musical information about *obscure* (not generally known) bands.

Figure 4.7

Learn about up-and-coming bands from the Internet Underground Music Archive.

can often give you ideas to draw from to create your own style. For example, growing up near an ocean may influence an artist's style or even the subjects of his or her art.

Tip

You can use Veronica to find other Gopher servers that have Smithsonian collections. Check the Resources Appendix in the back of the book for Gopher sites that have Veronica available to the public.

Artistic Collaboration

Art does not have to be created by only one person. In fact, it takes hundreds of people to create a musical play or to design and build a beautiful church or temple. These are a few examples of collaborative works of art that reflect an entire community of people.

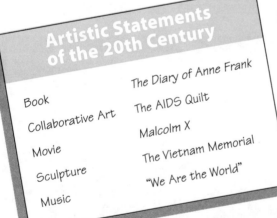

Artistic Statements of the 20th Century

Book	The Diary of Anne Frank
Collaborative Art	The AIDS Quilt
Movie	Malcolm X
Sculpture	The Vietnam Memorial
Music	"We Are the World"

Do you have a community of artists? Are you in a drama club? Do you and your friends like to paint? Use the talents and strengths of all your friends to create an artistic expression of the group's feelings.

The most important thing you can do with your own artistic creations is to share them with others. Let people see and experience your art. Perhaps your library or museum displays art from local artists. You may even want to see if a gallery will display your work. People might buy your art because they understand the feelings expressed in it.

Music is another common way for people to express their feelings. Songs are found in every culture in history. On the Internet, there are different music resources you can explore to find out how other musicians have used music for social action. In the 1980s, there was a song called "We Are the World." Famous musicians came together to create this song, which sold many records. The money was then sent to Africa to help feed starving children and adults. That's just one example of using music as a means of social action; see what else you can find.

Visions of the Future

Note

Kids everywhere have fantasies about what school will be like in the 21st century—will there be computers instead of teachers? Will the subjects be the same? Why not be a part of the change in learning and teaching now by taking part in *Visions of the Future*? In this project, you can join the ranks of youth leaders from all around the world to share your ideas for how to best use networks for learning. You and other kids can show teachers, parents, principals, and others about the benefits of global networking and how telecommunications breaks down barriers to learning. Some of the things you can do are participate in online projects, share your experiences with others, and get involved with a group that supports the use of telecommunications in education.

7:00 A.M. Tony and Angela are arguing about who will be first on the home communications center—a combination of television, phone, and computer—to see if they have received any e-mail messages from their friends in New Mexico. Ever since their family moved to Michigan over the summer, they use e-mail to stay in touch with their friends.

8:30 A.M. Tony is in his humanities class and needs to find the unemployment rate of the Ukraine for his group project. Because the books in the libraries don't even show the Ukraine as its own country, Tony turns to his computer and modem to help him find the answer. Within ten minutes, Tony has the answer for his group as well as the types of jobs that are most available in that country.

11:15 A.M. Angela is typing a letter in Spanish to a new netpal from Bogota, Columbia. This is one way that she will keep learning the language even though she has moved away from the Spanish-speaking community in New Mexico. She and her netpal are preparing for a video teleconference with scientists from Antarctica who are studying a hole in the ozone layer.

2:30 P.M. Tony and Angela take the bus to the local library to use a public communications center. They want to send a video they made of their new home to their friends and teachers in New Mexico to show them what their life is like in Michigan. The public communications center has a fast connection to the national telecommunications network, which is better for sending video files than their system at home.

The way Tony and Angela are learning is very different from their grandparents' and parents' experience. Instead of looking up answers in a textbook, they now use telecommunications to find answers to their questions.

The Internet feature you will use for this project is e-mail.

Note

Adding Yourself to the Numbers

Your opinion counts! You can participate in changing the way people learn by getting involved in any one of three different projects. Send a message to the e-mail address of your choice listed in *For More Information*.

For More Information

I*EARN	send an e-mail message to **iearn@igc.org**
Academy One	send an e-mail message to **a002@nptn.org**
Global Classroom Youth Congress	send an e-mail message to **rsch281c@cl.uh.edu**

I*EARN

Become a regular participant in I*EARN (International Education and Resource Network). There are several young people who run their own projects on this network. For example, David Marzilai, an 18-year-old from Massachusetts, moderates an online conference called I*EARN.YOUTH, which is accessed by 10,000 students and adults worldwide. It's easy to get connected to the projects on I*EARN, which are focused on involving youth international service organizations in meaningful projects.

Academy One

Get connected to a project on the Academy One network. There are projects for students of all ages that can be found on many of the freenet affiliates of the National Public Telecomputing Network (NPTN). Freenets are community networks that are popping up in towns all around the country that are free (or at least very inexpensive) to the residents of the community. The NPTN helps connect these freenets together. Mia Sillanpaa, a 15-year-old from Finland, has participated in many projects through Academy One, like *Save the Beaches* and *A Day in the Life of a Student*. Like the rest of Academy One's projects, students across the country are linked together to achieve a common goal. Five to ten different projects run at any given time. Send your e-mail message to see what's happening now.

Global Classroom Youth Congress

Many of the kids who are leaders on I*EARN and Academy One are also members of the Global Classroom Youth Congress. The Congress is a group of students that makes recommendations for using global networking as a tool for learning. In 1993, this group held its first meeting in Washington, D.C., during the annual meeting for the World Future Society. Send an e-mail message to find out how you can join and what you can do.

Creating Your Own Vision of the Future

What you do today will have an impact on what tomorrow looks like. If you have an idea about how learning should take place in the next century, speak up! Find out what UNICEF, the United Nations International Children's Education Fund, thinks about kids' futures by checking out *The UNICEF Gopher.* Work with other students to tell people about how telecommunications can be used to break down barriers to learning. Recommendations can be a lot more influential if there are many people suggesting the same thing.

The UNICEF Gopher

You can learn about UNICEF, an international organization dedicated to the future of children, by gophering to `hqfaus01.unicef.org`.

The people who make decisions about how young people learn need to hear about your experiences and suggestions. They're counting on you because yours is the first generation that knows what it is like to grow up learning about life through the Global Village.

Guten Tag
German

Bonjour
French

Buon Giorno
Italian

Hello
English

Boker Tov
Hebrew

Jambo
Swahili

G'day
Australian

Konnichi Wa
Japanese

Looking for Answers

When you've got a burning question and you need to find the answer, where do you go, who do you call? You've checked the library. You've asked your teacher. No one seems to know the answer to your question. This is the time to use the Internet.

This chapter has projects that direct you to helpful resources to answer specific questions and to explore a variety of interests. With *Trivia Treasure Hunt*, you and your friends can learn how to find information on the Internet by creating scavenger hunts. *Inquiring Minds Want to Know* provides you with step-by-step instructions for conducting research on the Internet. *Writer's Corner* gives you ideas for jump-starting your brain with new and interesting ideas for writing. *Hobbyist's Delight* adds to your delight on the Internet by giving you new places to play. You can find information on anything from sports to cooking to art. Whatever your question or interest may be, answers and information can be found on the Internet.

You can also participate in these activities by using the NetCruiser software that came with this book. Turn to Appendix C to find out more about NetCruiser.

Note

Trivia Treasure Hunt

Note

In *Trivia Treasure Hunt* you will learn how to create a scavenger hunt on the Internet. Hunting for information is a great way to learn interesting facts and to get used to moving around to new places online. In this project, there are two different hunts—one for words in the English language and another for countries around the world. These are just two examples of the kinds of hunts you can do yourself and create for your friends and family.

You have just been chosen as a contestant on "Jeopardy." You decide to practice before you go on by watching the show on TV. Here's the answer under Economics for $500: "The currency of Thailand." Your mind draws a blank as you hear yet another question you don't know. Where on earth do the creators of this game find all of this information? You thought you knew enough information to compete on the show, but they're asking some pretty far-out questions. What can you do to prepare yourself for your game? How about looking on the Internet?

Knowing answers to trivia questions would help you outwit your "Jeopardy" opponents, but this "trivia" could also be valuable information. For example, suppose you know a great deal about Africa—the different countries, tribes, and weather. While this may seem trivial to some people because they don't live in Africa, this information could turn out to be quite helpful in certain situations. For instance, if an African exchange student visits your school, you could begin a friendship by talking to the student about differences between Africa and America. Or perhaps a friend of yours traced her family roots to a certain part of Africa. You could share your knowledge and help your friend understand more about her family's heritage. You never know when you will have an opportunity to share your knowledge and help another person.

Note

The Internet feature you will use for this project is Gopher.

Word Trivia

Choosing the perfect word to describe what you are thinking can be difficult. Sometimes we use a similar word, a *synonym*, when we can't think of the right word. We use many different kinds of words every day. Here are a few:

synonym	*a word having the same—or nearly the same—meaning as another word (evil and wicked are synonyms)*
antonym	*a word meaning the opposite of another word (evil and good are antonyms)*
acronym	*a word composed of the first letters (or parts) of other words (the acronym "ASAP" means "as soon as possible")*

Finding the Reference Desk

Gopher to `gaia.sci-ed.fit.edu` and choose "Reference Desk" from the menu.

There are several resources on the Internet that you can use to solve a word trivia puzzle. Word puzzles are fun to do and make up with Internet sources like the Gopher at Florida Tech University where they have a "reference desk" with the American English and Webster dictionaries, an acronym dictionary, and *Roget's Thesaurus*. To get there, follow the directions in *Finding the Reference Desk*.

Tip

If you receive a message back from your search that says "Nothing Available. Gopher Error," it probably means the service has reached its user limit and is busy. You may need to try again later—late at night or early in the evening—when not as many people will be trying to use the service.

As you can see in Figure 5.1, there are many reference materials on this Gopher. The Thesaurus will help you find antonyms and synonyms, the dictionary contains definitions, and the acronym dictionary will help you decipher common acronyms.

```
┌─────────────────────────────────────────────────────────────────┐
│              ┌─────────────────────────────────────────┐          │
│              │ Internet Gopher Information Client v1.12S │          │
│              └─────────────────────────────────────────┘          │
│            Reference Desk (Dict., Thesaurus, zip/area codes)       │
│    -->   1. Search the Reference Menu Tree <?>                     │
│          2. ACRONYM Dictionary/                                    │
│          3. CIA World Factbook <?>                                 │
│          4. Congressional Directories/                             │
│          5. Country Codes (by Code).                               │
│          6. Country Codes (by Country).                            │
│          7. Dictionary  American English Dictionary (searchable) <?>│
│          8. Dictionary  Webster's Dictionary <?>                   │
│          9. Electronic Reference Books (UCSC)/                     │
│         10. General References (U. Michigan)/                      │
│         11. Geographic Name Servers (Info about US cities)/        │
│         12. Library and Research Information from USC/             │
│         13. Local Times Around the World/                          │
│         14. National Archives Gopher/                              │
│         15. Reference (Library of Congress)/                       │
│         16. Roget's Thesaurus (1991)/                              │
│         17. Search Many WAIS Indices/                              │
│         18. U.S. Telephone Area Codes/                             │
│                                                     Page: 1/2      │
└─────────────────────────────────────────────────────────────────┘
```

```
┌─────────────────────────────────────────────────────────────────┐
│    -->  19. U.S. Zip Code Directory (via U Oregon) <?>            │
│         20. US Census Information (1990)/                          │
│         21. VIRTUAL REFERENCE DESK - from UC Irvine/               │
│         22. World Country & Area Telephone Codes Index (Not USA or CANADA) <?>│
│         23. World Telephone Code Information/                      │
│                                                                    │
│    Press ▯ for Help, ▯ to Quit, ▯ to go up a menu     Page: 2/2    │
└─────────────────────────────────────────────────────────────────┘
```

Figure 5.1

An entire reference collection in one place!

Word Hunt: Complete the Sentence

To complete the sentence below, you will need to answer questions 1–8. All of the answers can be found in the dictionary, thesaurus, or acronym dictionary. Once you find the answer to #1 in Figure 5.2, you are on your own! (If you get stumped, you can find the answer at the end of this project.)

> #1_____
> though we are #2_____
> #3_____ #4_____
> from one another in miles,
> we are #5_____
> #6_____ of the
> #7_____ #8_____
> community.
>
> *Rachel, Seventh Grade*

Puzzle Questions:

1. What is an antonym of "odd?"

2. What is a synonym of "everyone?"

3. What is an antonym of "close?"

4. What is a synonym for "distant?"

5. Same answer as for question #2.

6. What is an antonym for "whole?"

7. What is a synonym for "equivalent?"

8. What is a synonym for "worldwide?"

```
Internet Gopher Information Client v1.12S

                  Roget's Thesaurus (1991)

-->  1.  Introduction.
     2.  License.
     3.  Roget Intro.
     4.  Search Roget's 1911 Thesaurus <?>
     5.  newroget.txt.
```

Figure 5.2

Roget's Thesaurus *gives you instant access to thousands of words.*

The questions for this puzzle are for Internet beginners, but as you and your friends become more advanced users, you can create puzzles with more difficult questions.

rnational Agent

If you like geography more than English, try making your own trivia puzzle with facts about countries and time zones. This information is interesting and easy to find on the Internet. For example, the Central Intelligence Agency (CIA) regularly collects data about foreign countries for the U.S. government and posts many of its findings on the Internet—see Figure 5.3 for an example. You can become a special CIA agent by using the information to create trivia questions for your friends and family.

Figure 5.3

You can use the CIA World Factbook to find out almost anything about any country in the world!

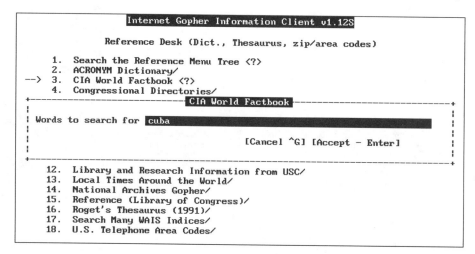

```
        Internet Gopher Information Client v1.12S

            Reference Desk (Dict., Thesaurus, zip/area codes)

        1.   Search the Reference Menu Tree <?>
        2.   ACRONYM Dictionary/
  -->   3.   CIA World Factbook <?>
        4.   Congressional Directories/
    +---------------------------- CIA World Factbook ----------------------------+
    :
    : Words to search for cuba
    :
    :                                      [Cancel ^G] [Accept - Enter]
    :
    +----------------------------------------------------------------------------+
        12.  Library and Research Information from USC/
        13.  Local Times Around the World/
        14.  National Archives Gopher/
        15.  Reference (Library of Congress)/
        16.  Roget's Thesaurus (1991)/
        17.  Search Many WAIS Indices/
        18.  U.S. Telephone Area Codes/
```

```
0000000057CIA
920120
CIA World Factbook 1991
Cuba

Geography
Total area: 110,860 km2; land area: 110,860 km2


Comparative area: slightly smaller than Pennsylvania


Land boundary: 29.1 km with US Naval Base at Guantanamo;
note--Guantanamo is leased and as such remains part of Cuba


Coastline: 3,735 km
```

What Country...?

The purpose of the Central Intelligence Agency is to keep our political leaders, like the President, informed about what is happening in different countries throughout the world. When you hear the acronym "CIA," you probably think of spies trying to locate secret information. But much of the information collected by the CIA is not secret. In fact, it's put on the Internet so everyone can learn about different countries around the world.

The CIA World Factbook is a great resource for helping you make a geographic trivia puzzle. Here are some sample questions to get you started:

> ? What is the land area of Albania?
>
> ? When an Afghan girl is born, what is her average life expectancy (the average number of years a person will live)?
>
> ? How many total kilometers of railroads are in Cuba?

What Time Is It?

If you're interested in time changes around the world, you should investigate "Local Times around the World" from the main menu of the Reference Desk. As you explore, you will see references to GMT, or Greenwich Mean Time. This is a measurement of time that begins in Greenwich, England, because it is located on the 0° meridian. A *meridian* is a giant imaginary circle that goes from the North Pole to the South Pole. Every city on the same meridian has the same *longitude* (a measurement of how far any city is from the 0° meridian). GMT is calculated from 0 to 24 hours, with midnight representing 0 hour. So, instead of saying it is 3 o'clock in the afternoon, you would say it is 15 hours, which is 12 hours (noon) plus 3 hours.

Here are a few sample questions about time zones that will help you begin to create your time-zone hunt:

 What time would it be in Australia if it is 4:00 P.M. in Chicago, Illinois?

 How many hours difference is there between Torino, Italy, and Greenwich Mean Time? How about Dublin, Ireland, and GMT?

 How many hours difference are you from GMT? (Clue: compare your city's time zone to GMT.)

Expanding Your Hunting Grounds

As you can see from the main menu of the Reference Desk in Figure 5.1, we have used only a few of the resources offered at this Gopher site. Once you have become familiar with those used in this project, you can take on the "Internet Hunt" trivia challenge. See *Where to Find the Internet Hunt* for directions to the game. The Internet Hunt is posted once a month across the Internet (Figure 5.4 shows what some of one month's questions might be like). There are prizes for those people who submit all the correct answers in the shortest amount of time. It's like "Jeopardy" on the Internet.

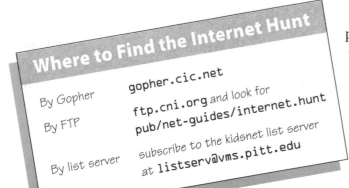

Where to Find the Internet Hunt

By Gopher   gopher.cic.net

By FTP   ftp.cni.org and look for pub/net-guides/internet.hunt

By list server   subscribe to the kidsnet list server at listserv@vms.pitt.edu

Follow all of the directions for completing and submitting your answers to the Internet Hunt. This is a very popular event, and you have a chance to win each month. Maybe you can work on hunts with your friends. Many brains are often better than one!

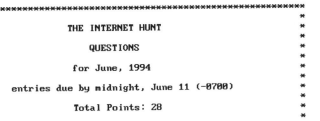

```
XXXXXXXXXXXXXXXXXXXXXXXXXXXXXXXXXXXXXXXXXXXXXXXXXXXXXXXXXXX
*                                                         *
*                  THE  INTERNET  HUNT                    *
*                                                         *
*                      QUESTIONS                          *
*                                                         *
*                   for June, 1994                        *
*                                                         *
*      entries due by midnight, June 11 (-0700)           *
*                                                         *
*                  Total Points: 28                       *
*                                                         *
XXXXXXXXXXXXXXXXXXXXXXXXXXXXXXXXXXXXXXXXXXXXXXXXXXXXXXXXXXX
```

Figure 5.4

By participating in the Internet Hunt, you can learn to move around the Internet and even win prizes.

```
As mentioned in previous announcements, this is a first-time novices
Hunt.  So if you (or your team), has entered the Hunt before, or if
you're quite comfortable surfing the Nets, take a well-deserved month
off.  We're cooking up something quite challenging for next month.
```

```
This summer I'd like to go whitewater rafting with some
friends. I need to get some gear - what information can
I get about whitewater outfitters on the Internet?
XXXXXXXXXXXXXXXXXXXXXXXXXXXXXXXXXXXXXXXXXXXXXXXXXXX
Question 2  (3 points)
(question designed by Carol and Neil Enns)

I have just started to use the Internet, and notice
that people use lots of funny symbols at the end of
their sentences. Someone told me these are smilies.
Is there a list of them on the net somewhere?
XXXXXXXXXXXXXXXXXXXXXXXXXXXXXXXXXXXXXXXXXXXXXXXXXXX
Question 3  (3 points)
(question designed by Dee Baldwin, Gerard Egan,
Bill Wilson, and Laura Windsor)

How can I find out what the requirements are for US
citizens traveling to Belize?
```

Answer to the Word Trivia Puzzle: "Even though we are all far away from one another in miles, we are all part of the same global community." (Rachel, Seventh Grade)

Note

Inquiring Minds Want to Know

This activity will help you perfect your research skills using the Internet and show you some ideas for developing a research presentation that contains reliable and useful information.

Note

Have a question that you want or need to answer? Chances are very good that you can answer it with a few keystrokes on your computer while connected to the Internet. In fact, you may become overwhelmed with the amount of information you receive. When this happens, it is important to make decisions about which facts relate most directly to your original question and which sources provide you with the most *reliable* (true) information.

Note

The Internet features you will use for this project are e-mail, Gopher, anonymous FTP, WWW, and WAIS.

Directing Your Research on the Internet

Quite often you start a research project with a very focused topic, such as "The Aftermath of the Los Angeles Earthquake of 1994," only to find yourself overwhelmed with information. You find information about the history of earthquakes in California, geological explanations of eighteenth century earthquakes, and the reactions of the Japanese to a recent earthquake in Tokyo. While it is possible to include all of the information you find, it is important to remember that a good research project is not defined by the *quantity* of information but by the *quality* of information.

Research is most successful when you break it down into steps. It is not until *after* you have gathered all the information you can that you actually make the decision as to what information is high quality. To help you with these and other decisions, here is a list of suggested steps to take in your own research:

1. *Choose a topic and describe it in one sentence (called a thesis statement).*
2. *Gather information from a variety of sources.*
3. *Group the information you found by different categories related to your topic.*
4. *Present your research in a format—written report, video, or even a speech—that you can share with your family, friends, or teachers.*

You can add your own steps depending on the type of research you are doing. For example, it might be interesting to include an interview with someone who has direct experience with your topic. There are many ways to gather information, and there are a lot of resources available.

1. Choose a topic for your research.

In school, your topic may be assigned to you—the teacher tells you exactly what to write about. But in this project, you get to choose your own topic. Your research can be about anything you want. Here are a few ideas:

> 👉 How are underwater tunnels built?
>
> 👉 Why has the president become more (or less) popular since he or she took office?
>
> 👉 What were the most important events in Louisa May Alcott's life?

Starting with a question helps you stay on track and not get distracted by all the other interesting information you may come across while doing research.

Once you know what question you want to ask, you will need to write it in the form of a thesis statement, which should include both your question and the answer you've come up with. For example, a thesis statement for the second question in the list might read, "The president's popularity has plummeted since his election due to rising unemployment and inflation." You may need to do preliminary research before you can write your thesis statement.

Using the Internet for Research

- Use Veronica to search different Gopher titles. If you do not have access to Veronica, check the resources in the back of the book to find out where you can telnet to use Veronica.

- Use Archie to search document names at different FTP sites. If you don't have access to Archie, check the resources in the back of the book to find out where you can telnet to use Archie.

- Submit a specific question to AskERIC in an e-mail message to askeric@ericir.syr.edu or explore the ERIC resources at ericir.syr.edu by using either

  Gopher ericir.syr.edu or
  WWW   http://ericir.syr.edu

  Search the WAIS source called "dowvision" for articles about current events (see Chapter 1 for the WAIS log-in procedures).

2. Find research articles, statistics, and information.

People who read or hear about your research will want to know the facts about your topic. You can use the Internet in a variety of ways to find these facts and supporting information. Check *Using the Internet for Research* for suggestions about how to gather all kinds of information.

To help you find places on the Internet that are relevant to your research topic, you can use the AskERIC service. ERIC stands for Educational Resources Information Center. This service is dedicated to helping students and teachers find and access learning resources of all kinds. All you have to do is send an e-mail message to AskERIC briefly describing your research topic. Within 48 hours you will receive a list of articles and Internet resources. You can also gopher to AskERIC and browse through the listings; if you were looking for earthquake information, you might follow the path shown in Figure 5.5.

```
┌─────────────────────────────────────────────────────────────┐
│         Internet Gopher Information Client v1.12S             │
│                                                               │
│           Root gopher server: ericir.syr.edu                 │
│                                                               │
│      1.  News and Information about ERIC and AskERIC/         │
│      2.  Map of the Library/                                  │
│      3.  Search AskERIC Menu Items <?>                        │
│      4.  Frequently Asked Questions (FAQ's)/                  │
│  --> 5.  AskERIC InfoGuides/                                  │
│      6.  Lesson Plans/                                        │
│      7.  Education Listservs Archives/                        │
│      8.  ERIC Clearinghouses/Components/                      │
│      9.  ERIC Digests File/                                   │
│     10.  ERIC Bibliographic Database (RIE and CIJE)/          │
│     11.  ERIC Full Text Prototype (Experimental)/            │
│     12.  Bibliographies/                                      │
│     13.  Other Education Resources/                           │
│     14.  Professional Organizations/                          │
│     15.  Education Conferences (Calendars and Announcements)/ │
│     16.  Electronic Journals, Books, and Reference Tools/     │
│     17.  Internet Guides and Directories/                     │
│     18.  Gophers and Library Catalogs/                        │
└─────────────────────────────────────────────────────────────┘
```

Figure 5.5

AskERIC has a variety of services and resources.

```
┌─────────────────────────────────────────────────────────────┐
│                    AskERIC InfoGuides                         │
│                                                               │
│     19.  deaf_resources.                                      │
│     20.  disabilities.                                        │
│     21.  disabled_students.                                   │
│     22.  distance_education.                                  │
│     23.  drama_1.                                             │
│     24.  drama_2.                                             │
│     25.  dyslexia.                                            │
│     26.  earthquakes_1.                                       │
│  -> 27.  earthquakes_2.                                       │
│     28.  ecology.                                             │
│     29.  electronic_journals.                                │
│     30.  freeware.                                            │
│     31.  french.                                              │
│     32.  french_lang_ed_K12.                                 │
│     33.  gender_stereotyping.                                 │
│     34.  geography.                                           │
│     35.  hazard_materials_2.                                 │
│     36.  hazardous_materials.                                │
└─────────────────────────────────────────────────────────────┘
```

```
┌─────────────────────────────────────────────────────────────┐
│  Gopher Sites:                                                │
│  -------------                                                │
│                                                               │
│  USA Gophers/Oklahoma/Oklahoma Geological Survey Observatory: │
│                                                               │
│  USA Gophers/California/University of California at Berkeley/National │
│  Info. Service for Earthquake Engineering (NISEE)/Other information │
│  resources/Earthquake Engineering Information Gopher          │
│                                                               │
│  USA Gophers/Texas/University of Texas at El Paso, Geological Sciences' │
│  Geogopher/Earth Sciences Resources (geogopher)/Other Earth Sciences │
│  gophers OR Seismology OR Internet.Resources.Earth.Sci        │
│                                                               │
│  USA Gophers/Illinois/Northwestern University, Department of Geological │
│  Sciences/Seismology Resources                                │
│                                                               │
│  USA Gophers/California/University of California - Santa Barbara │
│  Geological Sciences Gopher/Geology Research/USGS Geological Survey │
│  Gopher OR Seismology Resources OR USENET NEWS:sci.geo.geology. │
└─────────────────────────────────────────────────────────────┘
```

Tip

Focusing your search and sticking to your topic is easy if you remember which sites contain what *type* of information. Here are two clues to figuring this out:

1. Use the three letters at the end of an Internet address to tell you what kind of information you might find. For example, if an address ends in **gov**, you can be pretty sure you will find government reports and documents there. Check Chapter 1 for the list of all of the three-letter codes.

2. The type of Internet feature you use determines the type of information you will receive. For example, an FTP site contains documents, but a list server usually has first-hand accounts of an event. Review Chapter 1 for descriptions of these and other Internet features.

3. Group the information you gather into different categories.

You may be overwhelmed by all of the information you have collected during your research. The first step to organizing the information is to sort each piece of information into different categories. For instance, your research on the aftermath of the Los Angeles earthquake may be sorted into three subtopics:

 Geological explanations for the earthquake

 Physical damage and clean-up efforts

 Principles of constructing buildings to withstand earthquakes

Once you have sorted your information, be sure to determine whether or not each piece of information is reliable. To help you choose only the information that is reliable, ask yourself these questions:

 Does this information come from a source that is known for providing factual information?

 Does this information help explain my thesis statement?

Presenting Your Research

Now that you've completely researched a topic that interests you, you should present what you find to others rather than keeping it a secret. You can share it with family, hometown friends, teachers, and especially your friends on the Internet. Share your final presentation with the people on the Internet who helped you with your research. Keep a list of names as you are gathering information so you can send the results to everyone who helped.

Creative Presentation Ideas

Creating presentations from your research is a way to show others what you have found. Here are a few sample projects for the earthquake topic:

- Create a map that indicates different levels of earthquake damage to compare the effects of the earthquake in different parts of Los Angeles.

- Create a table detailing the relief efforts of various emergency organizations (for example, the Red Cross, local and national governments, and religious charity service). You could create your table using a spreadsheet program on your computer.

- Write a report describing the physical destruction of buildings, roads, and homes by the earthquake.

- Give a speech to a group of business-people in your city to convince them of the need to prepare for a possible natural disaster in your city.

- Create a newsletter with messages from people who lived through the earthquake that describe their personal experiences.

Writing Your Research Report

Writing about your research helps you bring the information together in an understandable way. When you write, you have to organize your thoughts on paper so that another person can read it and understand it. Writing can be a challenge, but it's one that brings a feeling of satisfaction when it is completed.

Using Your Unique Skills

If you want to try a different approach to presenting your research, look in *Creative Presentation Ideas* for a few creative ideas. Use your unique talents to *showcase* (exhibit) the information you have collected.

Writer's Corner

Note

There's a corner of the Internet reserved for all aspiring writers that is filled with works by famous authors from different historical eras. After reading a few stories, you may be inspired to take new and different approaches to your own writing. The corner has many resources to help your mind soar.

You're in the middle of writing an exciting story about one of your favorite characters, who is caught in a seemingly hopeless situation. You've thought about many things she could do to save herself, but none of them seems just right for your heroine.

One way to figure out what to do is to visit the *Writer's Corner* and read the writing of other authors. Here you will find the works of famous authors such as William Shakespeare, Harriet Beecher Stowe, and Anne Frank. Let your mind relax and relive the wild adventures other authors have shared before you put the wheels of your own mind into motion.

The Internet features you will use in this project are e-mail, FTP, WWW, and WAIS.

Note

Journey of the Mind

There are hundreds of stories through which your mind can wander before you even begin to write down your ideas. Follow these steps:

Finding Literature on the Internet

Gutenberg Project	anonymous FTP to **mrcnext.cso.uiuc.edu** and look for **pub/etext**
Wiretap	anonymous FTP to **130.43.43.43** and look for **/Library**
On-line Books Page	WWW to **http://www.cs.cmu.edu:8001/Web/books.html**
Poetry Archive	WWW to **http://sunsite.unc.edu/dykki/poetry/home.html**
poetry and poetry index	These WAIS sources include full text and reference information for past and present poets (see Chapter 1 for instructions on logging into WAIS sources).
Oxford Archive	anonymous FTP to **ota.ox.ac.uk** and look for **pub/ota**

1. **Find out what books are available through the Internet.**

For each of the places listed in *Finding Literature on the Internet,* there is an index or catalog of the books and poems you can find at each site. Look for files that may be named "README" or "index."

As you can see from the directory list of Wiretap in Figure 5.6, all of the electronic books are grouped by type—humor, classic, article, music, zines (magazines), fringe—making it a little easier to find something you know you will enjoy reading.

Figure 5.6

On Wiretap, you will find all kinds of electronic books and articles.

```
drwxr-xr-x   2 9013      42          512 Jul  1  1993 .cap
-rw-r--r--   1 9013      42         2197 May  9  1993 .dirs
-rw-r--r--   1 9013      42          505 May  3  1993 .files
-rw-r--r--   1 9013      42           73 Apr  5  1993 .links
drwxr-xr-x  20 9013      42          512 Jun 17 22:19 Article
drwxr-xr-x   9 9013      42         4096 May  9 21:28 Classic
drwxr-xr-x   3 9013      42         1024 Jul  1  1993 Cyber
drwxr-xr-x   3 9013      42          512 Jul 15  1993 Document
drwxr-xr-x   9 9013      42          512 Jul  1  1993 Fringe
drwxr-xr-x   7 9013      42          512 Jul  1  1993 Humor
drwxr-xr-x  11 9013      42          512 Jul  1  1993 Media
drwxr-xr-x   3 9013      42          512 Jul 11  1993 Misc
drwxr-xr-x   7 9013      42          512 Jul  1  1993 Music
-rw-r--r--   1 9013      42           98 Apr  2  1993 README
drwxr-xr-x  13 9013      42          512 Jun 19 00:03 Religion
drwxr-xr-x  16 9013      42          512 Jul  1  1993 Techdoc
drwxr-xr-x   3 9013      42         1024 Jul  1  1993 Untech
drwxr-xr-x   8 9013      42         1024 Aug  3  1993 Zines
```

2. Select one book to download to your computer.

Try this suggestion to get you started with a good short story. Select the file called `magi.txt`, which is O. Henry's *The Gift of the Magi*. Once you have found this selection in the directory, write down the exact file name and download it to your computer. When you have it on your computer, you can print it out or read it right from the computer screen. Either way, sit back and enjoy the story!

3. Brainstorm ideas for your writing.

Now that you have stimulated your creativity by reading, you might have a few ideas about how you could take one idea from the story you read and make it your own—a sort of "spinoff" story. Maybe you liked the character Delia in *The Gift of the Magi* so much that you want to write a new story in which she continues her experiences, or you could tell the same story but from the perspective of a neighbor, or even the gifts themselves could talk.

4. Choose a style of writing for your story.

There are many different types of writing—fiction, plays, nonfiction, poetry, essays, journals—that you can use to tell your story. Each type has unique qualities that lend themselves to a particular type of story. Plays, for example, consist of *dialogue* (spoken words) between different characters and an "acting out" of the story. This is very different from a poem where images are created with words and sometimes with their sounds. To get ideas for plays, you can start with the screenwriters and playwrights home page in Figure 5.7.

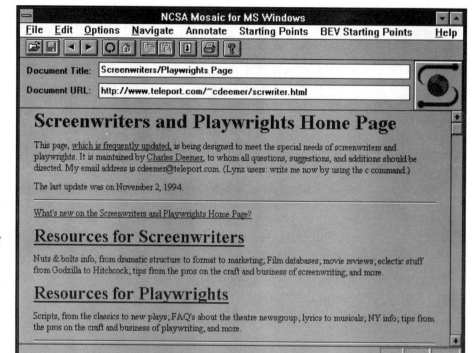

Figure 5.7

The Screen-writers and Playwrights Home Page will point you toward many playwrighting resources found on the Internet.

Begin Writing!

Now that you've developed some new ideas, you can return to your story or start a new one.

As you write, new ideas will surface, and those creative juices will begin to flow. To begin your story, you might want to look at the list of *Story Starters.*

Sharing Your Writing

Once you have finished writing, you should share it with other writers and readers. It can be a little scary to share your writing, but it is very interesting to hear what people have to say about your story. Each person will find something different and unique based on their own experiences.

Here are a few *Story Starters* for *The Gift of the Magi*:

- Write a modern version of the sacrifice and exchange of gifts (perhaps Delia sells her CD player to buy John a fancy bike seat, and he buys her favorite CDs by selling his mountain bike).

- Update the story and rewrite it through the eyes of each character.

- Change the format of the story to read like an exchange of letters between the characters or as various journal entries of either character.

- Write it from a third character's perspective, maybe a nosy neighbor who sees what's going on and gives a running commentary on what he or she sees.

To learn how to share your writing through the Internet, try the *Paperless Publishing* project in Chapter 7, which will help you find writing contests you can enter.

You're a Writer!

Congratulations! You have not only explored the writing of great writers, tapped the resources of the Internet, but also written your own story. *Writer's Corner* offers great resources for locating hard-to-find books. If you have a book assigned to you at school, you now know where you might get it easily without searching all over town for it. And, as with everything you do on the Internet, you now have a wealth of ideas for your own writing.

Hobbyists' Delight

Note

What do you do when school is out, your homework is done, and you're ready to kick back and have a good time? Are you a diehard football fan? A horse lover? A cycling nut? Maybe you prefer collecting stamps or autographs, or perhaps your idea of fun is to grab your camera and head out in pursuit of the perfect shot. Regardless of what your interests are, the Internet lets you experience them in ways you never before dreamed possible. Statistics and trivia about your favorite hobby… updates on soap operas…your favorite music group's touring schedule—a world of information is at your fingertips. And best of all, you will learn how to meet others who share your delights!

What delights you? What is the one thing you love to do above and beyond everything else? Is it playing a sport like tennis or football? Is it making things like kites or masks? Do you like to collect things like sports cards, coins, or stamps? Whatever your interest or hobby, you can find information and people to talk to about it on the Internet.

The Internet features used in this project are list servers, FTP, and Usenets.

Note ....

Pursuing Your Hobbies

Hobbies are as unique as people; they come in different varieties. You probably have a hobby of your own. Follow these steps to learn how to pursue your hobby on the Internet:

1. Focus on one hobby.

Before you begin pursuing all of your interests on the Internet, you may want to narrow down your preferences as much as possible. For example, if you search the Internet for everything that deals with music, you will come up with a list of hundreds of Internet sites and resources. Instead, focus your search with the name of a specific group or artist, or maybe one type of music. Similarly, if you want information on a sport or television show, be very specific. The "Simpsons" and "Star Trek" are just two of many shows that have their own Internet list servers. The Internet is also full of resources for sports fans, so be sure to target your main interest. That way you won't have to plow through lists of every sport from archery to volleyball when you want to find out about soccer.

So you say you don't have a hobby? Or that your hobby is so unusual that surely no one else will share your interests? Take a look at the variety of topics you can explore on the Internet in *Popular Hobbies*—and these aren't the only ones!

Popular Hobbies

Animals
Arts and crafts
Auto racing
Bagpipe playing
Baseball card collecting
Building models
Cooking
Dance
Ferrets

Guitars
Movies and movie stars
Motorcycles
Photography
Riding Rollercoasters
Science Fiction
Scouting
Trains
Travel

Tip

> You can even learn about a new hobby on the Internet. Choose an unfamiliar topic, and you will open up a whole new world!

If your hobby is very specialized or unusual, you might have to use a bit of detective work to find resources. Try broadening your search or looking for related hobbies. If you keep coming up with a dead end, ask other users for advice. It's perfectly okay to make mistakes and ask for help. Other Internet users are usually happy to help you find your way.

2. Explore the resources.

Finding resources on the Internet can be challenging and fun. As you explore, you will run across all kinds of interesting places you will want to go back to later.

You can begin your search with the places listed in *Some Places to Try* even if they do not match your topic. Try downloading the list of list servers, but be warned; it's a long file and might take a while to download! It's well worth the time, though, because the file contains a listing of all available list servers and what the discussion on those list servers is all about. You can also check out the Usenet groups that are organized around people's interests. If you need help learning about Usenet groups, read about them in Chapter 1.

COOL STUFF

Some Places to Try

List of list servers — anonymous FTP to `ftp.sura.net` and look for `pub/nic/mailing.lists`

Neon-Sign Baseball Statistics League (Rotisserie Baseball) — subscribe to the list server STATLG-L at `serv@sbccvm.bitnet`

Soap Opera Updates — Usenet group: `rec.arts.tv.soaps`

The Running Page — WWW to `http://sunsite.unc.edu/drears/running/running.html`

Science Fiction Archive — anonymous FTP to `elbereth.rutgers.edu` and look for `pub/sfl` or WWW to `http://gandalf.rutgers.edu/pub/sfl/sf-resource.guide.html`

Ceramic Arts and Pottery — subscribe to CLAYART at `listserv@ukcc.uky.edu`

You may need to brainstorm and be creative about where you look. If college sports teams is your interest, search for collegiate Gophers. These will probably have information about their sports teams—schedules, records, and maybe even awards.

3. Set a goal.

Sometimes having a goal helps focus your search. Try to find one of each of the following:

> A list server where you can exchange opinions and ideas about your hobby with others.
>
> A database of statistics, records, historical background, or trivia.
>
> A collection of files or past online discussions.

Tip Be sure to write down the places you go or keep a session log so that you can return to useful resources in the future. You can read more about session logs in Chapter 1.

4. Gather related information.

Now that you are familiar with some of the resources available for your particular area of interest, you can put your Internet skills to work by broadening your knowledge. The more you know about your hobby, the more you will enjoy it!

If you like cycling, try branching out. See if you can tap into a list of upcoming races. Pick an athlete and track his or her racing history.

Baseball fans will be delighted with the various rotisserie leagues available to Internet users. In rotisserie baseball, you pick a "dream team" of major league players, decide on starting lineups and batting orders, and send your players out to compete against other dream teams. How well your dream team players do depends on their performance in real life. If your star outfielder gets put on the injured list in real life, he has to sit out during rotisserie play, too.

If you're a fan of a certain actress, search around for information on her background. What do the critics say about her performances? What was her first role? Has she ever won an Oscar? Which other movies can you see where she has a part?

Golfing fans may find that their Internet search leads them on a journey to Scotland, the birthplace of the sport. The sky is the limit. Have fun, explore, and become an expert in the process!

Turning Your Hobby into a Business

As you learn more about your hobby, you may find that it can become a moneymaker. Many collectors, for example, meet other collectors who are looking for opportunities to buy and sell items. You can research your collectibles over the Internet and consult guides or experts for pricing information.

The Internet can get you started in the world of business; just check the places listed in *Setting Up Your Business*. Ideas for advertising, advice for small business owners, and tips for getting started are available.

As you can see, you can indulge any hobby by exploring the Internet.

Usenet Groups about Setting Up a Business

`alt.business.misc`
This group includes general discussions about managing your business, including how to start a business.

`misc.entrepreneurs`
This Usenet group includes discussions about operating a business.

`misc.forsale`
You can post messages to this group about anything you want to sell.

Guten Tag
German

Bonjour
French

Buon Giorno
Italian

Zdrastvitsye
Russian

Hello
English

Boker Tov
Hebrew

Jambo
Swahili

G'day
Australian

Konnichi Wa
Japanese

Salam Aleikum
Arabic

Adventures in Cyberspace

People, places, and events capture the adventurous side of our imagination. Whether it's a sports event, a trip to the South Pole, a political victory, a historical anniversary, or a royal wedding, everyone can identify an event that fascinates them. With the projects in this chapter, you will learn how to travel through cyberspace—the world of the Internet—to participate in special events. *Virtual Excursions* puts you in touch with people going on unique field trips or family vacations. *Challenging Contests* demands your best to compete with people all over the world in writing, problem solving, and other areas of expertise. *The Main Event* engages you as a participant, not simply a viewer. *Worldly Adventures* connects you to scientists who are on expeditions to find answers to puzzling questions. With the projects in this chapter, you can be a part of these special events, some of which may even go down in history books!

The NetCruiser software that came with this book offers an alternative way to do these activities. See Appendix C for more about this software.

Note

Virtual Excursions

Note

Virtual Excursions is a project that invites you on trips to distant and unique places with the help of the Internet and sometimes the television. ("Virtual" describes experiences that are provided by a computer, like a video game. A "virtual" excursion is a trip you experience without physically going anywhere.) With this project, you will visit exciting new places and invite others to share your own travel experiences.

People have always searched for new ways of traveling to distant lands. The Wright Brothers wanted to fly. The professor from the movie *Back to the Future* wanted to travel through time. Now, in the age of the Internet, you can travel through the computer.

On the Internet you can experience different worlds by reading descriptions about other people's trips with their class or family. The uniqueness of a particular destination is revealed to you through your discussions with other people and their own personal reports.

As you become a well-traveled passenger on these "virtual" trips and learn about different places in the world, you will discover you have a few favorites that you will want to revisit. These "virtual" travels will prepare you for any real traveling you might do.

The Internet features you will use for this project are e-mail and list servers.

Note

Joining the Trip

The only ticket you need for this field trip is an account on the Internet. With an exchange of e-mail messages, you can learn about the art collection of a museum, the geography of a distant city, or the history of a battlefield. Just follow these steps to begin your "virtual" field trip.

1. Find out what field trips you might want to join.

Before you join a field trip, you need to know where people are going. Post a brief message on a few list servers, such as the `k12.ed.science` Usenet group, which you can see in Figure 6.1. (The ones listed in *Educational List Servers* are very popular with teachers, who are the people organizing and coordinating most field trips.) Make it a

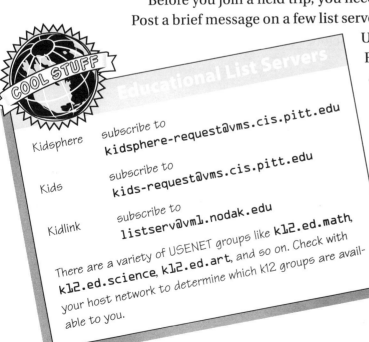

Educational List Servers

Kidsphere	subscribe to `kidsphere-request@vms.cis.pitt.edu`
Kids	subscribe to `kids-request@vms.cis.pitt.edu`
Kidlink	subscribe to `listserv@vm1.nodak.edu`

There are a variety of USENET groups like `k12.ed.math`, `k12.ed.science`, `k12.ed.art`, and so on. Check with your host network to determine which k12 groups are available to you.

```
┌─────────────────────────────────────────────────────────────────────────┐
│        Group Selection (news.itd.umich.edu  59)              h=help       │
│  17   1377  comp.sys.mac.misc        General discussions about the Apple Ma│
│  18   4318  comp.sys.mac.programmer   Discussion by people programming the A│
│  19   1415  comp.sys.mac.system      Discussions of Macintosh system softwa│
│  20   1073  comp.sys.mac.wanted      Postings of "I want XYZ for my Mac."   │
│  21     15  k12.chat.elementary      Casual conversation for elementary stu │
│  22    170  k12.chat.junior         Casual conversation for students in gr │
│  23  33612  k12.chat.senior         Casual conversation for high school st │
│  24    103  k12.chat.teacher        Casual conversation for teachers of gr │
│  25    633  k12.ed.art              Arts & crafts curricula in K-12 educat │
│  26      4  k12.ed.business         Business education curricula in grades │
│  27     47  k12.ed.comp.literacy    Teaching computer literacy in grades K │
│  28      2  k12.ed.health-pe        Health and Physical Education curricul │
│  29      2  k12.ed.life-skills      Home Economics, career education, and  │
│  30     26  k12.ed.math             Mathematics curriculum in K-12 educati │
│  31   2592  k12.ed.music            Music and Performing Arts curriculum i │
│  32     24  k12.ed.science          Science curriculum in K-12 education.  │
└─────────────────────────────────────────────────────────────────────────┘
```

Figure 6.1

As you can see, this Usenet group is quite active, which means you will probably get a good amount of responses to your posting.

```
┌─────────────────────────────────────────────────────────────────────────┐
│           k12.ed.science (19T 24A 0K 0H)                    h=help        │
│   1   +     Science Collaboration Project Addresses?     Ed Byrnes        │
│   2   +     ANNOUNCEMENT:  Fidonet echomail area - SpaceS Chris Rowan      │
│   3   +     Speaking of teaching chemistry               Greg King        │
│   4   +     JASON project                                Lori Gildow      │
│   5   +     Fall Mini-Med School                         Elizabeth K. Blatt│
│   6   +     NASA Eclipse Bulletins available via Internet Joseph B. Gurman │
│   7   +     Student Experiment Exchange                  Ed Andros        │
│   8   +     Those funny little quotes                    Tony Toews       │
│   9   +     JPL Comets conference moves to JPL           JPL Public Informa│
│  10   +     1-800 FOR SK                                 Alan Gould       │
│  11   +     VIRUS                                        CKSundberg       │
│  12   + 3   Natural Forces                               Victor Nguyen    │
│  13   + 2   Science Calendars?                           Ed Byrnes        │
│  14   +     H.S. Students Attend OSU Summer Institute at  Beth Johnston    │
│  15   +     Wanted: Best hands o                         John Tant        │
│  16   +     Sense of Balance                             Rose Woodruff    │
└─────────────────────────────────────────────────────────────────────────┘
```

short message that includes the following information:

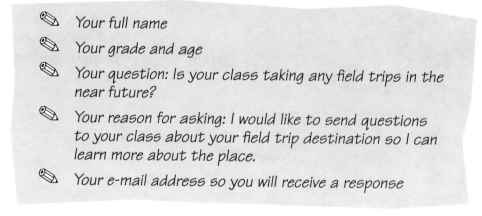

✎ *Your full name*

✎ *Your grade and age*

✎ *Your question:* Is your class taking any field trips in the near future?

✎ *Your reason for asking:* I would like to send questions to your class about your field trip destination so I can learn more about the place.

✎ *Your e-mail address so you will receive a response*

Before you send your message, read it to make sure you have asked everything you want to know.

2. Select a trip and read about the area or site.

Once you receive one or more responses to your posting, select the trip that you find most interesting. Maybe it is a place that you have never been. Maybe it is a place that you have visited but want to learn more about. No matter which trip you select, you are bound to have fun and learn something new.

Knowing a few facts about the class' destination will help you formulate questions that you can pose to the kids who are actually going on the trip. You can use the encyclopedia in your library or search the Internet for information. As you read about this new place, write down the major points of interest or sites that you want to explore. Identify specific places, such as Coit Tower in San Francisco or the Jefferson Memorial in Washington, D.C.

Sample Message

Hello, my name is Sandy. I am very interested in zoos. Because you are visiting the San Diego Zoo, would you answer these questions for me?

1. I have heard that the San Diego Zoo is not only a zoological garden but a botanical garden as well. Can you tell me some of the interesting plants that are in the zoo?

2. We've heard a lot about Gorilla Tropics and Tiger River. Can you describe these exhibits and tell me if you think they are better for animals than cages?

3. What was your favorite animal and why did you like it?

4. Do you think the San Diego Zoo is really doing anything to save endangered species? If so, what?

5. What are some of the endangered species the zoo has, and how do you think keeping them in zoos is saving them?

6. Should zoos be places to exhibit animals, or protect them, or both?

3. Send questions to the people who are going on the field trip.

Send your questions to the class before they go on their field trip so they'll be looking for the answers. You can ask detailed, factual questions such as, "In what year was the Jefferson Memorial built?" Or you can ask students for their opinions by asking questions such as, "Do you think Jefferson's ideas of democracy still exist today?" (Look at the *Sample Message* for ideas of the kinds of questions you might include in your message.)

In addition to your questions, introduce yourself, describe where you live, and explain why you are interested in their field trip.

You might want to ask the class when you can expect a response. You could also ask them to send you a postcard from their trip so you will have a picture along with the facts.

4. Share the information with people in your community.

You may be surprised by the answers you receive to your questions. There are probably other people in your community who would be interested in learning about your virtual field trip. Think of unique ways that you could share your questions and answers with others. Maybe your local newspaper would like you to write a guest editorial describing your experiences. You could also create a computer presentation using pictures, graphics, sound, and even digital movies to show what you learned. Or use the postcards you received to create a collage poster.

Strike up a conversation or debate with someone in the class. You could continue e-mail discussions about your questions as more issues arise.

You Can Be the Virtual Travel Agent

Now that you have learned from the travels of others, invite people to join your own trips in the same way. You can also become a virtual travel agent, matching virtual travelers with real trips, by creating a calendar of class trips and family vacations.

Invite Others to Join Your Trip

If you are going on a field trip with your school, post information about your trip to one of the list servers described earlier in *Educational List Servers*. You will need to post the information well in advance of the trip date so other people will have enough time to send you questions before you go. Look at *Posting Field Trip Information* for a simple way to submit your field trip information.

When you are answering the questions sent to you, try to respond as completely as possible. You are their eyes on the trip, so be as descriptive as possible. For example, you could write, "The Statue of Liberty is on an island," but it would be more descriptive and interesting to write: "The Statue of Liberty is on Liberty Island in New York Harbor, southwest of

Posting Field Trip Information

Your full name:

Your e-mail address:

Grade:

Subject of class (math, science, etc.):

Where is your excursion destination?

What are the tentative dates of your visit?

Describe the kinds of things you will see on your trip and what you think you might learn from the excursion.

Manhattan Island. She is 151 ft. (46m) high from the base she stands on to the top of the torch in her uplifted right hand. Her dress is draped like an ancient Roman toga; she also wears a crown and holds a book with the inscription 'July 4, 1776.'"

Create a Calendar of Family Travels

While field trips usually happen during the school year, families tend to take trips in the summer or during the winter holidays. By collecting and organizing information about family vacations into one calendar, you become a travel agent and can match individuals to trips they find interesting.

Post a notice of your project on a few list servers and include directions for submitting trip information. Tell people you will keep a calendar of all the trips that are sent to you. Then, ask people who want to be virtual travelers to request the calendar. They can select a trip and send their questions to the e-mail address listed. In this way, you can bring people together to see the world.

Challenging Contests

Note

In *Challenging Contests*, you will find and participate in contests related to what you like to do. For example, if you like to write, enter a sonnet-writing contest. If you like to think about the future, enter a space-colony design contest. Many groups sponsor contests through the Internet so the competition includes people from many different places.

Five intertwined rings symbolize the greatest contest in the world: the Olympic Games. Each summer or winter game happens only once every four years, and athletes dream about becoming Olympic competitors.

The Olympics provides the ultimate contest—one where training, determination, luck, and energy come together to produce Olympic champions.

Athletes who compete in the Olympics have competed in other events on the way to the top. City competitions, state competitions, regionals, nationals: the Olympics follows a long string of other contests.

The Olympics is about skill, ability, and physical challenges. But contests can be about any activity—writing, acting, painting, building, problem solving, and others—which means that there is a contest you can enter for almost anything you enjoy doing.

The Internet is full of notices about many different types of contests, which makes it possible for you to compete against people in places other than your school or city. For example, there is a contest called "Tele-Olympics" that includes participants from many different countries. Each April, kids compete in athletic events in their hometowns and then use the Internet to send their results to international judges. Later, after all of the results have been collected, the scores are combined and the final winners announced in an e-mail message. With Tele-Olympics, you can actually be a competitor in Olympic games!

> The Internet features you will use for this project are list servers, Gopher, and e-mail.

Note

Being a Contestant

The word "contestant" refers to a person participating in a contest, which is the root of the word. You usually hear the word "contestant" on television game shows and the word "competitor" at athletic events, but they mean the same thing. Regardless of what you are called during the contest, you always become a winner by participating in an event because you challenge yourself by competing. Follow these steps to find the right contest for you.

1. Use the Internet to find out about contests.

Many contest organizers post notices of upcoming contests on the Internet so the information will get to a large number of people in a variety of geographic areas. It would be easy to find contests if there were one big list of them, but unfortunately, as of the writing of this book, a list of contests did not exist. So, you will need to hunt contest notices down in different places on the Internet.

Contests that are educational, like the sonnet-writing contest, can be found on educational list servers and educational networks, such as Academy One. Contests dealing with a particular subject area, like science, can be found on subject-area list servers and special Gophers, such as NASA Spacelink. Check *Where to Search for a Contest* for a few places to begin your search.

Where to Search for a Contest

Learning Village
telnet to **nptn.org** and log-in as **visitor**; look in the "special events" menu

Educational List Servers
check the list in Virtual Excursions

One of the most well-known and popular contests on the Internet is *The Internet Hunt.* In this contest, you are given a list of questions that can be answered by getting information from different Internet resources. The challenge is to find the answers in different places on the Internet. People all over the world play it every month. Winners receive prizes for being the first to send in a perfect set of answers. You can find the contest's most recent posting in *The Internet Hunt.*

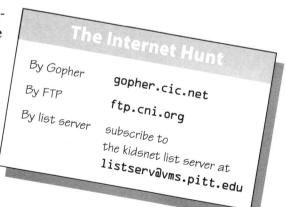

The Internet Hunt

By Gopher   `gopher.cic.net`

By FTP   `ftp.cni.org`

By list server   subscribe to the kidsnet list server at `listserv@vms.pitt.edu`

2. Read the requirements of the contest.

One of the keys to winning a contest is to find out exactly what the judges are looking for. In addition to the contest deadline, there may be other rules you need to know, such as:

- ✓ Registration Procedures
- ✓ Submission Formats
- ✓ Contest Deadlines

Challenge yourself. Try something new. You may be the winner of the next Internet Hunt.

3. Enter a contest.

Once you find a contest that you want to enter, plan your strategy. For instance, after reading the *Sonnet-Writing Contest* posting, you might make the following plan:

1. Learn about the structure of sonnets and the difference between Petrarchan and Shakespearean sonnets by Feb. 28.

2. Read three sonnets written by different authors by Mar. 15.

3. Write a first draft of my own sonnet by Mar. 22.

4. Ask two people whose writing I respect to review my sonnet by Mar. 30.

5. Make revisions and type up the final draft of my sonnet by Apr. 15.

6. Submit my sonnet (and any additional information required) to the contest by the deadline: Apr. 30.

Notice that the sample plan includes dates that are mini-deadlines. By making these, you help yourself plan ahead.

Sonnet-Writing Contest

LEARNING VILLAGE/ACADEMY ONE
INTERNET SONNET CONTEST
FOR STUDENTS AGES 13-19

Academy One invites entries from students for original sonnets written within the last 3 years. Sonnets may be submitted in the Petrarchan (Italian) or Shakespearean (English) sonnet forms. All entries must be submitted by e-mail on or before April 30. Judging will take place in early May. Sonnets will be judged on the basis of conformity to the meter and rhyme of the sonnet form, imagery, and originality of expression.

For further information, send e-mail to aa005@nptn.org.

Here Comes the Judge

In this activity, you can be the judge by creating your own contest and offering prizes or recognition. Maybe you are interested in space travel. What kind of contest based on this topic might be interesting? Perhaps something like the Space Colony Contest, which asks people to submit designs for a human colony in space, would be intriguing. The winning design might help scientists create a real space colony. Check *Contest Ideas* for suggestions of contests you might want to sponsor.

Contest Ideas

- Create a set of crossword puzzles or word games for people to solve.
- Ask for skits written about a historical or current situation and judge them on how humorous and creative they are.
- Collect short science fiction stories and choose the best based on the creativity of the story and the logic of the author's predictions.
- Hold a competition for computer-designed artwork.

Create Your Own Contest

You can sponsor your own contest with a little planning and creativity. Decide on contest requirements *before* you invite people to participate.

Here are some questions to ask yourself:

> ❓ *What is the topic?*
>
> ❓ *What do you want people to submit?*
>
> ❓ *What is the deadline?*
>
> ❓ *If you are collecting written responses, are there limits to how long they can be?*
>
> ❓ *If people are searching for answers to specific questions, how will they get access to the questions at the same time and in a fair way? (You could use the trivia hunt you created if you did the project Trivia Treasure Hunt in Chapter 5.)*

Before you post anything on the Internet, try the contest out on your friends. This way, you can check to make sure you've included all the steps.

Note ..... When you subscribe to a list server, you are adding yourself to a list of e-mail recipients. When you post a message on a list server, you are sending an e-mail message to everyone else who has subscribed to the list.

List Servers for Posting Your Contest

KIDZMAIL	subscribe to listserv@asuacad.bitnet post to kidzmail@asuacad.bitnet
KIDCAFE	subscribe to listserv@ndsuvm1.bitnet post to kidcafe@ndsuvm1.bitnet

Prizes and Recognition

Everyone loves competing for a prize even if you aren't offering cars, diamonds, or free trips! Think about what would be meaningful to your contest participants. For example, one of the prizes for Internet Hunt winners is a free subscription to an Internet magazine. It is pretty certain that anyone playing the Internet Hunt will enjoy this prize. Or maybe you want to create recognition certificates to send across the network. You can type up a one-page document that includes the name of the contest, the person's name, and a sentence that describes what they did in the contest. Perhaps you'll find you have as much fun competing in contests as in creating them. Keep in mind the old saying: "By challenging others, you challenge yourself."

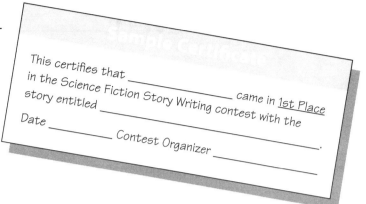

This certifies that _____ came in <u>1st Place</u> in the Science Fiction Story Writing contest with the story entitled _____.

Date _____ Contest Organizer _____

The Main Event

Note

What big events capture your imagination? The Super Bowl? The Oscar awards? Presidential elections? People all over the world eagerly follow these and many other events. The Internet is a great tool that lets you obtain information and talk to people before, during, and after *The Main Event*. For many of these big events, people create online resources that you can tap into for background information, daily or hourly updates, and connections to people who rank up there with you as fantastic fans.

You have read all the magazine articles, you have watched all the preview television shows, you have seen all the nominated films—you are fully prepared for an evening at the Oscars. It is going to be a long night in front of the television, so you have a stock of snacks and sodas ready to go. Some people might say you are obsessed with the Oscars, but you look forward to the event all year because you enjoy movies and dream of becoming a famous director. The Oscars help you learn the ropes of the profession and the secrets of film style.

Sound familiar? Maybe you look forward to a different kind of big event—sports championships or musical concerts—but chances are it is related to a favorite hobby that you may have explored in the project called *Hobbyist's Delight* in Chapter 5. You may be a big fan of the people who are well known and successful in your area of interest.

Fans are very important. They show support, they share their enthusiasm, and they help attract more people to the event. This project offers you new ways to express your "fanatical" feelings and meet others who share them.

Note

The Internet features you will use in this project are Gopher, telnet, list servers, and WWW.

Your Connection to the Big Events

In every month of the year, there is some kind of big event happening somewhere in the world. While you may only know about those that happen in America, such as the Grammy awards for music, important events happen all around the world. For example, soccer's World Cup takes place in a different country every four years with teams from many different countries competing to be the best in the world. Another main event occurred in South Africa when Nelson Mandela became South Africa's first Black president—a stunning achievement for a country that for so long supported the policy of apartheid, which discriminates against people of color. His inauguration was televised around the world.

You can tune into current world events by following these steps.

1. Find an upcoming event that interests you.

You will want to find an event that is happening in the near future. The nearer in time the event is, the more attention there will be. The media—newspapers, magazines, and television—are good sources of articles that preview upcoming events.

Big Events in the World

Space Shuttle Launch

Nobel Prize Awards

The 200th Anniversary of the U.S. Constitution

Baseball's World Series

Solar Eclipse

Wimbledon Tennis Championships

Earth Day

The Grammy Music Awards

The Iditarod Dog Sled Race

Many events are seasonal, such as the Super Bowl, which always happens in January. Spring signals spring training for baseball. Summer brings musical concert tours. In election years, fall is election time. Think about what season it is now and what events are typical of the season. *Big Events in the World* will provide you with more event ideas.

2. Locate information about the event and find people who are also interested in it.

Once you have chosen an event to explore on the Internet, look for resources that were created only for that event as well as for permanent sites that include a variety of special

Special Event Information

Academy One, special events section
telnet to **yfn2.ysu.edu** and log in as **visitor**

The Scout Report
gopher or telnet to **is.internic.net**
and look in "Internic Information Services"; or WWW to
http://www.internic.net/infoguide.html.
This report offers a regular update of all new sites and
resources on the Internet.

List of list servers
anonymous FTP to **crvax.sri.com** or
128.18.30.65 or anonymous FTP to **ftp.sura.net**
and look in the directory **pub/nic** for the file named
interest-groups.txt.

event resources. Check in *Special Event Information* for the addresses of the permanent sites. Many times notices of event activities on the Internet will be posted on list servers that are related to the subject of the event, such as politics, sports, science, literature, and others.

If you subscribe to the Scout Report—a weekly report sent to you through electronic mail—it will inform you of the newest sites on the Internet that may focus on an upcoming event. The report includes list servers, WWW pages, menu items on a Gopher, or even a new telnet site.

Tip

If you are at a loss for where to look for information about an event, do a Veronica search of Gopherspace (see Chapter 1 for a review of Veronica). Another idea is to find a WWW page related to the event that has links to other Internet resources.

3. Check for daily updates.

Once you locate a resource, write down the address and any log-in instructions. You will want to consult these resources before, during, and after the event for all kinds of updated information. If you have subscribed to a list server, there will be new messages from other Internet users. If you're using a Gopher, there may be updated results or background information. If you've found a WWW page, there may be new images you can download.

Through some of these resources, you have a chance to share your opinions and feelings about what is happening with people who care about the event as much as you do. If the winner of a sports event is a surprise to everyone, share your theory about why that happened through a list server. If you absolutely loved the new blockbuster movie,

tell people why. You will probably get some interesting responses to your opinions. You may want to track results of sporting events or election results and share them in a report at school. You can enhance the facts with the opinions you and your online *correspondents*—the people you communicate with—have shared about the event.

Events Bring People Together

Because soccer's World Cup was in the United States for the first time ever in 1994, there were many opportunities to see and meet people from other countries. Many people traveled to the United States for the first time to watch the games. More than soccer matches took place: people saw each other's traditional dress, they heard a variety of languages, and television programs included pictures and scenes from other countries. While the focus may have been on soccer, the World Cup experience went far beyond the game.

Figure 6.2 shows another sports passion that has made it onto the Internet: hockey.

Figure 6.2

Hockey mania on a WWW page

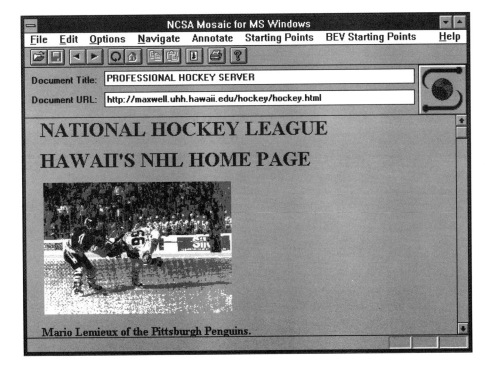

Make an Internet Event Guide

Perhaps you have built quite a collection of Internet event resources. Consider sharing it with others; they will appreciate your help. An Internet Event Guide prepared by someone who cares about certain events and has taken the time to pull online addresses together into one list can be quite valuable. See the Professional Hockey Server entry in the *Internet Guide to the National Hockey League* for an example of how to type it up.

> **Internet Guide to the National Hockey League**
>
> Professional Hockey Server   WWW to
> http://maxwell.uhh.hawaii.edu/
> hockey/hockey.html

Big events attract attention. Using the Internet to track the event lets you become an active participant rather than a passive bystander. Sharing your information encourages more sharing and lets you meet other enthusiasts. Enjoy the experience!

Worldly Adventures

Note

Are you an adventurer? Do you want to travel the world, braving physical challenges, to find answers to scientific questions? If so, *Worldly Adventures* is the project for you. Through the Internet, you will connect with scientists who are out there right now in the midst of a scientific expedition. Whether it is a journey across Antarctica or a dive to the bottom of the sea, you can use the Internet to communicate with scientists, read articles that describe the purpose of the expedition, and give daily updates of the scientists' progress to your friends.

When most people hear the word "science," they think of people in white coats in laboratories handling glass beakers and petri dishes on spotless countertops. However, this is only one vision of science. There are also scientists that pursue adventurous and sometimes dangerous expeditions that take them into previously unexplored territory. They go to the depths of the sea, the tops of mountains, across deserts and tundra, and through jungles to find answers to questions they have about how the world works.

While laboratories provide controlled environments for experiments, not every scientific question can be answered in a lab. This is why some scientists go on expeditions to collect data and samples from the field. For instance, if an Alaskan scientist is trying to figure out why the antelope population is declining in the Alaskan interior, the answer can only be found by going out into the wilderness and observing the behavior of the antelopes; this is called "field research."

Scientists doing field research often face interesting challenges. They may have to learn how to be prepared campers, how to survive in extreme weather conditions, and how to transport the data they have collected safely back to their laboratories.

Now that you know a few general facts about scientific expeditions, follow the steps in this project to get connected to a real scientific expedition happening right now.

The Internet features you will use in this project are e-mail and list servers.

Note

Scientists in Training

It takes a great deal of preparation and training to become a scientist. But with the Internet, you can join the team from your home and learn "on the job."

1. Find out what expeditions are currently underway or upcoming in the near future.

Because there isn't one calendar for all scientific expeditions, you will need to contact a few organizations and projects that help connect scientists with people who are interested in their mission. Here are four organizations that offer current information about many different scientific adventures.

Academy One

While you may be familiar with Academy One's ongoing projects, you may not know that they also support scientific expeditions. In 1994, they worked with a team of French scientists who studied the austral ocean (the ocean in the Southern hemisphere) and the continent of Antarctica. The organizers at Academy One established two list servers specifically for this project, one for English-speaking participants and one for French-speaking participants.

Live From...Other Worlds

As a joint project of the National Aeronautical and Space Administration (NASA) and the Public Broadcasting Service (PBS), *Live From...Other Worlds* uses television and computers to connect people with scientific expeditions. Television shows are aired on local PBS stations, and discussions and background information are available through the Internet.

The Jason Project

This project was started by the scientist who discovered the Titanic, Dr. Robert D. Ballard, because he received so many letters from students asking how he made his discovery. Each year students around the country join scientists on a variety of adventures through computer communication and satellite links. The most recent expedition was a trip to the country of Belize in Central America to study the health of planet Earth by exploring a rainforest and the largest barrier reef in the Western Hemisphere.

National Education and Technology Alliance (NETA)

NETA promotes networking in all grades from kindergarten to 12th grade. Recently they supported an expedition called Project EarthTrek, which was the first global surface *circumnavigation* (going completely around the globe) attempt ever made. The scientific team created an *amphibious* vehicle, one that operates on water and land.

These organizations may provide e-mail access and even satellite connections that you can coordinate with your school or local public station. You will find the addresses for the organizations in *Organizations Supporting Scientific Expeditions.*

2. Learn about the scientists' mission.

After you have selected an expedition to follow, collect information to learn more about it. Each expedition will have a unique purpose. Find out why the scientists are working in a particular part of the world. Many times you can find background information about the mission, the type of research, and the scientific team, as well as how you can participate in the expedition through the computer.

Organizations Supporting Scientific Expeditions

Academy One	send an e-mail message to **a-1@nptn.org** for information about current expeditions.
Jason Project	for more information, call the Jason Foundation for Education at (617) 487-9995.
Live From... Other Worlds	subscribe to the list server, livefrom, by sending a subscription message to **listmanager@quest.arc.nasa.gov**.
NETA	send an e-mail message to **neta@pipeline.com** for more information.

Every project will be designed a little bit differently. Some people will create a list server that they will use to distribute messages from the field, background materials, and questions from subscribers to the list server. Other projects will establish a Gopher or telnet site to organize all of the information and communication. Because each situation is different, pay close attention to the instructions you receive when you sign up to participate.

Ask questions.

Hopefully, the expedition you find interesting will provide a way for you to send questions for the scientists to answer. As you read the background information and the updates from the scientists in the field, develop questions to help yourself better understand what is happening. Be as specific and detailed as you can so the scientists can fully answer your question.

- What kind of containers do you keep your samples in?
- How do you record your observations?
- What are you hoping to learn through this expedition?
- Why did you choose this location for your expedition?

4. Update your class or friends as the expedition progresses.

Share the expedition adventure with your class and friends by providing regular updates on the progress of the scientific mission. Sometimes there will be good news and sometimes the scientists will have setbacks. There also may be opportunities to help the mission.

In a recent adventure to Antarctica, a small plane carrying several members of the team and a great deal of equipment crashed in Chile, a country on the west side of South America. Thankfully, there were just a few minor injuries. However, the equipment was destroyed. Without more money, the expedition would have ended. When students heard about this, they collected money from local communities to help the scientists. Instantly they became part of the team.

You may want to provide updates in the form of a daily or weekly newsletter. You can include a review of the day's or week's activities, copies of messages sent by other people, profiles of team members, and anything else you think might be interesting about this expedition. Use your computer to type the stories, draw pictures or maps, and organize the information. Then print it out for everyone to read.

Planning a Local Expedition

The best way to understand the purpose of scientific expeditions is to try one yourself. What is unique about where you live? Are there special plants or animals? Are you near the mountains or the sea? Answering these questions will help you create a scientific question that you and your friends can research. For instance, if you live by the sea, you might want to explore whether sea turtles lay eggs on a nearby beach.

The Research Trip

Once you have a question, plan an expedition to observe and collect data. Think about the supplies you'll need for your expedition and how you will collect the information you need to answer your question.

Keep a Log or Journal

All scientists keep a log or journal filled with descriptions of their observations. While something may seem insignificant at the time, a week later it may help answer a key question. Your notes will become very valuable for you, so keep them in a safe place, away from damaging elements like water.

Hopefully, you were able to answer your scientific question through your work on your expedition. If not, think about changing your question or gathering different data. Many times scientists have to go on four or five expeditions before they find an answer. All scientists have one thing in common: They never stop searching for answers.

Guten Tag
German

Bonjour
French

Buon Giorno
Italian

Ní Hâo Mà
Mandarin

Zdrastvitsye
Russian

Hello
English

Boker Tov
Hebrew

Jambo
Swahili

G'day
Australian

Buenos Días
Spanish

Konnichi Wa
Japanese

Salam Aleikum
Arabic

Chapter Seven

Share Your Ideas

How do you tell the world about your great ideas? Maybe you've thought of getting them published in a book or a magazine, recorded onto a CD, shown in an art gallery, or broadcast on the news. Now the Internet makes this even easier by offering all kinds of electronic journals, zines (magazines), galleries, and news services. Experience the *Gallery of the Future* by exhibiting your art on the network. Become part of a world-wide news team in *Networked News*. Compose the music that's playing in your head by accessing the *Musical Outlets* of the Internet. Share your writing electronically with *Paperless Publishing*. Now that the Internet is here, your ideas can fly high and soar around the world.

Note

You can also participate in these activities by using the NetCruiser software that came with this book. Turn to Appendix C to find out more about this software.

Gallery of the Future

Note

The computer and the Internet have changed many aspects of society, including how art is created and displayed. Many artists are now using computers instead of paintbrushes and pens to create their art. They also are using the Internet to send their creations to a worldwide audience. How might Internet access change the way that art is displayed in galleries? What will the gallery of the future look like? In this project, you will find images of art on the Internet, create your own computer art, and contribute your creations to a *Gallery of the Future*.

Art galleries have existed for hundreds of years. In earlier centuries, galleries took the form of personal art collections displayed in private homes. Galleries now are places that are open to the public, many times with frequently changing displays of different artists with a range of media (materials) and presentations.

Today you can find art galleries almost anywhere. In large cities there are often many galleries that support a range of artistic styles. Artists work very hard to prepare a collection of their work for exhibition at a gallery.

A new type of gallery is now being created on the Internet. Online collections of artistic images can be found, viewed, and even printed from your computer. While there are many images of art made from a variety of materials—oil paints, clay, watercolors—there is also a new kind of art finding its way into these online galleries. *Computer-generated art* describes a new approach that artists use to create beautiful and interesting pictures and images. To create computer-generated art, artists use computer programs—ranging from simple graphics to elaborate art studio programs—that provide tools for creating art on your computer. Other examples of computer-generated art include holograms, 3-D illusions, and any other type of computer graphics.

Note

The Internet features you will use in this project are list servers, Usenet, Gopher, WWW, and anonymous FTP.

Creating and Displaying Computer Art

Tapping into the galleries of the future and even contributing your own art is a fun and interesting experience. Just follow these steps.

1. Collect art images from the Internet.

Finding art on the Internet is great fun because there are so many different places to go. Each site listed in *Online Galleries* has one or more types of art. Look for files with names like README or Index to learn the exact instructions for downloading the images into your computer.

Online Galleries

3-D graphics	http://www.mcs.net/~wallach/freeart/buttons.html.
ASCII Library	gopher to **cs4sun.cs.ttu.edu** or **gopher.cs.ttu.edu**. This site includes many image libraries, not only the ASCII one. Look in the "Art & Images" menu.
The OTIS Project	anonymous FTP to **sunsite.unc.edu** and look in the directory path **pub/multimedia/pictures/OTIS** or anonymous FTP to **aql.gatech.edu** and look in the directory **pub/OTIS**. This is a library of hundreds of images, animation, and files of artist information.
Smithsonian Museum	anonymous FTP to **sunsite.unc.edu** and look in the directory **pub/multimedia/pictures/smithsonian**.
Dallas Museum of Art	gopher to **gopher.unt.edu** but send any questions through e-mail to **dma@gopher.unt.edu**. Look in the Dallas Resources menu; instructions for downloading images are included.
The Andy Warhol Museum Home Page	http://fridge.antaire.com:80/warhol/. This includes a tour of the museum and samples of various works by the artist.

For instance, in the ASCII Library you will find images, like those in Figure 7.1, that were created using the regular keys on the keyboard. ASCII is the most basic computer language, one that every computer speaks. So, art created in ASCII can be viewed by all machines without any special software.

Figure 7.1

Many creatures and designs can be found in the ASCII Library (see Online Galleries for information on finding this resource).

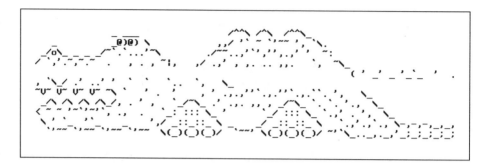

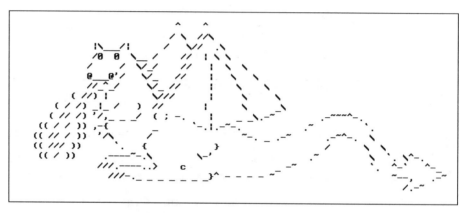

In the Dallas Museum of Art, you will find images of famous paintings and pieces of sculpture that are in the museum's collection; you can see an example in Figure 7.2. (These are in GIF89a format, so make sure your viewing software reads this format. If it doesn't, you can download a program called Compushow from this site.)

There are a number of different computer formats for graphic files, such as TIFF, PICT, and ASCII. You don't need to be too concerned about which format the art files are in because most graphical-viewing software programs include a number of translators. These computer utilities translate files into formats readable by your viewing program.

Tip

To view many of the image files you find in an online gallery, you will need some type of viewing software. The University of Texas provides many of these programs and other picture-related resources on their FTP site. Anonymous FTP to **bongo.cc.utexas.edu** and look at the files in the directory called **gifstuff**. Download the files you need.

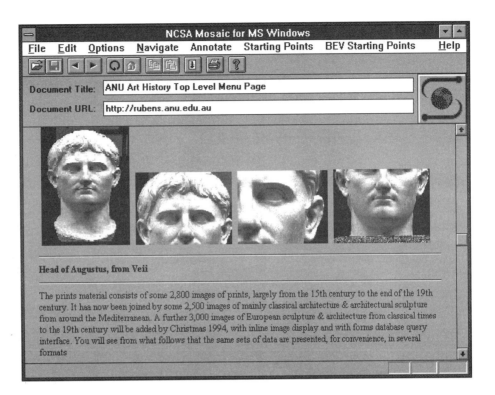

Figure 7.2

Artserve, from the Australian National University, has a collection of digitized art.

2. Create your own art using your computer.

As you start to explore your own artistic talents, ask yourself some questions about the images you have already collected from online galleries. Which one really attracts your attention? Why? What quality is the most intriguing? Challenge yourself to include this quality in the art you create.

To create art using your computer, it is helpful to have a computer drawing or painting program that includes a set of artistic tools. However, it is also possible to use a basic word processor to create ASCII art. No matter what you use to create your art, be sure to save it in a common format such as ASCII (also called "text"), PICT, or TIFF. (Use PICT or TIFF formats to save a picture created with a draw or paint program.) This process will help you when you get to Step 4 and upload your art to an online gallery.

3. Work with another person to create a collaborative work of art.

Sometimes it's fun to collaborate with an artistic keypal and create a unique work of art together. It's easy to do, too! Just have one person begin the creation with a simple artistic design. Then send it over the Internet to the other person who can add more elements—such as color or 3-D effects—to the design. Keep sending it back and forth until you both are pleased with your work of art.

If you don't already have a keypal who is interested in collaborating with you, post a message on one or more of the list servers or Usenet groups listed in *On-line Art Discussions* for a list of art groups and list servers. Then you can make a new friend and new art at the same time.

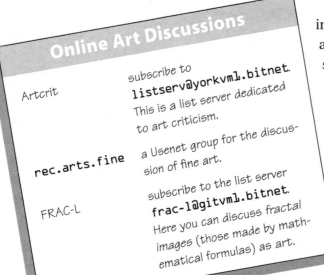

Online Art Discussions

Artcrit	subscribe to **listserv@yorkvm1.bitnet.** This is a list server dedicated to art criticism.
rec.arts.fine	a Usenet group for the discussion of fine art.
FRAC-L	subscribe to the list server **frac-l@gitvm1.bitnet.** Here you can discuss fractal images (those made by mathematical formulas) as art.

4. Contribute your art to an online gallery or image library.

It's time to get your artistic creation out into the public domain. Begin with a well-established site such as the one in *Where to Send Your Art*. As you find others on the Internet, add them to your list. Once you've contributed your creation, people from all over the world will be able to download and view your individual or collaborative art.

Also check with the people or organizations that maintain the image libraries you visited in Step 1. Several of them may be looking for new art to add to their collection. When you log in, look at the initial screen for an e-mail address where you can send a message asking if you can submit your art and how to do it.

Where to Send Your Art

alt.binaries.pictures.fine-art.graphics
a Usenet group for submitting and distributing computer-generated art.

Local Exhibition

To expand your artistic vision and skills, it helps to get honest and constructive comments from family, friends, and other viewers of your work. If you organize a local exhibition of what you've done, you can get feedback from people in your hometown. It might be interesting to compare comments from people who know you to those from the worldwide Internet audience.

Create a Personal Portfolio

Prepare several works of art before you have an exhibition. As you finish each one, keep it in a safe place, such as an artist's *portfolio* (a large case or folder) or two large pieces of cardboard taped together to make a large folder. Each time you add another artistic image to your collection, you are enlarging the portfolio from which you can choose the best pieces to include in your exhibition.

Use one of your computer-generated art pieces in a flyer inviting people to your exhibition. Because the art has been saved on disk, you

can copy and paste it into the flyer. (Look in the user's guide of your word processing program for copy and paste instructions.)

The flyer will give people an idea of what they can expect. Be sure to include the correct date, time, and place.

Transform a Regular Place into a Gallery

Look around. Any regular place—the garage, your bedroom, the porch, or even the bathroom—can be transformed into an art gallery. All you have to do is find a place that lets everyone easily see your work.

Be as creative with the space as you were with your art. For instance:

Hang pictures across the space with fishing line. Fishing line is made out of clear nylon, so it would look like the pictures were suspended in midair.

Attach pictures to all sides of a cardboard box.

Attach pictures to the ceiling so people have to lie down to look at them.

Networked News

Note

Do you think you want to be a journalist? With *Networked News* you can create your own news bureau with your friends and be a regular source of news for several different youth news wires.

Every night around 6 or 7 P.M., you can watch at least one hour of news on television. Approximately every 90 seconds, a news anchorperson describes a different event. Did you ever wonder how the television news agencies know about the things that are happening? Or how newspaper publishers find information about the stories they cover?

Most news agencies have several news *bureaus* (offices) scattered around their area of interest—a city, a state, the county, or even the world. These bureaus have a news *staff*, a collection of employees, that monitors

the events in their local area and sends in reports to the main news agency.

If a news agency is too small to support many different bureaus scattered around an area, they may use stories available through news wires. These computer networks transmit stories from news staffs all over the world. The news agency can then decide which stories to use in their newspaper or television news program.

With the Internet, many new wire services are being developed with special types of stories. For example, some wires carry stories about a single country. Others have stories written only by teenagers. These wire services are always looking for new sources of stories, so here's your chance to be a reporter, editor, or even the founder of a local news bureau.

Note The Internet features you will use in this project are e-mail, anonymous FTP, telnet, WWW, and Gopher.

The News Bureau

Although a news bureau can include hundreds of people, you can create one with only one person: yourself. Or if you happen to have some friends who want to form a news bureau, invite them to participate as well. The bureau can be as big or small as you like. (The advantage to having more people is that there will be more stories to send.) Once you are ready to go, follow these steps:

1. Decide which jobs everyone wants.

There are three basic jobs in a news bureau: editor-in-chief, copy editor, and reporter. The editor-in-chief decides which stories are newsworthy and meet the guidelines of the news agency. The copy editor reads stories to correct spelling and grammatical errors and to make sure that the writing is understandable. And the reporter researches and writes the story.

If you are the only person in the bureau, then your choice is easy. You do every job: You write the stories, you edit them, and you send what you've written to the news agency. If you are working with a team of friends, you and your friends can decide which role each of you really wants to have. You can figure out which jobs you like by trading jobs from time to time.

2. Contact youth news services about being a bureau for them.

Follow the directions for contacting several news services in *News Agencies for Youth* and ask for instructions for establishing your news bureau. You will need to get directions and guidelines for the format of a story, which might include the maximum or minimum length, appropriate story topics, and how to type it up (double-spaced lines, for instance). You may want to subscribe to the news services and read the stories for a few weeks to become familiar with the type of news distributed by each agency. Then you can decide which agency you want to write for. Figure 7.3 shows an example of a student-run newswire.

News Agencies for Youth

Project NEWSDAY

for information and a registration form, send e-mail to **newsday@bonita.cerf.fred.org**. Project NEWSDAY is an annual project sponsored by the Global SchoolNet Foundation.

WYN (World's Youth News)

send e-mail to **wyn@freenet.hut.fi**. You will get back information about subscribing to WYN and establishing a news bureau.

KNSO, a joint effort of
Operation Uplink II and *The Knoxville News-Sentinel*

telnet to **use.usit.net** and use the log-in and password **knso**. This is an experimental noncommercial news service loosely targeted at junior high and high school students. It includes articles and information drawn from *The Knoxville News-Sentinel* as well as other sources. To send comments or suggestions, send e-mail to **knsoedit@use.usit.net**.

The Global Student Newswire Project

WWW to **http://www.jou.ufl.edu/forums/gsn**.
This is a multimedia source of formal news stories on the Internet by student journalists and media scholars.

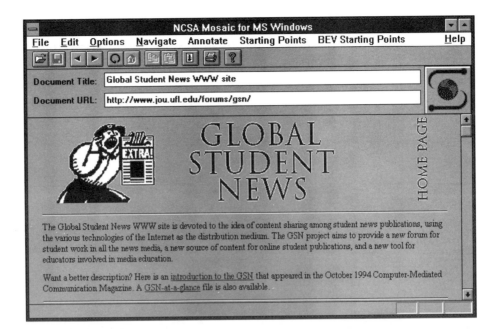

Figure 7.3

The Global Student Newswire Project is a great example of a student-run news bureau.

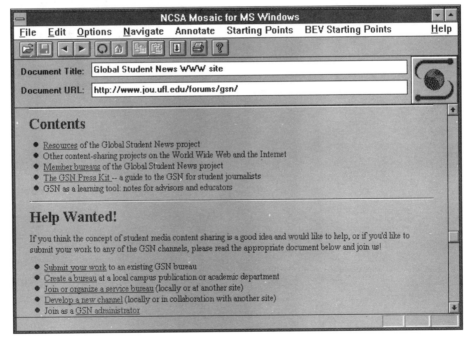

3. Set a schedule for sending stories to the news service you have selected.

Once you have the information you need to establish your news bureau, you will need to create a list of story assignments and submission deadlines. If you are working with a team of journalists, you will need to include several mini-deadlines so that the copy editor and the editor-in-chief have time to read and correct the story. If you are working on your own, leave yourself some extra time to proofread your story before sending it to the agency. Waiting until the night before the due date often gets the creative juices flowing, but this strategy may not produce a well-written story.

It's also a good idea to read other news articles to analyze writing styles and story ideas. There are several newspapers that make their articles available over the Internet. Check one of those listed in *Newspapers on the Net.* Figure 7.4 shows some *USA Today* pages.

Newspapers on the Net

Columbus Dispatch	gopher to **gopher.freenet.columbus.oh.us** and select "News, Weather, Calendar." You can read a daily newspaper from Columbus, Ohio.
French Language Press Review	gopher to **gopher.tc.umn.edu** and select "News." The French embassy in Washington, D.C., delivers a free daily review of the French press.
Norfolk Virginian-Pilot	WWW to **http://www.infi.net/pilot/vpls.html**.
Palo Alto Weekly	WWW to **http://www.service.com/PAW/home.html**. The Palo Alto Weekly carries news, real estate information, movie and restaurant reviews, and more.
USA Today	telnet to **freenet-in-a.cwru.edu** or **kanga.ins.cwru.edu** and log in as **guest**; only registered Freenet users have access to USA Today, but registration information can be found after you've logged on.

```
<<< NPTN/USA TODAY HEADLINE NEWS >>>

 1 About the Electronic News Center

 2 Headline News Summary
 3 Weather
 4 Snapshots

 5 NEWS
 6 MONEY
 7 SPORTS
 8 LIFE
------------------------------------------------
h=Help, x=Exit Free-Net, "go help"=extended help
```

Figure 7.4

USA Today is one of many newspapers available online.

```
TAR HEELS REMAIN NO. 1:
   North Carolina had an easy time in its only game of the week
and an even easier time holding on to the top spot in the USA
TODAY:CNN college men's basketball poll Sunday. The Tar Heels
(6-0) routed Virginia Military 129-89 Saturday. They also secured
31 of 34 first-place votes in the balloting to grab No. 1 for the
third straight week. UCLA got two first-place votes and Arkansas
got the other.

ARIZ. ST., VILLANOVA ARE UPSET:
   Phillip Chime's layup with 10.7 seconds remaining in overtime
Sunday night lifted Texas-San Antonio to an 87-85 upset of No. 15
ArizonState. The Sun Devils (5-2) led by 10 points in the second
half. Then-No. 25 Villanova (4-3) dropped out of the USA TODAY:CNN
college men's basketball poll after losing to Philadelphia-rival
St. Joseph's 60-57 Sunday afternoon.

JAZZ WIN 8TH STRAIGHT ON ROAD:
   Karl Malone scored 27 points and Jeff Hornacek 20, including
nine late in the fourth quarter, to lead the Utah Jazz to a 101-98
victory over the Milwaukee Bucks Sunday. It was Utah's team-record
eighth consecutive road win. Also: New Jersey 103, Miami 102;
Shown 50%, press <SPACE> for more, 'q' to quit, or 'h' for help
```

4. Find and write the news stories.

You've got your news bureau up and running, you know your deadlines, and you are reading other news stories. Now it's time to go out and find a story to write about. It may help to ask yourself some questions:

> *What is going on in my community?*
>
> *What are people talking about?*
>
> *What aren't people talking about that I think needs to be discussed?*
>
> *What good things do I see happening?*
>
> *What stories fit the topic guidelines of the news agency?*

Creating Your Own Newspaper

To expand your work as a news bureau, think about creating your own local newspaper with the stories you've written. Because you are covering local events and people, your community will be interested in your stories. You've already got the stories, now all you need is to print your paper and give it to people.

Laying It Out

There are many desktop publishing and word processing programs that can help you lay out your stories in columns like a newspaper. Check the program's user guide to find out how to make columns and how to cut and paste the text of your story into the layout.

Getting It Printed

You may need to do a little bit of research to find a printer or copy shop that will give you a discount on the printing of your newspaper. They may even donate their services. If you aren't able to arrange this, you may want to ask a few businesses to advertise in your paper for a small fee. Then you can use this money to pay for printing costs.

Journalistic Resources

John Makulowich's JList:
anonymous FTP to `ftp.clark.net` in directory
path `pub/journalism/jlist2b.txt`. This is a
compendium of Internet resources for journalists.

If you get stuck, check *Journalistic Resources*. Maybe you'll find an answer to get you back on track. With all the newsworthy stories in the world, a journalist's job is never over; there's always another story.

Musical Outlets

Note

Whether you like rock, jazz, funk, rap, or classical music, the Internet is a great place to find musical discussions, resources, and even sound files of musical recordings. While the *Musical Outlets* project will get you in touch with these musical sites, composing a new number-one hit is up to you.

Do you hear music when you daydream? Do you tap your pencils against the table? Are you ever seen *without* a Walkman on your head? If you fit this description, use this project to develop your talent as a musician. Take small steps towards composing your own song with help from other musicians and musical resources on the Internet.

Writing original songs is a creative process similar to writing a story or painting a picture. It takes a combination of talent, motivation, and skill. You can't be taught talent or motivation, but you can learn certain skills that will give you new ways of applying your creative ideas.

As a composer, you decide the tempo of the song, the instruments to be used, and even the lyrics. While it may seem a little overwhelming, you can take it one piece at a time and end up with a great original song.

Note

The Internet features you will use for this project are e-mail, list servers, Usenet, WAIS, and anonymous FTP.

Composing an Original Song

If you talk to a group of songwriters, each person in the group will describe a different technique for writing an original song. Some may wake up in the middle of the night with an inspiration and write an entire song in one hour. Some may start with a few bars of music and slowly complete a song. The following steps provide you with suggestions for exploring the process. Using these resources, you can find your own special way of putting it all together.

1. Analyze your favorite music.

Begin by analyzing the musical compositions you love; this will give you a deeper understanding of your musical preferences. Look at them from different perspectives by asking yourself questions like:

> *How does it begin? Why does it make me want to listen?*
>
> *What is the primary instrument? What instrument is strongest?*
>
> *Is there a major, abrupt change, or does the volume or intensity slowly increase?*
>
> *Does it make me want to dance or close my eyes and dream?*

COOL STUFF

Parkside Music Archives

To get to the University of Wisconsin, Parkside Music Archive, anonymous FTP to **ftp.uwp.edu** and look in the directory **pub/music**. This archive offers lyrics for more than 15,000 songs by more than 1,100 artists, as well as guitar tablatures (music notation based on an instrument's design), pictures of musicians and album covers, and a classical-music buying guide.

The University of Wisconsin supports a large music archive in which you can find all kinds of information about thousands of songs by hundreds of artists. Use this archive to collect information about some of your favorite songs and musicians. Figure 7.5 shows three screens you might see while searching for songs by the Rolling Stones.

Figure 7.5

Here's what you'll find when you search the Lyrics Archives of the Parkside Music Archives for the Rolling Stones.

```
artists/           =   Artists- Archives by Artist name
classical/         =   Classical Buying Guide
composition/       -   Articles of Music Composition
contest/           -
database/          =   Music Database program
faqs/              =   Frequently Asked Questions files
folk/              =   Folk Music Files and pointers
guitar/            =   Guitar TAB files from ftp.nevada.edu
help/              -
info/              =   rec.music.info newsgroup archives
kurzweil          14   Kurzweil K2000 Archives
lists/             =   Mailing lists archives
lyrics/            =   Lyrics Archives
lyrics.tar   59115520
midi/              -   Some midi files
misc/              -   Misc files that don't fit anywhere else
pictures/          =   GIFS, JPEGs, PBMs and more.
programs/          =   Misc music-related programs for various machines
releases          13   USA release listings (now info/releases)
reviews/           =   rec.music.reviews archives
sizes            319
uap/               -   Usenet Artist Polls
cs.uwp.edu:/pub/music
```

```
8192 Feb 17  1994 robin.leo
8192 Feb 17  1994 robinson.smokey
8192 May  6  1994 rockapella
8192 Apr 29  1994 rocky.horror
8192 Feb 17  1994 rodgers.richard
8192 May  6  1994 rodriguez.amalia
8192 Sep 17 03:42 rodriguez.silvio
8192 Mar 28  1994 rogers.and.hammerstein
8192 Feb 17  1994 rogers.kenny
8192 Feb 17  1994 rogers.sally
8192 Feb 17  1994 rogers.stan
8192 Nov 27 02:36 rolling.stones
8192 Nov 19 02:52 rollins.band
8192 Feb 17  1994 romantics
8192 May  6  1994 ronettes
8192 Feb 17  1994 ronstadt.linda
8192 Feb 17  1994 ross.diana
8192 Feb 17  1994 roth.david.lee
8192 May  6  1994 rotting.christ
8192 Feb 17  1994 rowwen.heze
8192 Nov 19 02:52 roxette
8192 Feb 17  1994 roxy.music
8192 Feb 17  1994 royal.guardsmen
```

```
goats.head.soup        11943
honky_tonk_woman         572
jumping_jack_flash       782
lady_jane                584
let.it.bleed           11153
paint_it_black          1083
respectable             1244
rewind                 16012
ruby_tuesday             833
salt_of_the_earth       1343
satisfaction            1321
steel.wheels           11611
sticky.fingers         10373
stray.cat.blues         1374
sympathy_for_the_devil
                        2177
time_is_on_my_side
                        1038
under_my_thumb           951
wild_horses              674
you_cant_always_get_what_you_want
                        1581
cs.uwp.edu:/pub/music/lyrics/r/rolling.stones
```

Tip

If you don't already know how to read music, you can try to learn by listening to a song as you follow along on the sheet music. However, it may be faster to learn from someone who knows how to read music for a particular instrument. Check with a local music store or the music teacher at school for information on classes or private lessons.

2. Identify the features of different musical instruments.

As a composer, it helps to understand the design and special qualities of different instruments, because it is the harmony of the instruments that gives a composition a distinctive and appealing sound.

As you can see from the list of Internet sites in *Instrument Resources*, there are places to go to learn about almost any instrument. If you don't see it in the list, be sure to check the *Music List of Lists*.

By subscribing to one list server and following the discussion for one week, you will learn more than you can imagine. For example, several of the sites offer guitar tablatures for many songs. Tablature is a system of musical notation used most often for stringed instruments in which the lines represent the strings, and the notes or letters on them represent finger placement. You can follow the tablature as you listen to the composition. This will help you learn how to play the piece on a guitar.

COOL STUFF

Instrument Resources

Drum/Percussion Mailing List	subscribe by sending an e-mail message to **drum-request@elof.mit.edu**. It offers discussions of everything related to percussion instruments.
Percussion Talk	join by sending e-mail to **rec.music.makers.percussion**. It is a Usenet group with discussions about percussion instruments.
Acoustic Guitar Archive	anonymous FTP to **casbah.acns.nwu.edu** and look in directory **pub/acoustic-guitar**. It carries the Acoustic Guitar Digest, an electronic magazine, and song transcriptions.
Guitar Chords and Tablature	anonymous FTP to **ftp.uwp.edu** and look in the directory **pub/music/guitar**. You will find guitar tablature and chords for old, electric, and acoustic songs. In the "R" directory, for example, you'll find both REM and the Ramones.
Lute Playing	gopher to **cs.dartmouth.edu** and select "Lute Files." You will find discussions of lute playing and performance.
Bagpipes	gopher to **cs.dartmouth.edu** and select "Bagpipe Archives." It has archived files and discussions of bagpipes and other related instruments.

3. Read the lyrics for several different songs.

You may have already found the lyrics to a few songs in the music archive at the University of Wisconsin. If not, search the archive for lyrics to a few of your favorites. You will see that the lyrics are actually poems. Sometimes it's easier to think about writing a poem in *stanzas*, or verses, than writing a song's words and music all at once. See if this works for you.

Have an online conversation with someone or a group of people interested in *a cappella* music (find the address in *Lyrical Resource*). This is music where the only instruments used are voices. In addition to words, singers will often make unique sounds or sing nonsensical words, called *scatting*, in an effort to create the illusion of many instruments.

Lyrical Resource

`rec.music.a-capella`
a Usenet group for those who enjoy performing or listening to a cappella (voice-only) music.

4. **Put your own ideas for instruments and lyrics together to create new melodies.**

During your research of different songs, instruments, and lyrics, you may have developed a few ideas of your own. Begin by combining a lyric idea with a few bars of musical notes. Start small—just a bar or two. Then keep adding to your song.

If you get stuck or want to talk with other musicians about your song-writing, join one of the list servers or Usenet groups listed in *Musical Discussion Groups*. There is always someone who will listen to your situation and offer you a new perspective or idea to keep you going. You can also provide this kind of support for others as you continue to be a contributing member of the group.

Musical Discussion Groups

Allmusic

subscribe to `listserv@auvm.american.edu`.
This list server offers discussion on all forms of music. Topics include composition, musicology, jazz, classical, funk, acoustics, and performance.

`rec.music.compose`

a Usenet group with discussion about notation and composition software, sources of inspiration, getting published, book reviews, and computer hardware used in composition.

Music List of Lists

send an e-mail message to
`mlol-request@wariat.org`
or anonymous FTP to `cs.uwp.edu` and look in directory `music/info/mailinglist`.

Starting a Band

The best way to test your new songs or musical ideas is to get a group of musicians together to play your composition. As you play what you have created, you can make adjustments as you go. Hearing a song inside your head can be very different from the way it sounds when it's played with real instruments. That's the great thing about composing. Until you hear something you like, you just keep trying—and have fun in the process.

As you continue to create new pieces, you will become a more experienced composer and may not need to make many adjustments at all. You may want to stay in touch with new happenings in music and what is available through the Internet by subscribing to the sites listed in *Staying Up to Date*. Be on the lookout for new places on the Internet to send a file of your music; these places will begin to become popular with the growth of the World Wide Web, and they will offer a great way to let others hear your music.

Staying Up to Date

Update Electronic Music News
subscribe to `listserv@vm.marist.edu`
and type in the message body:
subscribe upnews *<your full name>*

Music Resources
join by sending e-mail to `rec.music.info`.
It is a Usenet group with information about music resources on the Internet:
FTP sites, music newsgroups, mailing lists, discographies, concert dates, chart listings, and new releases.

Note Sound files are just like files of text or graphics, and you can upload them to the Internet in similar ways. Check with your local computer store to find out what sound utilities you need on your home computer so you can send, receive, and hear music files.

Paperless Publishing

Note Are you looking for a way to publish your essays and stories? The Internet provides many new online journals and *zines* (slang for "magazines") that are looking for all types of writing to distribute around the world. Enter the world of *Paperless Publishing* to learn how to send your writing through online connections.

Before the Internet, publishers of magazines, newspapers, and books decided whose writing to include in the company's publications. Because it takes a great deal of money to put these publications together, authors have had to compete to be selected as writers of the articles and books that actually get printed. However, this situation is changing rapidly as more and more people are discovering the Internet as a place to share ideas and resources and to get published. For example, there has been an explosion in the number of online literary journals.

As an author, you can take advantage of this explosion by submitting your writing and possibly getting it distributed electronically. You can also subscribe to these electronic journals.

> The Internet features you will use for this project are e-mail, list servers, Usenets, anonymous FTP, telnet, and WWW.

Note

The Publishing Desk

You already have everything it takes to become a published author. You have creativity, motivation, and, by following these steps, directions for submitting your work.

1. Begin a new piece of writing or adapt something you have already written.

Obviously you need to have something to submit to an online journal or zine. You may already have written a story, poem, or play by doing some of the projects in this book such as *Awesome Authors* or *Writer's Corner*. If so, pull it out, read it over, and make any changes or enhancements you think will make it a stronger piece.

If you haven't tried these projects yet, you will need to develop a written piece of work or adapt something else you've written. It can be any type or style—news, fiction, essay, poetry—and can be about anything.

2. Share your story with others before submitting it to an online journal.

Once you have a final version of your written piece, you're ready for the next step: finding someone to publish it.

However, before you start submitting your story to different journals and zines, you may want to have a few people read it and give you their

Online Writing Workshops

KID-LIT	obtain an account on the Youngstown Free-net by telneting to `yfn2.ysu.edu` and using the log-in: **visitor**. Once you are registered, go into the student bulletin board and find "KID-LIT." This is a place in Academy One where you can post your writing. There are two categories: one for kids up until the age of 12 and one for juniors ages 13-18.
The Fiction Writers Workshop	subscribe to `Fiction@psuvm.psu.edu`. This is a list server that encourages writers to submit writing and participate in a discussion about it.
`alt.prose`	a Usenet group where you can submit your writing. Discussions about the submissions occur on the Usenet group `alt.prose.d`.

impressions and comments.

There are student discussion areas on the Internet where you can send your manuscript to other aspiring writers. Use the sites listed in *Online Writing Workshops*. Asking for direct comments will give you new ideas for how to make your piece stronger and more interesting.

Learning to give, receive, and use "constructive" feedback—comments that help you improve your writing—are important skills for a writer to have. Use the tips in *Giving Literary Criticism* and *Receiving Literary Criticism* to help you identify those comments that are most helpful and apply them to your work.

Giving Literary Criticism

• Tell the author what you really like about the writing.

• Ask the author what he or she feels are the strengths and weaknesses so you can focus on these points in your comments.

• Offer specific suggestions on how the author can make the writing better.

Receiving Literary Criticism

• Before asking for feedback from others, let them know the aspects of your written work with which you are struggling.

• Keep in mind that the comments are about your writing, not about you personally.

• As the author, you should consider all suggestions given to you about your writing; however, only you decide which changes are made.

3. **Submit your writing to the appropriate resources.**

Now that your story is in final form, send it to as many online publishers listed in *Electronic Literary Journals and Zines* as possible (the home page from *Cyberkind*, one of these zines, is shown in Figure 7.6). You'll

Electronic Literary Journals and Zines

Young Authors send e-mail to **JMM12@psuvm.psu.edu**. Include your name, address, and phone number as well as your school's name, address, and phone number. This is an electronic journal that publishes student work.

CORE anonymous FTP to **etext.archive.umich.edu** and look in the directory **pub/Zines/Core_Zine**. Send e-mail to **core-journal@eff.org** to subscribe to the zine and to receive instructions for submitting your writing. This is a zine for poetry, essays, fiction.

InterText anonymous FTP to **etext.archive.umich.edu** and look in the directory **pub/Zine**. Send e-mail to **jsnell@ocf.berkeley.edu** to subscribe to the zine and to receive instructions for submitting your writing. This is a short fiction bimonthly zine.

Cyberkind **http://sunsite.unc.edu/shannon/ckind/**. This is a WWW zine of fiction, nonfiction, poetry, and prose related in some way to the Internet, cyberspace, computers, or the networked world in general.

Global Literary Magazine send e-mail to **coldspring@igc.apc.org** to get the current schedule. This is an annual I*EARN project, organized by Cold Spring Harbor High School.

The Vocal Point WWW to **http://bvsd.k12.co.us/cent/Newspaper/Newspaper.html**. This is a monthly newspaper created by the students of the Boulder Valley School District. It covers a significant local or national topic.

Figure 7.6

The home page for Cyberkind, an online literary magazine.

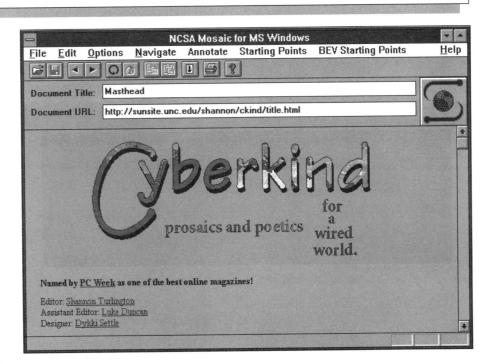

always want to keep your eyes open for new places to submit your work. If your story doesn't get published on the first try, don't get discouraged! You might need to make a few revisions or just be persistent and continue to submit your writing.

Become a regular subscriber to the online journals as well. This way you will see your writing when it appears in an issue of the journal or zine. As a subscriber, you also have the opportunity to read other people's writing and observe different styles and perspectives. Figure 7.7 shows the table of contents for *Cyberkind*.

Figure 7.7
Cyberkind *offers a variety of poetry, prose, and other literary selections.*

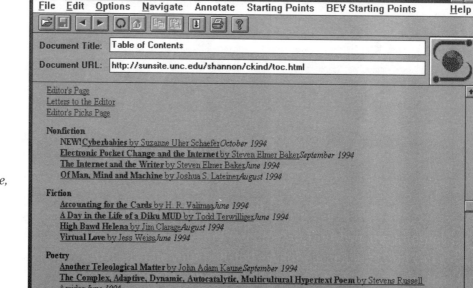

You Be the Publisher

Once you become familiar with the online world of publishing, you will know all you need to about creating your own electronic journal or zine. You will need to collect writing, determine which pieces will be included, create the issue, and distribute it to all who subscribe. All of these tasks can be done with the most basic Internet feature of e-mail. The best part about being the publisher is that you get to decide the theme of your zine: essays by teenagers, new poetry, etc. It's up to you!

Creating the Zine

Once you post a message asking for people to send you their writing by e-mail, you should have plenty of things to choose from to include in your new zine. Create a word processing file, paste in the pieces you have chosen, and save it as a file in text format. (Check the user's guide of your word processing program for instructions on pasting and saving.) Give your zine a title, and it's ready to be sent to all of your subscribers.

Managing the Subscriptions

In addition to new pieces of writing, you will also receive messages from people wanting to become subscribers to your zine. You will need to check with your system administrator to learn how to create a mailing list to which you can add all of the subscribers' e-mail addresses. Then, once your issue is ready to be sent, you can send it to the list, and the computer will take care of getting it to each individual address.

The Internet makes writing and publishing more accessible and fun, so don't hold back...just go for it!

Guten Tag
German

Bonjour
French

Namaste
Hindi

Buon Giorno
Italian

Ní Hâo Mà
Mandarin

Zdrastvitsye
Russian

Hello
English

Boker Tov
Hebrew

Ya'teh
Navajo

G'day
Australian

Jambo
Swahili

Buenos Días
Spanish

Konnichi Wa
Japanese

Salam Aleikum
Arabic

The World Is a Lab

When you hear the word "laboratory," do you think of glass tubes, white coats, and safety goggles? With these projects you can include trees, lakes, soil, and air in your definition. You can learn the secrets of *Predicting the Weather*. Or you can find out how people feel about different issues by *Polling for Answers*. If you enjoy reading and watching the news, you can challenge the news industry as a *Media Watchdog*. Research how to preserve nature by conducting *Environmental Experiments*. You'll soon see how the world is your laboratory.

The NetCruiser software that came with this book offers an alternative way to do these activities. See Appendix C for more about this software.

Note

Predicting the Weather

Note

Think you can predict the weather? Give it a shot with this project by learning about different factors that alter weather patterns. There are several resources on the Internet where you will find current data on weather, including temperatures, images of weather events and weather patterns, and the predictions of people who observe the weather. With a little practice, you can anticipate what the weather is going to be in the near future.

 If there is ring around the moon, it's going to rain tomorrow.

 If the sky is orange, a tornado is on the way.

 If a dog squeals and is restless, a lightning storm will happen soon.

 You can tell how many miles away a storm is by counting the number of seconds between a stroke of lightning and a boom of thunder.

What other weather sayings do you know? Most of the sayings listed above are myths that try to explain natural *phenomena* (events). Before the study of weather—*meteorology*—became a popular science, people used these sayings to predict and forecast the weather.

Now there are many weather monitoring and research stations that assist meteorologists in developing weather predictions and forecasts for television news, newspapers, and radio news. Their work and the information they provide is very valuable. It may take one meteorologist many hours of research and observation to create an accurate five-minute weather forecast.

Because there are many different factors that affect the weather—like wind forces, moisture levels, land formations, and ocean currents—making predictions can be difficult. However, it's important to meet the challenge, because weather conditions have a *profound* (extensive) effect on farming, construction, and our everyday lives.

Note

The Internet features you will use in this project are telnet, Usenets, anonymous FTP, and WWW.

Becoming an Amateur Meteorologist

Even though it takes many years of training in school to become a meteorologist, you can begin as an amateur weather observer.

1. Choose several locations in the world to monitor.

Weather happens 24 hours a day, everywhere in the world. At any given time, there are places that have sunshine, rain, snow, freezing temperatures, high winds, and other weather conditions.

Using a world atlas or a map of the United States, choose two or three locations to observe every day for some period of time; it may be for a week, a month, or even a year. Try to pick locations that are different from each other. Perhaps you'll want to select places with different climates. Take a look at a city's *altitude* (vertical distance from sea level), as

well as its latitude and longitude, to find its "global address." (A city's latitude is the distance, measured in degrees, from the equator. A city's longitude is the distance, measured in degrees, from the prime meridian, an imaginary vertical line that runs through Greenwich, England. For example, the global address for Washington, D.C., is 38 degrees North, 77 degrees West.)

Tip

Because many of the weather services on the Internet provide information for major cities around the world, it will be helpful to identify large cities with high populations as observation locations.

You may also want to choose places that are more likely to experience extreme weather situations. For instance, the Caribbean islands prepare for hurricanes during a season that lasts from May through November, while the coast of Thailand prepares for typhoons from June through September. In the United States, California is prone to earthquakes.

Where to Get Weather Data

Weather Underground	telnet to downwind.sprl.umich.edu 3000
Blue Skies	get the software by anonymous FTP from madlab.sprl.umich.edu in subdirectory pub/Blue-Skies. (You'll need a direct Internet connection to use this software.)

2. **Observe weather conditions on a daily basis.**

The Internet hosts many sites that provide daily and even hourly updates on weather conditions around the world. Begin by using the Weather Underground listed in *Where to Get Weather Data*; Figure 8.1 shows what it looks like. It is a very easy-to-use system, and it will familiarize you with meteorological terms and concepts.

Note

If you have a direct Internet connection that can support the use of the Blue Skies software (talk to your network administrator if you don't), use it to look at photographs of the inside of a hurricane. It is a sight you will hope you'll never see for real!

```
Press Return for menu, or enter 3 letter forecast ity code:

                  WEATHER UNDERGROUND MAIN MENU
                  ********************************
                  1) U.S. forecasts and climate data
                  2) Canadian frecasts
                  3) Current weather observations
                  4) Ski conditions
                  5) Long-range forecasts
                  6) Latest earthquake reports
                  7) Severeweather
                  8) Hurricane advisories
                  9) National Weather Summary
                  10) International data
                  11) Marine forecasts and observations
                  12) Ultraviolet light forecast
                  13) Michigan K12 schools program
                  X) Exit program
                  C) Change scrolling to screen
                  H) Help and information for new uers
                  ?) Answers to all your questions
                     Selection:
```

Figure 8.1

Find information about all types of weather in the Weather Underground.

```
SEVERE THUNDERSTORM WATCH NUMBER 816
NATIONAL WEATHER SERVICE KANSAS CITY MO
1118 AM EDT MON SEP 26 1994

 A..THE NATIONAL SEVERE STORMS FORECAST CENTER HAS ISSUED A
SEVERE THUNDERSTORM WATCH FOR

     MUCH OF CENTRAL AND NORTHERN VIRGINIA
     PARTS OF SOUTHWEST MARYLAND
     THE DISTRICT OF COLUMBIA
     DISTRCT OF COLUMBIA

EFFECTIVE THIS MONDAY MORNING AND AFTERNOON UNTIL 500 PM EDT.

LARGE HAIL...DANGEROUS LIGHTNING AND DAMAGING THUNDERSTORM WINDS
ARE POSSIBLE IN THESE AREAS.

THE SEVERE HUNDERSTORM WATCH AREA IS ALONG AND 50 STATUTE MILES
EITHER SIDE OF A LINE FROM 30 MILES SOUTH SOUTHWEST OF LYNCHBURG
VIRGINIA TO 20 MILES NORTHEAST OF WASHINGTON DIST OF COLUMBIA.

REMEMBER...A SEVERE THUNDERSTORM WATCH MEANS CONDITIONS ARE
   Press Return to continue, M to return to menu, X to exit:
```

Use the Weather Underground and other weather-related resources to find data about the locations you are observing. In addition to temperature highs and lows, you may also want to note the *barometric pressure* (air pressure), wind levels, and amounts of *precipitation* (moisture falling on the earth). Other facts, such as moon stages, tides, hours of daylight, and seasons, may be interesting to track as well.

You can keep your notes in a notebook or in a computer spreadsheet. (Check with your parents or teacher to find out whether you have access to a spreadsheet.) The advantage of using a computer spreadsheet is that it will be easy to create charts to show changes in and make comparisons of weather conditions.

If a storm is occurring, you can track its path using your map or atlas. On a regular basis—perhaps two times a day—stick a pin on your map to indicate the position of the storm. As it moves, your pins will illustrate the storm's path.

3. Identify weather patterns.

After you have recorded at least one week's worth of observations, you may be able to identify repetitive patterns in the weather. For instance, is there always a brief rain shower in the mid-afternoon in one of the cities you are observing? Or is there a consistent temperature range right before a thunderstorm?

After a full month of observations, you can look at other factors that may influence weather conditions. For example, do the stages of the moon (new moon, quarter moon, half moon, three-quarters moon, and full moon) affect the weather?

As you continue to observe changes in weather, ask yourself a few questions:

 How do latitude and longitude affect precipitation levels?

 How does altitude affect temperatures?

 Do storms move differently when they are over water or over land?

Several of the resources listed in *Additional Resources* provide images of weather events that you can download onto your computer. You may need some special software, so be sure to read any README files. (You can read more about this type of file in the FTP section of Chapter 1.)

4. Predict the weather for one location.

After you've identified a few patterns, your observations can help you predict future weather conditions. With one of the locations you have observed, predict what the high and low temperatures may be one day in advance. See if you can predict other aspects of the weather, such as when it will rain or snow.

As your predictions get closer to the actual weather conditions, try to extend your forecast for a few days in advance, although even meteorologists have a hard time predicting more than five days ahead. If your predictions are different from what actually happens, you can always try again the next day.

Share your predictions with your family and friends. They may begin to rely on you for the forecast rather than on your local news station.

> ### Additional Resources
>
> `sci.geo.meteorology`
> this Usenet group is a forum for discussing meteorological issues.
>
> NASA Weather Reports
> anonymous FTP to `ames.arc.nasa.gov` and look in `pub/SPACE/WEATHER`.
>
> Weather Image Archive
> anonymous FTP to `ftp.colorado.edu` and look in `pub/weather-images`.

Planning Ahead

How many times has an event that you wanted to attend been canceled because of rain or snow? Perhaps you are on a sports team that plays outdoors. Your ability to predict the weather could be a very valuable skill to your team. You could become a personal weatherperson for your family and friends. Suggest to people what activities they may want to prepare for as a result of your weather forecast. Here are a few ideas:

> ✓ Sailing is best on a windy day but not just before a storm is due.
>
> ✓ Skiing is best on a cold, but not freezing, day just after a fresh layer of snow has fallen.
>
> ✓ Football and cycling are best on crisp and sunny days.

You can also warn your friends about dangerous weather conditions:

✗ *Don't go skiing today because the temperatures are too cold and you may get frostbite.*

✗ *Don't go running today because both the humidity and temperature are very high and you could get heat exhaustion.*

✗ *Don't go in the water this afternoon because lightning has been sighted and lightning is attracted to water.*

Weather Prediction Contest

If you find that several of your friends are also interested in observing weather conditions, create a contest for predicting the weather. Identify one location and tell everyone to make a prediction for the next day's weather. Set a deadline, such as 5:00 P.M. Check the weather the next day and see who has the closest prediction.

If you have already explored the project *Map Mania*, you know that geographic land formations may also affect weather conditions. For example, mountain ranges often protect cities from adverse weather.

Weather can be very unpredictable, so always be on the lookout for unusual conditions. With practice, you will see some interesting patterns and perfect your meteorological skills.

Polling for Answers

Note

Sometimes it takes more than one person to answer a question. Sometimes it takes hundreds or even thousands of people all answering the same question to figure out how an entire community feels. With *Polling for Answers* you can take a poll of your family, friends, people on the Internet, and anybody else you want to include to find out how people feel about something that interests you.

Imagine this: The mayor of your town has just canceled the rock concert scheduled tonight at the civic center because she received tips that a group of kids from another town was going to come and cause trouble in the parking lot. Was this a good decision? Although you can predict that people with tickets to the concert will be upset by the decision, how does the rest of the community feel about it?

To find out, the local news show conducts a poll or a survey of what people think. While the poll may not lessen some people's disappointment at the canceled concert, it may give the mayor a better understanding of the people's thoughts on the issue.

In a poll, individuals answer questions about their opinions on various issues. Newspapers and many other groups and companies conduct polls in a variety of ways on all kinds of topics. For example, polls are very popular around election time; they tell the candidates how the voters feel about them.

Polls can be used to find out how any group of people feels about any one issue. Use this project to learn how to design a poll, get responses, and share the results with other people.

⋯⋯⋯⋯⋯⋯⋯⋯⋯⋯⋯⋯⋯⋯⋯⋯⋯⋯⋯⋯⋯⋯⋯⋯

The Internet features you will use for this project are list servers and Usenet.

Note ⋯⋯⋯⋯⋯⋯⋯⋯⋯⋯⋯⋯⋯⋯⋯⋯⋯⋯⋯⋯⋯⋯⋯

Making Your Name as a Pollster

There are people, called pollsters, who have the job of creating and analyzing polls of all types. They work for politicians, television news programs, and other groups that need to know how the public feels. Follow these steps to conduct your own poll and see what it's like to be a pollster.

1. Create your poll.

The main focus of a poll is the question or questions it contains. However, before you start writing your list of questions, you need to determine what issue you want to ask people about. If it is an election year, you can ask people about the different candidates or the most *controversial* (argued) issues in the campaign. Look at the list of *Sample Poll Topics* to set your brain in motion for your own topic ideas.

Sample Poll Topics

What do people think about…

- the use of animal hides in the making of fur coats?
- the use of metal detectors at movie theaters or schools?
- the government's plan to reduce the federal deficit?

Once you have your topic, you will need to create a set of questions to learn how people feel about this topic. Professional pollsters think hard about exactly how to phrase a question so that it draws the most honest answer from a person. If people don't answer truthfully, the results of the poll won't really reflect people's opinions.

You should keep your list of questions to five or less. Keeping it short will increase the number of people who decide to participate in your poll.

To make it easy to compare opinions, write questions that people can answer with a "yes," "no," or "maybe." As you collect answers, it will be easy to see the way most people feel about the question. For example, you may have 70 "yes" responses, 20 "no" responses, and 10 "maybe" responses to the question, "Do you think video games should be rated, like movies, for levels of violence?"

You can then convert each number into a percentage by dividing the number of responses of one type by the total number of responses. For instance, 70 + 20 + 10 = 100, so for the percentage of "yes" responses, divide 70 by 100. You get .70, which equals 70 percent, therefore you have 70 percent "yes" responses.

Places to Post Your Poll

Kidlink
subscribe to `listserv@ndsuvm1.bitnet`.

Kidsphere
subscribe to `kidsphere-request@vms.cis.pitt.edu`.

KIDZMAIL
subscribe to `listserv@asuacad.bitnet`.

Penpal-L
subscribe to `listserv@unccvm.bitnet`.

`alt.politics.election`
this Usenet group is a place to discuss local and state politics and election practices.

2. Distribute your poll.

As you can see in *Places to Post Your Poll*, the Internet is a great place to distribute your poll and ask for participants. You can get a wide range of opinions by sending your poll to several list servers. The key to getting responses from many people is to send it to people who will find the topic of the poll interesting. If you send out a poll that asks people about the candidates for the governor of Montana, you should probably send it to people who live in that state; Florida residents won't be too interested in your poll. You may want to get a list of list servers to find ones that attract people who have interests similar to the topic of your poll (find the instructions for this in Chapter 1).

3. Compile the results.

As you receive completed polls, you will need to log the answers onto one sheet. Because there are only three answers for each question, you can keep track of the responses with tally marks on a chart.

4. Analyze the results.

One of the most important aspects of a research project is the analysis of the results. To make an accurate analysis, you need to read each question and see which answer received the most responses. Ask yourself some questions about it:

> ❓ Did a lot of people agree, or did an equal number of people choose each answer?
>
> ❓ Do the results of one question help me understand the results of another question? For example, if you are conducting a poll about music, you may find that the older participants enjoy classic rock while the younger participants enjoy alternative rock.

Share the results of each question with everyone who participated in your poll. They will find it very interesting to see how popular or unpopular their opinions are. If the topic of your poll is a hot topic in the news, you may want to share your results with your local news station or newspaper. People are always interested in results from polls about current issues.

Polling for Others

Look around you. There are many organizations that need surveys conducted by trained pollsters. Talk to your school. Maybe the cafeteria wants to poll students about favorite food selections to help design future menus. Or perhaps the football team wants to survey the people who come to the games to determine appropriate ticket prices.

Your experiences as a pollster will not only help the groups gather the information they need to make decisions or plan programs, but they will also help you learn skills you can use throughout your life.

Media Watchdog

Note

This project will show you how to analyze the newspaper articles you read. As a *Media Watchdog*, you will use different strategies to examine what issues are being written about and where in the newspaper they are placed. You will decide what newspapers to survey, the length of time to spend on surveying, and what questions to ask. Once you have collected the information, you can share it with the rest of the world.

You can be a watchdog—not the kind that sits in front of a dark house at night, but the kind that surveys newspapers to report on how they are covering the events and issues in the world. As a watchdog, you can make daily observations about the length of articles, their placement on the page, or any other aspect you find interesting. After a certain length of time, you will pull all your observations together to make a few conclusions about how the media covers a particular issue.

Watchdogs help journalists and editors do their jobs better. They inform the journalistic community about problems or oversights in coverage. Your research may help reveal aspects of the issues that are not being covered in the paper.

The Internet features you will use for this project are list servers, Usenets, Gopher, telnet, and WWW.

Note

Surveying the Scene

Just as surveyors examine a piece of land for future construction, you can survey newspapers to examine how different issues are addressed.

1. Choose a few issues to survey.

To begin your survey of the media, you will need to choose no more than three issues to monitor. You want to limit the amount of information you are tracking so you can really concentrate on one or two areas.

While you may think you know which issues you want to monitor, spend a week making a list of what issues are on the front page of the newspapers you've selected to survey. As an issue is repeated, make a tally mark to indicate that it has been the focus of a story more than once.

At the end of one week, you will see on your list which issues have been the most popular news stories. Make your choices from this list. You may want to choose the most- and least-covered issues for your survey.

2. Identify the sources (newspapers) you will use.

Choosing too many newspapers to survey can be overwhelming, so limit the number of newspapers you are using to two or three. You will probably want to include your hometown paper or, if you have more than one, the newspaper with the widest circulation (the largest number of copies sold). You can choose another source from the newspapers available in *Newspapers on the Net*.

3. Choose one research perspective.

A research perspective can usually be expressed in the form of a question. Here are some examples for examining newspapers and the articles they contain regarding the coverage of the president's actions:

> ？ What is the length of all stories that contain information about the president? Does one newspaper have longer articles than another? Figure 8.2 shows an article from USA Today about the president's approval ratings.
>
> ？ Where are articles that contain information about the president positioned? On the front page? Third page of the business section?
>
> ？ What is the frequency of coverage, or how many articles are there that contain information about the president?

Once you have decided on the research perspective you want to take, try to write your own questions. Make the questions as clear as you can.

Newspapers on the Net

Columbus Dispatch

gopher to **gopher.freenet.columbus.oh.us** and select "News, Weather, Calendar." Daily newspaper from Columbus, Ohio.

French Language Press Review

gopher to **gopher.tc.umn.edu** and select "News." The French embassy in Washington, D.C., delivers a free daily review of the French press.

Norfolk Virginian-Pilot

WWW to **http://www.infi.net/pilot/vpls.html**.

Palo Alto Weekly

WWW to **http://www.service.com/PAW/home.html**. The Palo Alto Weekly carries news, real estate information, movie and restaurant reviews, and more.

USA Today

telnet to **freenet-in-a.cwru.edu** or **kanga.ins.cwru.edu** and log in as **guest**; only registered Freenet users have access to USA Today, but registration information can be found after you've logged on.

Figure 8.2

This article from USA Today *describes President Clinton's latest approval ratings for his job as the country's leader.*

```
Article #681 (681 is last):
From: AmeriCast-Post@AmeriCast.com
Newsgroups: americast.usa-today.news,usa-today.news
Subject: news Tue, Sep 271994
Date: Tue Sep 27 05:56:51 1994

DECISIONLINE: News
USA TODAY Update
Sept. 27, 1994
Source: USA TODAY:Gannett National Information Network

CLINTON'S APPROVAL RATING ISES:
   Americans are feeling better than they did a week ago about
President Clinton's handling of the Haiti problem, a new poll
says. A USA TODAY:CNN:Gallup Poll found Clinton got a boost in
verall job approval, from 39 percent before Haiti became a hot
spot to 44 percent now. But a majority, 57 percent, say Clinton
does not deserve re-election. The poll has a 3 percent margin of
error.

SANCTIONS LIFTED FROM HAITI:
   President Clinton told the U.N. General Assembly Monday he'll
lift U.S. travel and trade sanctions against Haiti. He urged
Shown 12%, press <PACE> for more, 'q' to quit, or 'h' for help
```

4. Monitor the coverage.

Now you are just about ready to begin your research by monitoring the coverage of an issue in several newspapers. The only decision you still need to make is when you are going to end the monitoring. Decide how much time you can spend on monitoring every day. Be realistic. Perhaps you'll spend an hour a day for one week, one month, or even a year (if you are a *really* ambitious watchdog).

Because you can always repeat this project by changing the issue, the perspective, or the sources, begin your first survey with a short length of time, such as one week. As you become a pro surveyor, you can increase the number of days you monitor the media. Every additional day will make your *findings* (the results of a research project) stronger.

5. Report your findings.

As with all research, it is important to report your findings to other people in the community who are interested in what the media is doing and how they are covering current issues. Share your observations with family, friends, and others on the Internet. Write a one-page description of your conclusions. Here are a few questions you may want to ask yourself before you write about what you found concerning coverage of the president's actions:

> *Were articles about the president always longer in one of the newspapers?*
>
> *Were articles about the president always on the front page regardless of other important events?*
>
> *Was there an article about the president every day in one newspaper and only once a week in another newspaper?*

As you look at your monitoring sheet, what conclusions can you make? In addition to your written description, you should be able to create a few graphs to demonstrate large differences. For example, a graph can show how many times each newspaper printed an article about the president.

Journalistic Forums

alt.journalism
this Usenet group is a forum for discussing journalism and any issues of interest to journalists.

alt.journalism.criticism
this Usenet group is a forum for debating media coverage of current and historical events.

Carr-L
subscribe to **listserv@ulkyvm.louisville.edu.** This list server focuses on the use of computers, including online research and graphics, in journalism.

Journet
subscribe to **listserv@qucdn.queensu.ca.** This online newsletter covers topics of interest to journalists and journalism educators.

In addition to the places on the Internet listed in *Journalistic Forums,* send a copy of your findings to your hometown paper. They may find it interesting enough to write an article about you and your research.

Exploring the Watchdog Frontiers

You can be a watchdog of many types of media: not just newspapers, but also television news shows, magazines, movies made for television…you name it. If people know that you and others are out there checking on what they are doing, they might think more carefully about what they write.

Create a Media Watchdog Team

Because there are newspapers in almost every city or town, you can enlist a whole team of watchdogs to survey the same issue across numerous sources. This is an excellent way to expand the reach of your surveying. People from different states and even different countries can explore how media coverage changes by region and country.

Environmental Experiments

Note

Experimentation is a process used by scientists to discover clues and answers to questions people have about the world. While many experiments take place in a laboratory, there are scientific questions that must be examined in the real world. The world then becomes a laboratory where scientists can observe people, animals, and nature to gather clues and answers. With *Environmental Experiments*, you are the scientist gathering clues and collaborating with other student scientists through the Internet to discover answers and new questions regarding environmental issues.

What is the quality of the water near a large factory? How fast is the ozone layer of the atmosphere deteriorating? How long does it take for the fish population to return to normal after a natural disaster, such as a flood?

To answer these questions, or at least discover a few clues, scientists conduct observations and experiments in the environment they are curious about. They may be gathering samples of water or tagging and counting fish. The method each scientist uses to examine a scientific question changes depending on the focus of the research. For example, you can conduct chemical experiments on water samples, but with living animals you will use the method of observation.

The Internet was originally designed in the 1960s as a tool to help scientists share the results of research and collaborate on ideas. Sometimes many scientists will pool (collect) everyone's data together to get a global perspective on a question. As a student scientist on the Internet, you can do this, too. You can work with an organization, such as the World

Wildlife Federation, to help answer questions with a team of scientific researchers from around the world.

The Internet features you will use for this project are e-mail, Gopher, and WWW.

Note ....

The Scientific Process

Scientists use a set of strategies to help them be efficient at finding answers. Think about when you lose something. You usually find what you lost faster when you try to retrace your steps or close your eyes and imagine where something is, rather than just running around looking in random places. By following strategic steps, you can scientifically and efficiently find answers or clues to questions about your world.

1. Design a research question.

There are several different ways to go about designing a research question. You may already have your own idea. If you don't, there are many organizations that would be pleased to have a team of volunteers to help with research questions they've already developed.

An example of working with an organization can be seen in one New Hampshire teacher's collaboration with National Science Foundation scientists. The Foundation wants to learn more about the ozone layer of the atmosphere, and the teacher has a class of students linked together to study the question. Through this project, called EnviroNet, the teacher and students are helping the National Science Foundation learn more about the environment, which can then help other scientists develop strategies to protect it.

National Science Foundation

For more information about collaborating with the National Science Foundation on science projects, you can call the Foundation at (703) 306-1620.

Check *Environmental Organizations* to find a group that shares a concern of yours or try using Veronica to find some environmental Gophers like those in Figure 8.3. Many of these organizations have a local office in your city, so check the business white pages of your phone book.

Environmental Organizations

The Audubon Society	This organization is concerned with the protection of all species of birds.
Environmental Protection Agency	This organization is a department of the U.S. government that protects many different aspects of the environment such as water, soil, and air.
Society for the Prevention of Cruelty to Animals	This organization monitors the safe treatment of animals and finds homes for homeless dogs and cats.
World Wildlife Federation	This organization monitors the status of animals around the world, especially those on the endangered species list.

```
┌──────────────────────────────────────────────────────────────────────────┐
│       Internet Gopher Information Client v1.11.I                            │
│                                                                            │
│                            Environment                                     │
│                                                                            │
│   --> 1.  CIESIN Global Change Information Gateway/                         │
│       2.  EcoGopher at the Unversity of Virginia/                          │
│       3.  EnviroGopher/                                                     │
│       4.  Go M-Link/                                                        │
│       5.  GreenGopher at University of Virginia in Charlottesville/         │
└──────────────────────────────────────────────────────────────────────────┘
```

```
┌──────────────────────────────────────────────────────────────────────────┐
│       Internet Gopher Information Client v1.11.I                            │
│                                                                            │
│   Information Center for the Environment - The ICE House gopher            │
│                                                                            │
│   --> 1.  Welcome to The ICE House gopher service (last updated 1994 July 25...│
│       2.  California Department of Parks and Recreation/                    │
│       3.  California Rivers Assessment (CARA)/                              │
│       4.  John Muir Exhibit/                                                │
│       5.  Long-Term Ecological Research (LTER)/                            │
│       6.  Man And the Biosphere (MAB)/                                     │
│       7.  U.S. National Park Service (NPS)/                                │
│       8.  Assorted Other Items Related to Environmental Protection/        │
│       9.  harvey's Cyberspace Jump Station (gopher edition)/               │
│      10.  Miscellaneous Documents/                                         │
│      11.  Software for PC, UNIX, and Macintosh/                            │
│      12.  The UC Davis gopher/                                             │
│      13.  Other Gopher and Information Servers (at University of Minnesota)/│
│      14.  Outgoing files ready for pick-up (files here only temporarily)/  │
└──────────────────────────────────────────────────────────────────────────┘
```

Figure 8.3

These environmental Gophers were found by using Veronica to search directories containing the word "environment."

2. Create a team of researchers.

The more data you gather, the more likely it is that your results will be accurate. This is why the Internet is such a powerful tool for scientific research. You can post a notice asking for volunteer scientists to assist with the project. Within days, your team of researchers can grow from one to a hundred.

You will need to create a notice that includes the following information:

- ✎ *a one-sentence description of the research question*
- ✎ *the length of the project*
- ✎ *any significant deadlines during the project*
- ✎ *guidelines for collecting and reporting information*
- ✎ *the benefits of participating in the project*
- ✎ *your name and e-mail address*

Ask someone you respect to look over your notice to make sure you have included all the necessary information. Once your notice is complete, post it on one of the places listed in *Online Environmental Resources*.

Online Environmental Resources

Environmental Learning Center (ELC)
send an e-mail message to **xx151@nptn.org**. There are three areas: resource information about the environment, safety and project information, and a discussion and announcement area. To access them, you must register as a Cleveland Freenet user.

Environmental Resource Center
WWW to **http://ftp.clearlake.ibm.com/ERC/**. The site has stored environmental data and information (see Figure 8.4 for some ERC pages).

The Collaboratory
send an e-mail message to **xx171@nptn.org**. This is an area where you can advertise your experiment and ask others to participate. A database is being kept of the different projects, past and present.

Interactive Frog Dissection
WWW to **http://curry.edschool.virginia.edu/~insttech/frog**. This site includes text, 60 images, 17 QuickTime movies, and clickable image maps.

NASA Goddard Space Flight Center
gopher to **gopher.gsfc.nasa.gov**. This Gopher offers a lot of NASA information.

Figure 8.4

The home page for the Environmental Research Center. Underneath, ERC's main menu gives you easy access to the extensive collection of information.

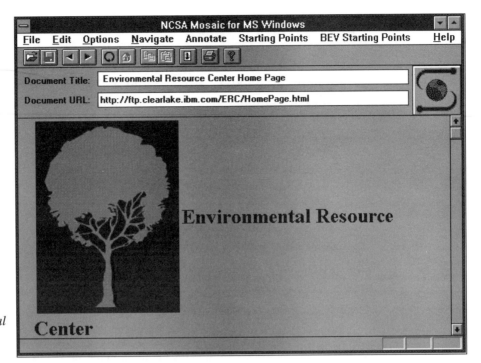

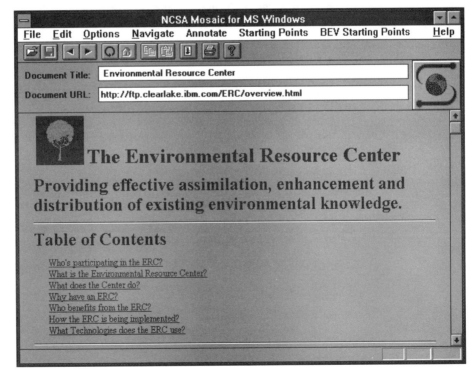

3. Conduct the experiment.

You've got a team of people and you know what the question is, so now it's time to go looking for clues and answers. You may need to gather samples of elements such as water or soil. Or the members of your team may need to observe animals, such as a flock of geese, for a certain period of time.

The process you use to do the research will have a tremendous impact on the outcome of the research. If you are working with an organization, they may be able to give you ideas about how best to gather the information. If not, ask a few people you know who are involved with science— perhaps a science teacher or someone at an environmental organization —to help you develop your plan for getting information that will help you answer your question.

Tip

In the project description you post, include specific instructions for collecting and reporting the information the student scientists find through their research, such as dates due, format for results, and so on.

4. Collect all of the results.

Once you are finished gathering data, you'll need to combine all the results to discover similarities and differences.

As project coordinator, you should create a master data sheet where you will record the information from individual researchers. By collecting the information on one sheet, you will be able to recognize patterns or gaps that will help you gain a new perspective on the problem.

5. Distribute the findings of the research.

Your description and analysis of the findings is important information that you should distribute to other scientists who might be interested in your research topic. This description should include the following:

- ✎ a one-sentence statement of the research question
- ✎ a list of the people and geographic locations involved in the project
- ✎ a brief description of how the information was collected
- ✎ a list of conclusions that the research team made based on the information or observations collected

For your conclusions, ask yourself and the other members of your research team what you learned from the project. What did you find interesting when you read the information from other researchers? Do you have enough material or the correct information to answer your original research question?

Be sure to share your findings with your research team as well as with other organizations that might find your research interesting. To find organizations that are active users of the Internet, use Veronica to conduct a Gopher search. Use the subject of your scientific research—such as environment, water, or animal—as your search word to find organizations that would be interested in your work.

Continuing Your Research

The wonderful thing about science is that there are always new unanswered questions. While some may come from the findings of your current research, they can also be new questions that you have about another topic. Here are some ideas for continuing your research.

Coordinate an Annual Research Event

Annual updates on your research are helpful to identify trends in the subject of your research. For example, is the water getting cleaner? Coordinate an annual research project on the same subject to determine if there are any long-term changes in the focus of your research.

Establish a Student Research Center

You can create your own local student research center in your community or school. While you can do this on your own, it might be fun and interesting to become a part of the *National Student Research Center*, which supports student research projects in several ways. In addition to helping and supporting your research, the Center also provides a database of findings from previous student research projects.

As you conduct research projects, you will see how much we still don't know about the world we live in. Your work is very important; it will help us expand our understanding and learn how to coexist with nature.

National Student Research Center

Send an e-mail message to **nsrcmms@aol.com**. Based at Mandeville Middle School in Louisiana, the NSRC facilitates the establishment of Student Research Centers in schools across the country. Students use the scientific method to study all kinds of problems that interest them. The NSRC publishes an electronic journal on a quarterly basis with abstracts of research projects. There is also an electronic library of student research and a database of information.

Namaste
Hindi

Guten Tag
German

Chào Bạn
Vietnamese

Bonjour
French

Buon Giorno
Italian

Ní Hâo Mà
Mandarin

Zdrastvitsye
Russian

Hello
English

Boker Tov
Hebrew

Kumustá
Filipino

Ya'teh
Navajo

Jambo
Swahili

G'day
Australian

Buenos Días
Spanish

Konnichi Wa
Japanese

Salam Aleikum
Arabic

Take a Walk on the Wild Side

Feel like living on the edge of reality? If your answer is yes, take a walk on the wild side of the Internet where only the curious ones venture. You can have fun *Playing in the MUD*. Or have a virtual experience with the project *Simulating Life*. Finally, you can test out the interactive WWW sites with *Weaving the Web*. No matter which project you choose first, you are bound for an experience you will never forget!

Note

You can also particpate in these activities by using the NetCruiser software that came with this book. Turn to Appendix C to find out more about this software.

Playing in the MUD

Note

Like to play in the MUD? Not the red, gray, or brown slimy stuff, but the wild places on the Internet called MUDs where you enter a new world and work with other people to explore it. MUD means Multi-User Dungeon. New MUD sites are popping up every day on the Internet. You won't get dirty by *Playing in the MUD*, but prepare yourself for an unusual and intriguing experience.

Do you remember when you used to make up games when you were a little kid? Maybe you used to pretend you were someone else, like a super-hero, and played with your friends on a far-off planet. You don't have to

stop pretending just because you are growing up. On the Internet, you can join sites called MUDs and create a new character that you become every time you log in to the MUD.

MUDs, or Multi-User Dungeons, are unusual places because many different people can be interacting with each other at the same time. A MUD usually has a theme or a common idea to guide what is happening online. Participants type commands to explore the environment and interact with others. In this project, you will learn about several different MUDs that you can join.

MUD is just one name for these multi-user environments. There are also MUSHs (multi-user simulated hallucinations), MOOs (MUDs, object-oriented), and MUSE-MUDs (multi-user simulated environments –multi-user dimensions).

The Internet features you will use for this project are telnet, anonymous FTP, and WWW.

Note

Joining a MUD

Getting connected to a MUD is pretty similar no matter what MUD you are trying to join. Below are the steps to join a MUD called The Never-Ending Story, which is designed for new users of MUDs (*newbies*).

1. Join one MUD.

MUDs are so different from other sites on the Internet that it is difficult to learn about them without actually getting into one and moving around. Several MUDs are designed for people who are new users of these sites. One of these is called The NeverEnding Story, as you see in Figure 9.1, which involves participants in a continuous set of adventures that include a variety of characters.

To begin your MUD experience, connect to The NeverEnding Story by telneting to the address in *MUDs for Newbies*. Once connected, you will need to type **connect guest**, which will establish you as a guest on the

```
The page peels back to reveal a scarlet light of soft ambience while white light
tears into the room where you stand.  Within that light you see a singularity,
so intense that it should vaporize you where you stand, but there is no pain...
no sensation.

You cast the book aside, frightened yet excited. You tell yourself as you tremb
le, "They're not real!  It's only a story!  That's impossible!"

<<------------------------------------------------->>>
  ** NES Mush is now a registration system **

    Contact: kris@paul.rutgers.edu   (Cuddles)

    Supply three different character names
    and a password. Valid e-mail address is
    required.

    Account "guest" is available with 15min
    login time limit. Do a "connect guest".
<<------------------------------------------------->>>
```

Figure 9.1

This is what you see when you connect to The NeverEnding Story.

system. As a guest you are given fifteen minutes to explore the different areas of The NeverEnding Story, but to participate, you will need to register by sending an e-mail message to `kris@paul.rutgers.edu`. In your message, supply the following information:

✔ Three different character names (in case your first choice is taken)

✔ A password

✔ Your e-mail address

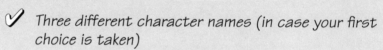

MUDs for Newbies

Diversity University
send e-mail to `mail@town.hall.org` or anonymous FTP to `town.hall.org` to learn about the DU campus and find out what address to telnet to. The DU campus is a fascinating place for anyone interested in learning and having a good time in cyberspace.

The NeverEnding Story
telnet to `snowhite.ee.pdx.edu 9999`. This is a place where you are a character in a never-ending story.

Wisney World
telnet to `levant.cs.ohiou.edu 5000` or `132.235.1.100 5000`. This is a wacky online world with many different areas to explore.

When you receive a reply message with your character name and password, you can telnet to The NeverEnding Story, type **connect**, your character name, and then, after the prompt, your password.

2. Explore a MUD.

Once you are connected to The NeverEnding Story, you can do several different things to get acquainted with how things work. To do anything, you will need to type in a command. Here is a list of a few to get you started:

help topics	*to get a list of general MUD and MUSH topics*
help commands	*to get a list of general MUSH commands*
+help	*to get a list of commands specific to The NeverEnding Story*

3. Interact with other people in the MUD.

There are many different ways to interact with people in a MUD environment. Most of the time you will need to use a combination of different commands. You will want to find out which other people are connected when you are so you can talk to them online. Each MUD may use different words, so get the list of commands the first time you connect to a new MUD.

Getting More MUDdy

The number of MUDs and other multi-user environments is increasing as more and more people find out how fun and interesting they can be. There are many different resources that can help you learn about new sites as well as offer tips for getting around in those that you have already joined. Some of these are listed in *Help Getting through the MUD*.

Help Getting through the MUD

The Almost-Complete List of MUSHes	WWW to `http://www.cis.upenn.edu/~lwl/muds.html`. This is a long list of multi-user simulated environments, but it provides addresses, short summaries, and links to appropriate FTP sites and home pages.
Current list of active MUDs	anonymous FTP to `caisr2.caisr.cwru.edu` and look in the directory `pub/mud` for old lists. Subscribe to `mudlist@glia.biostr.washington.edu` to have an updated list sent to you every Friday.
Frequently Asked Questions (FAQ) about MUDs	anonymous FTP to `ftp.math.okstate.edu` and look in the directory `pub/muds`.
MUD Information Usenets	`rec.games.mud.admin`, `rec.games.mud.tiny`, `rec.games.mud.announce`.

Subscribing to educational list servers may also keep you up-to-date because teachers who are creating special sites will often post announcements about what they are doing and how you can contribute. (See *International Survey* in Chapter 2 for some list servers to try.)

Extending Your Experience

Your experiences in a MUSE will be so exciting and unique you may want to find ways of sharing your adventures with friends and family. Here are a few ideas for showing them why you like it so much:

✔ Create a board game based on the experiences and adventures you encounter online.

✔ Help a friend connect to a MUSE and create an online character.

✔ Draw a map of the online environment if one isn't available online.

Most people who join MUDs find themselves getting addicted and have a hard time pulling themselves away from the computer to do anything else…even eat! So, be sure to eat—and have a wild time as you play in the MUD.

Simulating Life

Note

Each year a set of simulation projects are offered, each of which recreate an environment where you can explore and experience an activity without *really* doing it. Simulations are virtual reality experiences. If you did the project *Virtual Excursions* in Chapter 6, you have already simulated traveling to interesting places.

Would you like to be an astronaut in the next space shuttle mission? Or an Olympic athlete? A business whiz on the stock market? Or maybe you would like to explore an unknown planet and lead a new colony of people? Sound impossible to do? Not if you participate in one of several simulations offered through the Internet.

Simulation projects create an environment or experience that is similar to the real thing. For example, when teenagers are learning how to drive, they may simulate driving by using a machine similar to a video driving game rather than learning in a real car and risking an accident.

There are several different simulations available through Academy One on the National Public Telecommunications Network (NPTN) that might be of interest to you. You can be on a space shuttle as it launches, or you can trade commodities on the stock market, for example. While

your simulation experience won't be exactly the same as actually doing it, you will get a feel for what it might be like.

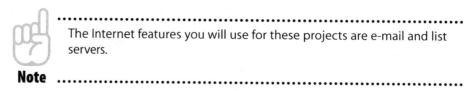

The Internet features you will use for these projects are e-mail and list servers.

Note

The Virtual Experience

The toughest part about joining a simulation is finding one that interests you at the right time. Most simulations have a time schedule because everyone involved must know when the simulation begins and ends. Follow these steps to find and join a simulation for the virtual experience of your dreams.

1. Find out what simulation projects are available.

You will be able to find several different simulations on the Internet. One group, the National Educational Simulations Project Using Tele-communications (NESPUT), offers a number of them every school year, like those shown in Figure 9.2. You can see the list from the 1994–1995 school year in *NESPUT Simulations*.

Figure 9.2

Through Academy One you can get a list of simulations as well as specific experiences included in each one.

```
<<< NESPUT: Telecommunicated Simulations >>>
            <go nesput>

1 About NESPUT and Telecommunicated Simulations
2 PROJECT: Simulated Space Shuttle Program (Centennial Launches)
3 PROJECT: Historic Space Missions (Feb., 1992)
4 PROJECT: The "Virtual Worlds" Simulation Project
```

```
<<< ACADEMY ONE SALUTES SPACE EXPLORATION >>>

1 About the simulation
2 List of participating schools
3 Simulation of Friendship 7 mission
4 Simulation of Apollo 11 mission
5 Simulation of the Hubble Telescope
6 Simulation of Challenger 2 Mission
7 Reports from simulated NASA stations worldwide
8 Space Trivia
9 What were you doing when...
10 The Press Box (Comments)
-----------------------------------------------------
h=Help, x=Exit Free-Net, "go help"=extended help
```

NESPUT Simulations

The National Educational Simulations Project Using Telecommunications (NESPUT) offered the following simulations through Academy One during the 1994–1995 school year:

Centennial Launches	Schools around the world will participate in a simulated space shuttle mission. Some schools will simulate the shuttle, others will be alternate landing sites, weather stations, solar flare observatories, Space Station Freedom, and others.
Salute to Space Exploration	This event pays tribute to all pioneers of the space programs around the world. The simulation will center around a historic space shuttle mission.
TeleOlympics	Individuals compete in a variety of track events in their own school yards and post the winning scores in each category to the computer network. Results are compared and international winners receive recognition.
Virtual Worlds Simulation	This space simulation allows every participant to be an astronaut who voyages to an unknown planet. A special NASA video is used to drive the liftoff and landing sequences. Students conduct a variety of experiments in flight and on the new planet.
Taking Stock Simulation	This interactive project is based on the inner workings of the stock market, where individuals buy and sell stock without risking real money.

List of Simulations

You can get an updated list of simulation projects in two ways:

- Send an e-mail message to **aa005@nptn.org** asking for the most current list of NESPUT simulations.

- Telnet to the Cleveland Freenet (**freenet-in-a.cwru.edu**) or the Youngstown Freenet (**yfn2.ysu.edu**) and select "Academy One." From Academy One's main menu, select "Projects Underway." If you're not already a registered user of this Freenet, follow the instructions on the screen to become one.

To get a current list of the simulations, connect to Academy One, which hosts these projects. Follow the directions in *List of Simulations* to do so.

2. **Ask about the project schedule and participation requirements.**

To decide which simulation you should join, ask yourself a few questions based on what you've learned from Academy One. Your answers to these questions will help you decide if a particular project interests you and works with your schedule.

> ❓ *What interests do you have?*
>
> ❓ *How much time is required?*
>
> ❓ *When does the project begin and end?*
>
> ❓ *Does the project accept both individuals and groups for participation?*
>
> ❓ *What Internet features do I need to participate?*

3. **Stick with the project.**

Once you make a commitment to a simulation project, stick with it. The other participants and project coordinators will be counting on you to perform your role in the simulation.

At the end of the simulation, you may want to continue corresponding with the other people in the project. You can talk about your experiences during the simulation and maybe even plan a future simulation for other groups of people.

Getting in on the Action

Because simulations usually require a group of people to work together within a set period of time, you'll need to find out about new simulations *before* they start. Most simulations won't allow people to join in the middle of the simulation. So how do you stay informed about new opportunities? You might want to check list servers such as those listed in *International Surveys* in Chapter 2, look at Academy One postings, and keep in contact with previous simulation participants. Don't forget: When you find out about a new simulation, share the information online!

Weaving the Web

Note

New World Wide Web (WWW) sites are being created every day, some of which let you try out some pretty amazing experiments. In *Weaving the Web*, you can dissect a frog and play games with moving geometric shapes and patterns. As you become a pro at using the Web, you can even make your own Web page to put on the Internet.

Just as a spider weaves its web to capture its food, you can weave yourself around the World Wide Web to capture a few wild experiences. No longer are Web pages just places to read and browse around. New pages are being developed that let you interact with the page, similar to how you interact with software games and programs.

People are excited about the potential of WWW and programs like Mosaic that let you easily interact online with them. The graphic capability that allows pictures and even movies to be sent across the Internet and viewed is pretty impressive. We're seeing the first step toward multimedia networks, and you're in on it!

Note

The Internet feature you will use for this project is WWW.

Frog Dissection Using a Computer

Do you think dissecting a frog would be interesting, but you don't like the idea of touching a dead creature? Does your school not have access to the laboratory equipment you need to dissect a frog? The Interactive Frog Dissection can help you learn what a dissection is all about, and you'll be able to see what's inside a frog. Figure 9.3 shows the main menu for the Interactive Frog Dissection.

1. **Connect to the Interactive Frog Dissection.**

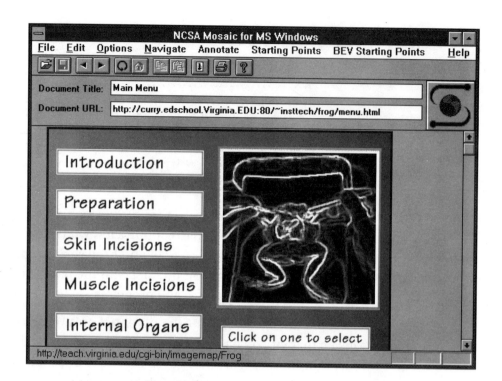

Figure 9.3

This is the main menu for the Interactive Frog Dissection.

Interactive Frog Dissection

You will need to open a new URL and type in
http://curry.edschool.virginia.edu/
~insttech/frog

Created by graduate students at the University of Virginia, this site takes you step-by-step through an actual dissection of a frog with pictures, movies, and written descriptions. Use the address in *Interactive Frog Dissection* to connect to this Web site.

Note

Be aware that these items, especially the movies, are big files that take time to download. Be patient. You will know that an item is being downloaded by the movement of two small circles on the Mosaic icon.

2. Explore each section of the main menu.

When you bring up the main menu for this project, you will see five different areas you can enter. Within each area you will be given information about the frog's different internal systems, shown different dissection techniques, and presented with activities to check how well you learned.

It will help you a great deal to begin with the Introduction. Included in this is a category called Conventions where you will find tips for interacting with this Web site.

Tip

As images or movies are downloading, use the scroll bar to read through all of the text. Then, when you can see the image or movie, you will already be familiar with what is being demonstrated.

Gallery of Geometric Games

The Geometry Center, a project of the University of Minnesota, is the home of a gallery of games, all of which incorporate geometric shapes or patterns. You don't have to be a geometry whiz to play the games. In fact, the games may help you learn different geometric principles and provide you with a better understanding than you would get just from reading about it in a textbook. The Geometry Center main menu is shown in Figure 9.4.

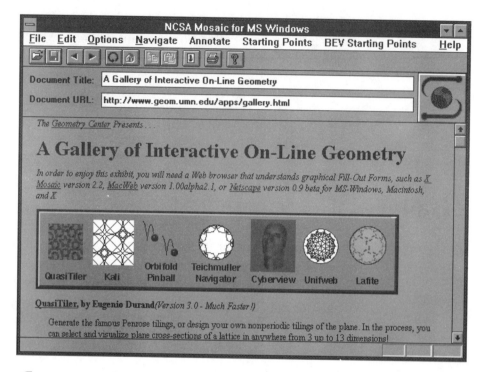

Figure 9.4

This is the main menu for the Geometry Center.

1. Connect to the Geometry Center.

While you can use any Web browser to connect with *The Geometry Center*, you will need specific browsing software to actually play the games:

- ☑ MacWeb for the Macintosh, or
- ☑ XMosaic for Windows

The Geometry Center

You will need to open a new URL and type
http://www.geom.umn.edu/apps/gallery.html.

If you don't already have one of these, you can easily download one by clicking on links provided on the Geometry Center's Home Page. These are public domain tools and they can be installed easily.

2. Play Orbifold Pinball.

In Orbifold Pinball you roll a ball on an unusual playing board. The game includes bumpers like a regular pinball game, but the board is

curved so a ball that barely misses a bumper will still be whipped around as if it had hit the bumper. The game gets its name from the board's shape, which mathematicians call an *orbifold*. In Figure 9.5 you can see information about Orbifold Pinball.

Figure 9.5

When you enter each game, you will see a description of the geometric principles and objectives of the game.

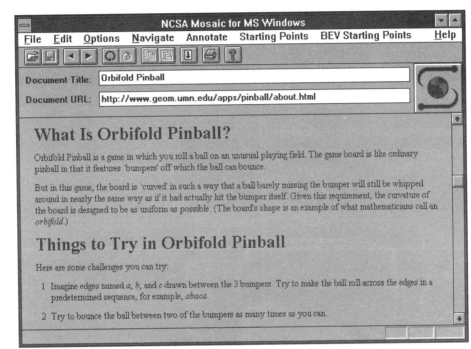

Games at the Geometry Center

QuasiTiler	create beautiful nonperiodic tilings of a space.
Teichmuller Navigator	manipulate tiles to create moving geometric patterns.
Cyberview	see images through an interactive 3-D object viewer for the WWW. The Geometry Center provides a library of images.
Unifweb	discover and visualize geometric surfaces by choosing different generators and relations.
Lafite	create symmetrical patterns, like those of M.C. Escher.

3. Try the other games.

This site offers many other games you can play—look at *Games at the Geometry Center* for some ideas. Each game was created by a different person, which makes each one special.

Adding to the Web

The World Wide Web is a collaborative creation of many people with different ideas. There are people just like you who are interested in trying new things and exploring new ways of learning.

Make Your Own Home Page

It's possible for you to make your very own Home Page that anyone on the Internet can explore. You create the document using ASCII text, the most basic computer language with commands that are specific to a language called HTML (hypertext markup language). The different tutorials listed in *Guides for Making Your Own Web Home Page* will take you step-by-step through the process. What you put in your page is up to you. You can make it focus on your favorite sport, your school or community, your favorite books, or anything else you think other people would find interesting.

There are several WWW sites designed for education which *might* house your Home Page for the entire Internet community to explore. While the sites listed in *WWW Sites for Education* do not currently house student pages, the organizers of these sites might know the address for a site that does.

Guides for Making Your Own Web Home Page

The NCSA Education Group's OnLine Tutorials
`http://www.ncsa.uiuc.edu/Edu/Tutorials/TutorialHome.html`.

The HTML Documents
A Mosaic Tutorial: `http://fire.clarkson.edu/doc/html/htut.html`. This tutorial will show you how to create and display Mosaic screens.

WWW Sites for Education

K-12 Resources
`http://www.nas.nasa.gov/HPCC/K12/edures.html`

Janice's K-12 Cyberspace Outpost
`http://k12.cnidr.org/janice_k12/k12menu.html`

NASA Ames Research Center K-12 World Wide Web
`http://quest.arc.nasa.gov/`

Subscribe to the Scout Report

To find out about new pages, subscribe to *The Scout Report*. It's a weekly update of new sites—all kinds of sites—and includes addresses and short descriptions of what you will find. At the end of the report is a Weekend Scouting section that lists the sites designed mostly for fun.

The Scout Report

There are several different methods of subscribing to the Scout Report:

By list server "Scout-Report"
subscribe to `majordomo@is.internic.net`

By WWW
`http://www.internic.net/infoguide.html`

By Gopher
`is.internic.net` and then select "InterNIC Information Services/Scout Report"

The Web will continue to expand, grow, and evolve. Be a part of the process by checking out new sites and creating and updating your own. You will truly be contributing to the world of tomorrow.

Networks: Where Have You Been All My Life?

In this appendix you'll find a lot of kids' responses to the question, "Networks, where have you been all my life?" Many of these responses were winners in an essay contest on that topic that was sponsored by the U.S. Department of Education's National Center for Education Statistics, the National Science Foundation, and the National Aeronautics and Space Administration (NASA).

Frank "Gib" Gibson

This essay was written by 1993 SuperQuest participant Frank Gibson of New Hanover High School in Wilmington, North Carolina. It won the 1994 "Networks: Where Have You Been All My Life?" essay contest. A hypertext version of this essay exists on the World Wide Web at: `http://www.tc.cornell.edu/Edu/SQ/Gibson/Gibson.essay.93.html`.

Midway through my junior year at New Hanover High School in Wilmington, North Carolina, an experience began for me that has re-routed the path of my entire education and learning adventures. I and three other students won a national scientific computing contest called SuperQuest, sponsored by the Cornell University Theory Center and the

National Science Foundation. SuperQuest was no ordinary science fair—rather, it was a "take a giant leap outside of your mind" contest. It was a fortuitous opportunity for us high schoolers. Our sudden introduction to the world of high-performance computers included IBM RISC clusters, an ES/9000 vector processor, and a KSR parallel processor.

One of the greatest benefits of participating in the SuperQuest program has been my exposure to computer networks and telecommunications. I delved into the online world for my first time, before we had won, when the team and I were constructing a science project the SuperQuest judges might deem a winner. We spent just one whole semester reaching consensus on the topic! Each of us had ideas—from investigating mag-lev trains, to orb spiderwebs, to pitching a baseball. Which of these were within our capability? And which should we perhaps leave to the Princeton researchers? We turned to the Internet to gather the advice and experience of more knowledgeable folks. Our first action was to post questions on as many science bulletin boards and online services as possible. The two we frequented were the SuperQuest home base at the Cornell Theory Center and the High-Performance Computing network (HPCwire). Both were the ideal sources to check the feasibility of modeling an orb spider web or the flight of a baseball on a supercomputer. Sometimes we received answers in a day—and sometimes within an hour. We were wowed not only by the speed of the knowledge transfer, but also by the altruism of the network community. Through our communications, we were able to quickly focus on the orb spider web as our project. It was within our scope.

In the archaic tradition of our twelve years of schooling, we trekked to the local library to research spider webs. This proved to be time-consuming. One of our teachers introduced us to WAIS, Internet's indexed database search function. Ecstasy! We sat with him as he logged onto the net from his desktop PC, called up WAIS, and ordered it to do both a worldwide search of indexes with the words "spider" or "web" in them, and a cross-reference follow-up. Within twenty minutes, the net had spewed twenty pages of information sources. We were filled with the sudden comprehension of the scientific process—the gathering of data and the elimination of possibilities.

As part of the SuperQuest prize, we attended a three-week summer seminar at the Cornell Theory Center. There we were introduced to LAN networks and file-sharing, mainframes and X-terminals, and the minute details of the Internet. Thus, we could suddenly access the libraries of each of the seven schools at Cornell as well as data from specialized projects such as the synchrotron and recent biomedical research. Again, the process of gathering data was accomplished primarily through using computer communications.

Upon our return home, we were able to use our Internet connection (which was another SuperQuest reward) to continue our research and also access the computer facilities back at Cornell. After two months of a maniacal pace, and with our interim report mailed, we decided to take a week-long break. However, I found myself drawn to the computer—there were so many interesting things to explore, and I was so curious. I logged into "sunsite" at the University of North Carolina at Chapel Hill and began browsing archives, just for the fun of it. I pulled up a picture of an ancient Vatican manuscript, with its crinkled brown pages and mottled writing. However, disappointed that I could not make out any of the words, I was about to close the window, when I had an idea! Using the XV software (also obtained from the net), I zoomed into one word and smoothed it—and suddenly it was legible! I had stumbled onto a combination of resources that allowed me to examine the document.

And I didn't stop there. My high school's current agenda involves the reforming of the traditional daily schedule; we may initiate "block" schedules in the coming year. As student body president, I represent my school on the Superintendent's Advisory Board (our mission: to investigate the pros and cons of block scheduling). We decided that most importantly, we needed to hear from students in other schools which had implemented the program. The nearest one was five hours away. A group of teachers had been bussed in the previous month to visit for an hour or two of questions—the only time available after travel time. No student on the advisory board wanted to repeat this exercise, and in fact, we were almost reduced to drawing straws for a victim, when I had a sudden flash. A bit of background: The state of North Carolina has, within the past five years, set up a fiber-optics network that enables a teacher at one school to simultaneously teach her home class as well as classes which are located across the county and even the state. My mother was

teaching an Oceanography class over the system, and I knew that at least one of those schools was block-scheduled. At the next advisory board meeting, I moved that we postpone our road trip and use the fiber-optics network for an after-school teleconference. Within four weeks, we had teleconferenced with two block-scheduled schools. We asked questions that mattered to students: what happens when you miss school, how are athletics affected, and how are advanced placement classes organized? Moreover, the two block-scheduled schools were able to discuss their own variations of block scheduling.

Computer technology has not simply affected my education; it has changed my personality. I have traveled from having a daydream about why spider webs are so strong, to performing concrete scientific research, to making an obscure document understandable (one which I did not know existed but for the Internet), and I initiated a solution to a real-life organizational problem. I'm feeling pretty good.

Randy Hammer, 11th Grade

Randy Hammer, a DO-IT Scholar at the University of Washington and eleventh-grader at Timberline High School in Lacey, Washington, was runner-up in the grade 10–12 category in a national essay contest on the Internet.

My name is Randy Hammer, and I am a junior at Timberline High School in Lacey, Washington. I am totally blind, with two glass eyes. I have been blind all my life, and never known anything different. I have been mainstreamed in schools all my life and have always had to depend on others to get me school materials. If I needed or wanted a book for class, it had to be transcribed into Braille or put on tape. However, in August of last year a whole new door was opened to me. I am a member of the DO-IT (Disabilities, Opportunities, Internetworking Technology) Program at the University of Washington. This program is funded greatly by the National Science Foundation. It gives high school students with disabilities the chance to overcome their challenges by the use of the Internet.

Getting Internet access was the best thing that ever happened to me. In a way, my computer and access to the net has become my eyes to the world. I can read a newspaper, talk to people around the world, and get materials for class papers, unlike before when I had to depend on others to get the resources I needed.

Upon receiving my access in August of 1993, I was able to read a newspaper for the first time in my life. This may sound trivial, but to me it was a great accomplishment. It was the *Washington Post*. I was not aware of the variety of topics covered by newspapers. I knew about the front page, feature articles, and sports section, for instance, but I did not know of the huge amount of stories in these sections. I was amazed. Before getting access, I had to get sighted people to read me the paper. However, with the help of a screen reader and a host at the University of Washington called UWIN (University of Washington Information Navigator), I browsed through the paper, found just what I wanted to read, and read it. I can even mail myself the articles and save them; somewhat like how you cut articles that you like out of the paper to save for future reference. This was amazing to me. And not only can I read the *Washington Post*, but also the *Moscow News,* and several other papers mainly used by scientists. So, the net has helped me get in better contact with the world via online newspapers.

Many of you know of IRC or some other type of chat system. This caught me by surprise when I first started on the net. I am taking German in high school and plan to be a foreign-language expert. If I want to try out my German on people, I just telnet to Germany and try it on actual Germans (who are really strict teachers, and who catch every mistake you make; I know, I have made many). Another aspect of the chat systems is talking to people about current events. I can telnet to a chat system and talk to people from California about the earthquakes there, or I can talk to people from Kansas City and ask about the Chiefs' chances in the Super Bowl. Thus, the net is a tool for me to get feedback from people all over the world on what they think of different things, and it's an interesting way to make new friends.

But the best aspect of the net is the ability to get information on any topic. There are a lot of ways to do this. First, you can join a list server and find out about a topic from experts. Though I haven't joined a list server yet, I may do so in the near future. Second, you can e-mail an expert in a field with a question and get an answer to your question quickly. But the best way to get materials is through Gopherspace. I recently needed information on Poland. I entered Gopherspace, moved to a server in Poland itself, and there I found all the information I needed on my subject. Also, there are encyclopedias, dictionaries, and thesauruses in Gopherspace. If a server does not have the information you need, you can just find either another that will have the exact material or one that will have some sort of information book that you can use to get the information that you need.

In closing, the Internet has become a great part of my life. In the seven months that I have had access to the net, I have built up over two hundred hours on it. I use it to find out about current events, do research papers for school, and just talk to people about everyday life. I would recommend the Internet to anyone that needs these services. It is hard now to remember how I lived without this wealth of materials and information at my fingertips.

Marcus Saylor, Age 6

Marcus Saylor, age six, is in the first grade at Delmar Elementary School in Mardela, Maryland.

Hi my name is Marcus. I am six. I like computers. I have a friend in Tasmania. His name is Glenn and he wrote to me. I know where that is on the map. It is far far away. I can see it on the map on the screen. It is dark on the screen where Glenn is, but it is light where America is. That's because Glenn is sleepy and I am in school. Tasmania is on the bottom of the world! The water might be falling because it is in the bottom. Glenn is not in school right now because it is summer, and he's asleep right now anyway. We are having winter and it is cold here but not where Glenn lives. I see his picture on my wall by the map of the whole big world. His teacher sent it to us. He has dark brown hair and he wrote to me and it is fun. Yeah, I like to do this real good.

I have another friend in England called Billy, but I don't have his picture. He told us that he likes his mummy and daddy and Merwin. He likes swimming, picnics, and riding horses. I never rode a horse. But I like to swim. I never went on a picnic. Billy goes to Stanley Infant School in London. That's funny because it doesn't seem the same name as our school. An infant is a baby, but that's what they call their schools in England for the little children.

I have a big friend in Finland who talked to me on the computer one day. His words came on the screen. I saw them coming fast. I told him that I can count up to 10…now I can almost count to 100! My friend is Mikael and he gave me his numbers in his language. We are writing big sentences today, and we are almost off the screen! My teacher gave me a copy of how to count up to ten in Finland.

I was in the newspaper because I was typing to Glenn on the computer. My messages go to Glenn and Billy and Mikael through that thing over there called a modem. The lights blink when we do this. It goes to the big network like a post office through the telephone wires. My letters get there fast.

There's a Rudolf and a snowman on our computer that blinks. I like it. It is real pretty. Our friend, Meike, in The Netherlands sent them to us. She made the pictures.

Our friend, Olya, in Russia sent us her picture through the wires, and she and her brother are there, but the picture is on its side! Olya sent us a little tune about a fir tree that the Russian children put in their house at New Year's.

I feel good when I come to the computer room and I play with numbers and stories and write to my friends. I come every day. I wish I had a computer at home. This helps me in school because it gets my mind better because you are reading and reading and that's good. I learn about other countries and maps and what time it is.

The chat that follows was held for a demonstration of the KIDLINK IRC chat capability. Lara Stefansdottir, sysop of the Icelandic Education Network, was presenting telecom at a European Conference on telecommunications and asked participants to join her. There were participants from Maryland, Finland, South Carolina, Chicago, Virginia, New Jersey, and Iceland. The chat has been edited for clarity. Note that when a participant gives his or her seat to a new participant, a message appears to notify others. ("Patti is now Marcus," for example, indicates that Patti has given her seat to Marcus.)

—..—..—..—..—..—..—..—..—..—..—..—..—..—.—

Excerpts from a real time IRC chat on Thursday, October 14, 1993

—..—..—..—..—..—..—..—..—..—..—..—..—..—.—

<A_JamieW> Hello first graders…

*** PattiW is now known as Marcus

<A_JamieW> Are you part of the group writing to England?

<Mikael> Hello Marcus

<A_JamieW> Hello Marcus!

<Marcus> hhhhhhhhhhiiiiiii

<RebeccaL> Hi Marcus

<BonnieT> My students are writing to England

<Marcus> ii aaam 66

<Marcus> oops! he's 6 (Patti)

<A_JamieW>Bonnie, is that in the vacation project or to Mike's group of kids?

<Mikael> =)

<BonnieT> It is the vacation project

<A_JamieW> Two of my students are also writing to England..in that project.

<BonnieT> The social studies are looking for other groups as well but the vacation
project is wonderful

<A_JamieW> Ben has been a busy boy!

<Mikael> Could I ask… when is the IRC Chat tomorrow?

<BonnieT> Yes, Ben has!!!!!!!

<Marcus>i like ssschhhhool

<BonnieT> I would like to know that as well

<A_JamieW> Mikael, it should begin about an hour earlier than right now, I think.

<RebeccaL> Marcus, where are you? Did I miss that?

<Mikael> Marcus, what is your favorite subject?

<A_JamieW> I will not be able to join anyone until after 1:00 however… :-(

<Marcus> I like math

<A_JamieW> Good for you Marcus.

<A_JamieW> What are you learning in Math now?

<Mikael> Marcus: That's great! That is my favorite subject, too =)

<Marcus> i can count to 20

<A_JamieW> Marcus, my little girl is in first grade, too.

<Marcus> i am in America

<RebeccaL> Marcus, that is GREAT!

<Marcus> i am in Delmar Maryland

<Mikael> Marcus, would you like to have the first ten numbers in Swedish
and Finnish?

<Marcus> yes!

<A_JamieW> So would we!

<Marcus> pleassseee

<RebeccaL> YES!

<Mikael> Then I will mail them to Patti and she can give them to you!

<RebeccaL> OHHHH I thought you were going to tell us now! My 7th graders
are excited!

<Mikael> ok. here they are:

<Marcus> thhhhhhhhank yyoouu

<Mikael> first in Swedish (my mother tongue), then in Finnish…

*** Marcus is now known as Heather

(Heather is another 1st grader who changed seats with Marcus at this
point, though Marcus got to see the numbers from Mikael.)

<Mikael> 1 = ett = yksii

<Mikael> 2 = tva = kaksi

<Mikael> 3 = tre = kolme

<Mikael> 4 = fyra = neljao

*** dwatson (dwatson@leo.nmc.edu) hasjoined channel #europe

<Mikael> 5 = fem = viisio

<Heather> i am 6 too

<Mikael> 6 = sex = kuusi

<Mikael> 7 = sju = seitsemanwwe

<Mikael> 8 = atta = kahdeksanike

<Mikael> 9 = nio = yhdeksan

<Mikael> There they are!

<Mikael> Some of the a and o have little dots over them =)

<Heather> wwe like your numbbers

<Mikael> Letters you don't have in English.

<dwatson> Mikael…Where are you?

<Mikael> dwatson: In Vaasa, Finland.

The chat continued. These kids may be among the youngest passengers on the Information Highway.

Rachel Weston

Seventh-grader Rachel Weston, who attends school in Arlington, Virginia, wrote this essay.

As I flipped through my e-mail messages one morning, I suddenly received a new one entitled "The Sydney Bush Fires." The mail was from my Australian key pal, and he was telling me and some of his other key pals what it was like to be experiencing the bush fires that were burning all round Sydney. Forgetting all about my other messages for the time being, I quickly wrote back and arranged to go with him to the KIDLINK IRC (Internet Relay Chat). On IRC, a place where, amazingly, people can talk back and forth, I was able to ask my friend all about the disaster. It turned out he was less than ten kilometers from the fires, he could see the flame-tinged sky and smell the smoke from his window, and he was able to tell me how far the fires were from the famous Opera House and the Taronga Park Zoo. During the next several days I communicated through e-mail several times more with my Sydney friend, and the fires got even closer to his house. Ultimately he was safe. However, all week long the information about the Sydney fires that I knew was more up to date than anything in the newspapers.

That is only one of my amazing network experiences, but it is one that illustrates the way being on a computer network and having access to the Internet has changed my life in wonderful ways.

I was one of the first students from my school to get an electronic address on CapAccess, a local public access network in the Washington, D.C., metropolitan area. Using CapAccess I have learned how to use the library section, which is very helpful with my school research projects. In this section I can search for information from a dictionary, a library card catalog, or an article database. This occurred recently when I wrote about the Blue Crab that lives in the Chesapeake Bay. While I couldn't always get the article that I needed, the network told me exactly where to look in my local library, and if I had a fax machine (which I don't), I could have asked for an article to be faxed to me for a small charge.

I have also used Gopher sections to look up interesting topics, gather information, and mail them to my electronic mailbox. A lot of places have a Gopher, and when you get to one Gopher, it is possible to travel from there to a lot of other Gopher locations.

Now that I have been on CapAccess for a few months, I am interested in registering at another Freenet, perhaps at the National Capital Freenet in Ottawa, Canada. One of the neat things about this network is that, being in Canada, it has information in French and in English. After visiting this network a few times, I believe it will give me some opportunities to develop my French skills and be a better French student.

Being on a network has also expanded my circle of friends. At my school right now there are not many girls who are as interested in network technology as I am, though there are quite a few boys. By joining a list server called Kidcafe, I have met a group of girls who are just as interested as I am (I have also met some more boys). At the beginning many of us used the list server a lot. Now we use our own electronic addresses and only use the list server on occasion. I still use the Kidcafe list server to make new acquaintances.

My friends write back and forth almost every day, and we carry on interesting conversations—sometimes about the networking and sometimes about ordinary middle school things. Sometimes we help each other learn how to do new technical things. For instance, my friends in England and Tennessee helped me get started and master IRC. As I get more confident about my networking skills, I hope to share them with my friends at school, encouraging them to discover the opportunities that are available.

I would also like to help my school develop its space on CapAccess. I think it would be fun to have a conversation area or, more importantly, a homework question-and-answer section. This would involve both teachers and students. Because a lot of students would be interested in using the homework section, they would master the basics of networking.

I think this is how a lot of people will eventually learn the skills they will need to do a particular task, and they will learn the networking part in order to do the job.

Although the Internet and CapAccess are a lot of fun and have expanded my horizons, there are some difficulties. In order to make some time each day to use the network, I have had to become more organized with my schoolwork. Sometimes that even means starting my homework at recess and really working in study hall. At other times, I rush to check and clear messages when I have a minute or two after school.

These days I cannot imagine how I used to manage without access to a network. The technology of the network and my activities have made me realize how small the world can be. When I communicate with someone in Slovenia or England or Argentina, I realize that the problems that they have are not very far away from me. So even though we are all far away from one another in miles, we are all part of the same global community.

Excerpts from Seth J. Itzkan's Interview with Chris Tanski

The interview, excerpted as follows, was conducted online with Chris Tanski, a fourteen-year-old Internet guru. Chris is the owner of three list servers and is on the Internet at least twenty hours a week managing discussion forums that feed around the world.

Seth: Who are you? What is your name? How old are you? Where do you go to school?

Chris: My name is Chris Tanski, and I am 14 years old. I am the owner of two Listproc lists and one Listserv list. I am also an associate at MapPower Corp., and I'm in the 9th grade at the Cortland Jr./Sr. High School in Cortland, New York. My hobbies include computers and cycling.

Seth: How long have you been working with networking, and particularly the Internet?

Chris: I have been involved with computers since I was seven years old when I used an Apple II+. Today I use a Mac LCII. I have been involved with networking since I was 13. That was also the time I started investigating the online world. Today I have one Internet acct., one Internet/bitnet acct., one bitnet/Internet mail-only acct., and one Internet mail and Usenet acct. along with my 14,400-bps modem.

Seth: What are the list servers that you are the owner of? Tell me a little about them.

Chris: The `GOLF-L` list, which is hosted by `LISTSERV@UBVM` or `LISTSERV@UBVM.CC.BUFFALO.EDU`, was popular from the start. About 15,000 postings later, the list currently has over 250 subscribers and sees about 70 to 90 postings per day. The list is also gatewayed to the `REC.SPORT.GOLF` Usenet group. The next list I started was the `BICYCLE` list, now hosted by `LISTPROC@YUKON.CREN.ORG`. There are almost 300 subscribers coupled with 30 to 50 postings per day. The third list I started was the `SKI-L` list, again hosted by `LISTPROC@YUKON.CREN.ORG`. This list has around 150 subscribers and sees 10 postings per month.

Seth: How long have you been the owner of these list servers? How did you set them up? Is there any cost? Are you sponsored?

Chris: Setting up the lists was easier said than done. The GOLF-L list was set up at the University of Buffalo, which graciously agreed to host the list despite the heavy load on their system. The GOLF-L list was difficult to manage at first due to my inexperience with Listserv. However after about 50 notes to the staff at the Univ. of Buffalo, I began to get the hang of Listserv. Perhaps the format below will summarize:

LIST NAME	ORGANIZATION WHICH SET UP LIST	SYSTEM ON WHICH LIST IS
GOLF-L	University of Buffalo	LISTSERV@UBVM LISTSERV@UBVM.CC.BUFFALO.EDU
BICYCLE	Bitnet (CREN) NIC	LISTPROC@YUKON.CREN.ORG
SKI-L	Bitnet (CREN) NIC	LISTPROC@YUKON.CREN.ORG

The process by which I started the golf list was this. First I got a list of all the list server systems geographically nearby. This included sites throughout New York. Next I used the RELEASE command to determine the list server postmaster at each site. I then wrote to each list server postmaster explaining that I wanted to set up a list about golf, and I asked if their list server could host the list. I received negative replies from most and so I wrote to the Listserv list owners' discussion list asking if any list server postmasters would consider hosting the list. I received a reply from the Univ. of Buffalo, and they agreed to host the list; however, due to low disk space, archives of the list could not be kept. That's how the GOLF-L list came to be. The BICYCLE list was formed basically the same way. I contacted local list server postmasters and the Bitnet (CREN) NIC agreed to host the list. The SKI-L list was formed by me contacting the Bitnet NIC and asking if they would mind hosting another list. Setting up the lists did not cost a thing, and I am not sponsored.

Seth: How many hours are you online?

Chris: I am online for 15 to 25 hours per week. This increases to 23 to 30 during the summer. The number of hours also increases steadily every year as I have more responsibilities (such as managing my lists) to carry out.

Seth: What are your responsibilities as a list server owner?

Chris: The main item which takes up the majority of my online time is diagnosing and responding to error messages generated by mailers and list servers. I take these messages and make entries in a log book I have. The log includes the address of the subscriber affected, which list is the error for, the number of error messages (which steadily increases), and a description of the error message and the action taken by me. When a certain number of error messages are received, the postmaster of the site on which the affected user is receives a note from me which details the fact that the user can't receive list mail for various reasons. The user for whom the error messages are being generated is then removed from the list and only allowed back on the list when the problem(s) causing the error message is corrected. On an average day, I receive at least 30 error messages, however, on some days I have received as many as 150. Another responsibility of a list owner is to deal with disputes which may arise on the list. These are commonly referred to as flame wars and start when one subscriber makes a personal attack on another subscriber based on something that was said. Flaming usually includes obscene language and/or racial slurs. Flames, as opposed to constructive criticism, are not welcome because of the negative tone they are associated with as well as the intent to embarrass a person. My policy, which is similar to that of most other list owners, is a one strike and you're out policy. If you flame someone, then you are taken off the list and not allowed back on.

Seth: What is MapPower? What do you do for them?

Chris: MapPower Corp. is my place of employment. I have been working there since September of 1993. My job ranges from office work (copies, filing, etc.), to working with 4th Dimension and MapGrafix software. MapPower specializes in linking electronic maps with powerful database software to create a custom management solution. I am proud to be able to work for the corp.

Seth: Do you help your teachers or school administrators with any networking or Internet-related issues?

Chris: I have no formal relationship with my school that involves answering questions about computers in general, the Internet, or networking. I do try and answer all questions teachers or administrators may have.

Seth: Where did you learn Internet commands and list server management? Did you teach yourself?

Chris: I taught myself Internet commands as well as list server commands. Every now and then I may have to refer to the manual or online help for exact command syntax and/or command arguments. I have a strategy for learning anything that has to do with computers—I try to learn the program, system, etc., without using the manual(s). I believe manuals are for referring to when you have a problem, not for learning a topic. It follows that I believe in learning from experience.

Seth: Do you know other "youth" list owners like yourself? If so, can you tell me a little about them?

Chris: No, I don't know any other youth Listserv owners.

Seth: Other than technical knowledge, what have you learned from being a list manager?

Chris: The majority of what I have learned has been technical, but there are a few things that I have learned other than that. First, a large percentage of the people who use the net are more likely to consider the person they are corresponding with as a machine rather than a person. This explains why flaming takes place; the flamer thinks of every other user as a terminal or computer. That is because people feel protected or shielded by their computer; people know that the person they flame can't get physical with them because of the distance factor. Another thing I have learned from being a list owner is that users of the net are much more apt to be friendly with a person over the net than they are when meeting face to face. This goes along with the reason for flaming; users know that they can be friendly with someone and not have to be embarrassed should the person replying decide to be over-friendly as well.

Seth: What do you see as the academic value of networking?

Chris: Networking has a very large academic value. However, I feel the context in which networking is currently used may be slightly off. The majority of students using the net under the direction of their teachers are using it for pen-pal purposes. While this may appear to work, I don't believe it does anything more than waste bandwidth. If students wish to pursue that area on their own, then fine, but they shouldn't be forced into it. I think the most appropriate use of the Internet is the sharing of resources. A student could access data from the NOAA for a report on Earth Science. A student could check Usenet groups for discussion about topics they are studying in class and correspond with real people instead of reading out of a textbook. But most of all, I think students need to be allowed time to explore the net on their own, at their own pace.

Seth: What suggestions do you have for helping to get more youth involved in networking?

Chris: The big problem with the Internet is that many people and businesses are trying to expand the resources for those already connected instead of providing access to those people not connected. I think connection providers need to recognize the fact that youth have as much right to open and unrestricted access as anyone else. If I had to offer advice to a district looking to get connected, it would be the following:

• involve students in the process; this will provide insight into the amount of usage, resources required, etc.

• look beyond the realm of obvious choices for Internet providers— check for those providers just starting out.

• hire an independent consultant, someone not affiliated in any way with your school district, state ed. department, etc.

Seth: What do you want to do in the future?

Chris: I hope to study networking at college and become either a network analyst, systems analyst, information specialist, or network designer. My goal is to receive my doctorate in some area of computing.

Chris Tanski:

ctanski@onondaga
captanski33@snycorva.cortland.edu

About the author:

Seth J. Itzkan is a writer and consultant in the area of global networking. Contact him online at Seth35@aol.com.

Resources

This appendix is a resource guide to all of the Internet sources you will find throughout the book. The resources are organized under the following categories and alphabetized by name.

Art and Music

Communications

Economics

Fun and Games

Geography and Environment

Government

Literature and Writing

Mathematics

Miscellaneous

Reference

Sports and Hobbies

Art and Music

3-D Graphics

An online gallery of three-dimensional graphics; it is used in *Gallery of the Future* (Chapter 7).

```
http://www.mcs.net/~wallach/freeart/buttons.html
```

A Cappella Music Discussion

A Usenet group that is a discussion of a cappella music; it is used in *Musical Outlets* (Chapter 7).

```
rec.music.a-capella
```

Acoustic Guitar Archive

An anonymous FTP site that is an archive of acoustic guitar music as well as the magazine *Acoustic Guitar Digest;* it is used in *Musical Outlets* (Chapter 7).

```
casbah.acns.nwu.edu and look in pub/acoustic-guitar
```

Allmusic

A list server about all types of music; it is used in *Artistic Reflections* and *Musical Outlets* (Chapters 4 and 7).

```
listserv@auvm.american.edu
```

Artcrit

A list server about art criticism and analysis; it is used in *Artistic Reflections* and *Gallery of the Future* (Chapters 4 and 7).

```
listserv@yorkvm1.bitnet
```

Artserve

A WWW site that contains an art history database; it is used in *Artistic Reflections* (Chapter 4).

```
http://rubens.anu.edu.au/
```

ASCII Library

A Gopher that contains ASCII-based graphical images; it is used in *Gallery of the Future* (Chapter 7).

```
cs4sun.cs.ttu.edu
```

or `gopher.cs.ttu.edu` and look in the "Art & Images" menu

Bagpipes

A Gopher that is an archive of information about bagpipes; it is used in *Musical Outlets* (Chapter 7).

`cs.dartmouth.edu` and select "Bagpipes Archives"

Ceramic Arts and Pottery

A list server that contains information about ceramic arts and pottery; it is used in *Hobbyist's Delight* (Chapter 5).

`listserv@ukcc.uky.edu` and subscribe to "CLAYART"

Composition Discussion

A Usenet group that contains discussions about composition; it is used in *Musical Outlets* (Chapter 7).

`rec.music.compose`

Computer-Generated Art Library

A Usenet group that contains a library of computer-generated art; it is used in *Gallery of the Future* (Chapter 7).

`alt.binaries.pictures.fine-art.graphics`

Dallas Museum of Art

A Gopher that contains images of art from the Dallas Museum of Art; it is used in *Gallery of the Future* (Chapter 7).

`gopher.unt.edu` and look in the "Dallas Resources" menu

E-mail questions to `dma@gophermunt.edu`

Drum/Percussion Mailing List

A list server for the discussion of drums and percussion; it is used in *Musical Outlets* (Chapter 7).

`drum-request@elof.mit.edu`

Film Gopher

A Gopher of a film database; it contains 6,500 movies made before 1986; it is used in *How Do I Use the Internet?* (Chapter 1).

`info.mcc.ac.uk` and look in `/Miscellaneous/Film Database`

Fine Arts Discussion

A Usenet group that contains discussions about fine art; it is used in *Gallery of the Future* (Chapter 7).

```
rec.arts.fine
```

FRAC-L

A list server that hosts discussions of fractal images as art; it is used in *Gallery of the Future* (Chapter 7).

```
frac-l@gitvml.bitnet
```

Guitar Chords and Tablature

An anonymous FTP site about guitar music and tablature; it is used in *Musical Outlets* (Chapter 7).

```
ftp.uwp.edu and look in pub/music/guitar
```

Jazz Information Server (WNUR-FM)

A WWW site that contains information about jazz music; it is used in *Artistic Reflections* (Chapter 4).

```
http://www.acns.nwu.edu/jazz/
```

K12 Art Education Newsgroup

A Usenet group where people discuss K-12 art in education; it is used in *Virtual Excursions* (Chapter 6).

```
k12.ed.art
```

Louvre Exhibits

A WWW site that contains various images from Louvre Exhibits; it is used in *Artistic Reflections* (Chapter 4).

```
http://mistral.enst.fr/~pioch/louvre/
```

Lute Playing

A Gopher that contains information about lute playing; it is used in *Musical Outlets* (Chapter 7).

```
cs.dartmouth.edu and select "Lute Files"
```

Movie Review Newsgroup

A Usenet group that contains a movie review newsgroup; it is used in *How Do I Use the Internet?* (Chapter 1).

    rec.arts.movies

Music List of Lists

An anonymous FTP site that contains a list of musical list servers; it is used in *Artistic Reflections* and *Musical Outlets* (Chapters 4 and 7).

> E-mail: `mlol-request@wariat.org`

> FTP: `cs.uwp.edu` and select `music/info`

Online History of Art

A WWW site that contains historical art files and images; it is used in *Artistic Reflections* (Chapter 4).

    http://life.anu.edu.au

OTIS Project

An anonymous FTP site that contains a gallery of original artwork; it is used in *Artistic Reflections* and *Gallery of the Future* (Chapters 4 and 7).

> `sunsite.unc.edu` and look in `pub/multimedia/pictures/OTIS`

> or `aql.gatech.edu` and look in `pub/OTIS`

Percussion Talk

A Usenet group that contains discussions about percussion instruments; it is used in *Musical Outlets* (Chapter 7).

    rec.music.makers.percussion

Smithsonian Museum

An anonymous FTP site that contains images of art from the Smithsonian Museum; it is used in *Artistic Reflections* and *Gallery of the Future*. (Chapters 4 and 7).

    sunsite.unc.edu

Star Trek Archive

An anonymous FTP site that contains a Star Trek archive; it is used in *How Do I Use the Internet?* (Chapter 1).

    ftp.uu.net

Underground Music Archives

A WWW site associated with the University of California at Santa Cruz that contains a music archive with information about obscure bands; it is used in *Artistic Reflections* (Chapter 4).

```
http://sunsite.unc.edu/ianc
```

University of Wisconsin, Parkside Music Archives

An anonymous FTP site located at the University of Wisconsin that contains music archives; it is used in *Artistic Reflections* and *Musical Outlets* (Chapters 4 and 7).

`ftp.uwp.edu` and look in `pub/music`

Update Electronic Music News

A list server that distributes an online newsletter, *Electronic Music News*; it is used in *Musical Outlets* (Chapter 7).

```
listserv@vm.marist.edu
```

The Andy Warhol Museum Home Page

A WWW site that contains the art of Andy Warhol; it is used in *Gallery of the Future* (Chapter 7).

```
http://fridge.antaire.com:80/warhol/
```

Communications

Academy One (Youngstown Freenet)

A telnet site for scientific exploration of a variety of projects; it is used throughout the book.

`yfn2.ysu.edu` and log in as **visitor**

E-mail: `a002@nptn.org`

or `a-1@nptn.org`

Carr-L

A list server that focuses on the use of computers in journalism; it is used in *Media Watchdog* (Chapter 8).

```
listserv@ulkyvm.louisville.edu
```

Cleveland Freenet

A telnet site to reach Academy One.

    freenet-in-a.cwru.edu

An alternate address is the Youngstown Freenet.

    yfn2.ysu.edu

Columbus Dispatch

A Gopher source containing the daily newspaper from Columbus, Ohio; it is used in *Networked News* and *Media Watchdog* (Chapters 7 and 8).

    gopher.freenet.columbus.oh.us and select
    "News, Weather, Calendar"

e.Club

A telnet site to find a net pal; it is used in *F³: Finding Foreign Friends* (Chapter 2).

    freenet-in-a.cwru.edu to register for an account with Cleveland
    Freenet, which will give you access to Academy One's e.Club

Educational (K-12) List Servers

Usenet groups related to K-12 education; they are used in *Virtual Excursions* (Chapter 6).

    k12.ed.science

    k12.ed.math

    k12.ed.art

French Language Press Review

A Gopher source for the *French Language Press Review,* it is used in *Networked News* and *Media Watchdog* (Chapters 7 and 8).

    gopher.tc.umn.edu and select "News"

Gerinet

An e-mail source for finding senior citizen pen pals; it is used in *Exploring the Past* (Chapter 2).

    listserv@ubvm.bitnet

The Global Student Newswire Project

A WWW and multimedia source of news stories; it is used in *Networked News* (Chapter 7).

> `http://www.jou.ufl.edu/forums/gsn`

I*EARN

An e-mail address for connecting to various student-run projects; it is used in *Visions of the Future* (Chapter 4).

> `iearn@igc.org`

John Makulowich's List

An anonymous FTP site that has a compendium of resources for journalists; it is used in *Networked News* (Chapter 7).

> `ftp.clark.net` and select path `pub/journalism/jlist26.txt`

Journalism Discussion

A Usenet group for sharing ideas with other journalists; it is used in *Media Watchdog* (Chapter 8).

> `alt.journalism`

Journet

A list server to receive an online newsletter that covers topics of interest to journalists and journalism educators; it is used in *Media Watchdog* (Chapter 8).

> `listserv@qucdn.queensu.car`

KIDCAFE

A list server for kids; it is used in *Challenging Contests* (Chapter 6).

> subscribe to: `listserv@ndsuvm1.bitnet`
>
> post to: `kidcafe@ndsuvm1.bitnet`

KIDZMAIL

A list server for kids; it is used in *International Survey, Challenging Contests,* and *Polling for Answers* (Chapters 2, 6, and 8).

> subscribe to: `listserv@asuacad.bitnet`
>
> post to: `kidzmail@asuacad.bitnet`

KNSO

This telnet site is a joint effort of Operation Uplink II and *The Knoxville News Sentinel*; it is used in *Networked News* (Chapter 7).

> `use.usit.net` and use the log-in and password: **knso**

> E-mail suggestions to: `knsoedit@use.usit net`

Norfolk Virginian-Pilot

Use this WWW source to reach one of the many newspapers on the net; it is used in *Networked News* and *Media Watchdog* (Chapters 7 and 8).

> `htpp://www.infi.net/pilot/vpls.html`

Palo Alto Weekly

Use this WWW source to reach one of the many newspapers on the net; it is used in *Networked News* and *Media Watchdog* (Chapters 7 and 8).

> `http://www.service.com/PAW/home.html`

Penpal-L

This list server helps people to find net pals; it is used in F^3: *Finding Foreign Friends, International Survey*, and *Polling for Answers* (Chapters 2 and 8).

> `listserv@unccvm.bitnet`

Project NEWSDAY

An annual project sponsored by The Global SchoolNet Foundation; it is used in *Networked News* (Chapter 7).

> `newsday@bonita.cerf.fred.org`

Senior Pen Pals

An e-mail address for finding a senior pen pal; it is used in *Exploring the Past* (Chapter 2).

> `elders@sjuvm.stjohns.edu`

USA Today

The telnet sites for the national newspaper *USA Today*; they are used in *Networked News* and *Media Watchdog* (Chapters 7 and 8).

> `freenet-in-a.cwru.edu`

> `kanga.ins.cwru.edu` and log in as **guest**

WYN (World's Youth News)

The e-mail address for obtaining back information about subscribing to WYN; it is used in *Networked News* (Chapter 7).

```
wyn@freenet.hut.fi
```

Economics

Business Newsgroup

A Usenet group that includes general discussions about managing your business, including how to start a business; it is used in *Hobbyist's Delight* (Chapter 5).

```
alt.business.misc
```

Dowvision

A WAIS source with a newsfeed from the Dow Jones News Service; it is used in *How Do I Use the Internet?* (Chapter 1).

Telnet to `wais.com` and look for "Dowvision"

Entrepreneurs Newsgroup

A Usenet group that has discussions about operating a business; it is used in *Hobbyist's Delight* (Chapter 5).

```
misc.entrepreneurs
```

Fun and Games

Chinese Chess

Telnet sites to access games of Chinese Chess; they are used in *Game Gurus* (Chapter 3).

```
coolidge.harvard.edu 5555
128.103.28.15 5555
```

Game Servers

Telnet sites that offer many interactive games; they are used in *Game Gurus* (Chapter 3).

> `herxl.tat.physik.uni-tuebingen.de` with user name: **games**
>
> `pavax3.iap.physik.uni-tuebingen.de` with user name: **games**

Go Server

A telnet site that allows you to access the game Go; it is used in *Game Gurus* (Chapter 3).

> `hellspark.wharton.upenn.edu 6969` and log in as **guest**,
> then type **help go**

Internet Hunt

A trivia game based on information found on the Internet; it can be reached through Gopher, FTP, or list server. It is used in *Trivia Treasure Hunt* and *Challenging Contests* (Chapters 5 and 6).

> Gopher: `gopher.cic.net`
>
> kidsnet list server: `listserv@vms.pitt.edu`
>
> FTP: `ftp.cni.org` and look for `pub/net-guides/internet.hunt`

Learning Village

A telnet site to help you find a contest; it is used in *Challenging Contests* (Chapter 6).

> `nptn.org` and log in as **visitor**

MUD Information Usenets

These Usenets will provide you with lists of MUDs. They are used in *Playing in the MUD* (Chapter 9).

> `rec.games.mud.admin`
>
> `rec.games.mud.tiny`
>
> `rec.games.mud.announce`

NESPUT—National Educational Simulations Project Using Telecommunications

An e-mail source for information about participating in simulations; it is used in *Simulating Life* (Chapter 9).

> `aa005@nptn.org`

The NeverEnding Story

A telnet MUD site; it is used in *Playing in the MUD* (Chapter 9).

snowhite.ee.pdx.edu 9999

Problem of the Week Club

An e-mail address to access a different challenging math problem each week; it is used in *Mission: Mathematics* (Chapter 3).

mspanswick@rmecco.cerf.fred.org

WISDOoM Crossword Server

A telnet source for crosswords and other games such as Scrabble; it is used in *Game Gurus* (Chapter 3).

next7.cas.muohio.edu 8888 and on the first line type **help**

Wisney World

Telnet addresses for a wacky online world; they are used in *Playing in the MUD* (Chapter 9).

levant.cs.ohiou.edu 5000

132.235.1.100 5000

Worlds of Conquest

A telnet address for a MUD for novice players; it is used in *How Do I Use the Internet?* (Chapter 1).

28.174.31.163 4000

Geography and Environment

Blue Skies

An anonymous FTP site with information about the weather; it is used in *Predicting the Weather* (Chapter 8).

madlab.sprl.umich.edu and look for pub/Blue-Skies

The Collaboratory

An e-mail service where you can advertise your experiment and ask others to participate—a database is also being kept of the different projects, past and present. It is used in *Environmental Experiments* (Chapter 8).

`xx171@nptn.org`

Earthquake Info

A telnet site with information about earthquakes; it is used in *Map Mania* (Chapter 2).

`geophys.washington.edu` and use the log-in and password: **quake**

Environmental Learning Center (ELC)

An e-mail address with three areas of environment learning: resource information about the environment, safety and project information, and a discussion and announcement area; it is used in *Environmental Experiments* (Chapter 8). To access it, you must register as a Cleveland Freenet user.

`xx151@nptn.org`

Environmental Resource Center

A WWW site with stored environmental data and information; it is used in *Environmental Experiments* (Chapter 8).

`http://ftp.clearlake.ibm.com/ERC/`

Geographic Server

A telnet site with geographic information; it is used in *Map Mania* (Chapter 2).

`martini.eecs.umich.edu 3000` and type **?** for directions

Global Land Information System (GLIS)

A telnet site with detailed geographical information; it is used in *Map Mania* (Chapter 2).

`glis.cr.usgs.gov` and log in as **guest**

Live From…Other Worlds

A list server that supports electronic field trips; it is used in *Worldly Adventures* (Chapter 6).

`listmanager@quest.arc.nasa.gov`

Meteorology Newsgroup

A Usenet group where meteorological issues are discussed; it is used in *Predicting the Weather* (Chapter 8).

```
sci.geo.meteorology
```

NASA Goddard Space Flight Center

A Gopher site that offers a lot of NASA information; it is used in *Environmental Experiments* (Chapter 8).

```
gopher.gsfc.nasa.gov
```

NASA Weather Reports

An anonymous FTP site that contains weather reports from NASA; it is used in *Predicting the Weather* (Chapter 8).

`ames.arc.nasa.gov` and look for `pub/SPACE/WEATHER`

National Oceanographic and Atmospheric Association (NOAA)

A WAIS database you telnet to; it is used in *How Do I Use the Internet?* (Chapter 1).

`wais.com` and look for "NOAA"

NETA

An e-mail address for the National Education and Technology Alliance, which supports scientific expeditions; it is used in *Worldly Adventures* (Chapter 6).

```
neta@pipeline.com
```

PARC Map Viewer

A WWW site where you can access a map program that creates a map for you based on information you type in; it is used in *Map Mania* (Chapter 2).

```
http://pubweb.parc.xerox.comm/map
```

Rocks-and-fossils

A list server for discussions about rocks and fossils; it is used in *Scientific Explorations* (Chapter 3).

subscribe to: `majordomo@world.std.com`

questions to: `sshea@world.std.com`

U.S. State Department Travel Advisories

An anonymous FTP site for the U.S. State Department that has travel advice for countries all over the world; it is mentioned in *How Do I Use the Internet?* (Chapter 1).

`ftp.stolaf.edu` and look for `pub/travel-advisories`

Weather Image Archive

An anonymous FTP site with weather images; it is used in *Predicting the Weather* (Chapter 8).

`ftp.colorado.edu` and look for `pub/weather-images`

Weather Underground

A telnet site with a wealth of weather-related information; it is used in *Predicting the Weather* (Chapter 8).

`downwind.sprl.umich.edu 3000`

World Factbook93

A telnet site for a WAIS database that has information about countries all over the world; it is used in *Map Mania* (Chapter 2).

`wais.com`, log in as **wais** and select "world-factbook93"

Government

Congressional Address Listing

An e-mail source for congressional addresses; it is used in *A Capitol Idea* (Chapter 4).

`comments@hr.house.gov`

Congressional Quarterly

A Gopher site for a magazine that has comprehensive information about current legislation; it is used in *A Capitol Idea* (Chapter 4).

`gopher.cqalert.com`

Election Politics Discussion

A Usenet group to discuss local and state politics and election practices; it is used in *Polling for Answers* (Chapter 8).

```
alt.politics.election
```

Global Classroom Youth Congress

An e-mail source for the coordinator of the Global Classroom Youth Congress; it is used in *Visions of the Future* (Chapter 4).

```
rsch281c@cl.uh.edu
```

HNSource

A telnet site offering access to historical events and documents; it is used in *Exploring the Past* (Chapter 2).

```
ukanaix.cc.ukans.edu
```
and log in as **history**

```
or 129.237.33.1
```

House of Representatives' Bills

A WAIS source for all of the bills of the 103rd session of the House of Representatives; it is used in *A Capitol Idea* (Chapter 4).

Telnet to `wais.com` and log in as **wais**. Look for `USHOUSE_house_bill_text_103rd`

Legi-Slate Gopher Service

A source of information about bills pending in congress; it is used in *A Capitol Idea* (Chapter 4).

Gopher: `gopher.legislate.com`

Telnet: `consultant.micro.umn.edu` and log in as **gopher**, choose "search gopher titles at UMN gopher" and type **legi-slate**

President of the United States

An e-mail address for sending mail to the president of the United States; it is used in *A Capitol Idea* (Chapter 4).

```
president@whitehouse.gov
```

Vice President of the United States

An e-mail address for sending mail to the vice president of the United States; it is used in *A Capitol Idea* (Chapter 4).

```
vice.president@whitehouse.gov
```

Y-Rights

A list server about the rights of youths; it is used in *A Capitol Idea* (Chapter 4).

`listserv@sjuvm.bitnet`

Literature and Writing

CORE

An anonymous FTP site for a magazine of poetry, essays, and fiction; it is used in *Paperless Publishing* (Chapter 7).

FTP: `etext.archive.umich.edu` and look for `pub/Zines/Core_Zine`

E-mail: `core-journal@eff.org`

Cyberkind

A WWW source for a magazine of fiction, nonfiction, poetry, and prose related to the Internet; it is used in *Paperless Publishing* (Chapter 7).

`http://sunsite.unc.edu/shannon/ckind/`

Fiction

A list server about fictional writing; it is used in *Awesome Authors* (Chapter 3).

`listserv@psuvm.psu.edu`

The Fiction Writers Workshop

A list server that encourages writers to submit writing and participate in a discussion about it; it is used in *Paperless Publishing* (Chapter 7).

`Fiction@psuvm.psu.edu`

Global Literary Magazine

The e-mail address of a literary magazine organized by Cold Spring Harbor High School; it is used in *Paperless Publishing* (Chapter 7).

`coldspring@igc.apc.org`

InterText

An anonymous FTP site for a short fiction bimonthly magazine; it is used in *Paperless Publishing* (Chapter 7).

FTP: `etext.archive.umich.edu` and look in the directory `pub/Zine`

E-mail: `jsnell@ocf.berkeley.edu`

KID-LIT

A telnet source for the Youngstown Freenet. Once registered, go into the student bulletin board and find "KID-LIT." It is used in *Paperless Publishing* (Chapter 7).

`yfn2.ysu.edu` and log in as **visitor**

Library of Congress Archives

An anonymous FTP site where you can access many of the archives of the Library of Congress; it is used in *How Do I Use the Internet?* (Chapter 1).

`ftp.loc.gov` and log in as **anonymous**

On-line Books Page

A WWW source to find out what books have been put online; it is used in *Writer's Corner* (Chapter 5).

`http://www.cs.cmu.edu:8001/Web/books.html`

Oxford Archive

An anonymous FTP site where you can access the Oxford Archives; it is used in *Writer's Corner* (Chapter 5).

`ota.ox.ac.uk` and look for `pub/ota`

Poetry

A WAIS site with poems and poetic commentary; it is mentioned in *How Do I Use the Internet?* (Chapter 1).

Telnet to `wais.com`

Poetry Archive

A WWW site with archived poetry; it is used in *Writer's Corner* (Chapter 5).

`http://sunsite.unc.edu/dykki/poetry/home.html`

Poetry Index

A WAIS site that indexes poetry; it is used in *Writer's Corner* (Chapter 5).

Telnet to `wais.com`

Project Gutenberg

An anonymous FTP site where you can access many online books. They are used in *Awesome Authors* and *Writer's Corner* (Chapters 3 and 5).

`mrcnext.cso.uiuc.edu` and look for `pub/etext`

or `128.174.201.12`

at first prompt type **cd gutenberg**

Prose Writer's Discussion

A Usenet group where you can submit your writing. Discussions about the submitted writing occur on `alt.prose.d`. It is used in *Paperless Publishing* (Chapter 7).

`alt.prose`

Science Fiction Archive

An anonymous FTP site and WWW source for accessing an archive of science fiction information; it is used in *Hobbyist's Delight* (Chapter 5).

FTP: `elbereth.rutgers.edu` and look for `pub/sfl`

`http://gandalf.rutgers.edu/pub/sfl/sf-resource.guide.html`

Smithsonian Institute's Office of Printing and Photographic Services

An anonymous FTP site for the Smithsonian Institute; it is used in *Artistic Reflections* (Chapter 4).

`photo1.si.edu`

Two files that will help you find your way around:

`smithsonian.photo.info.txt`

`photo1.catalog`

Spotlight on Authors (and Spotlight on People)

A feature of Academy One on Youngstown Freenet; it is used in *Awesome Authors* (Chapter 3).

`yfn2.ysu.edu` and log in as **visitor**

Teaching English as a Second Language, K-12

A list server about ESL for grades K-12.

    teslk-12@cunyvm.bitnet

The Vocal Point

A WWW site that contains a monthly newspaper created by the students of the Boulder Valley School District. The paper covers a significant local or national topic. It is used in *Paperless Publishing* (Chapter 7).

    http://bvsd.k12.co.us/cent/Newspaper/Newspaper.html

Wiretap

An anonymous FTP site that contains all kinds of electronic books and articles; it is used in *Awesome Authors* and *Writer's Corner* (Chapters 3 and 5).

    wiretap.spies.com

    or 130.43.43.43

    Look for /Library

Young Authors

An e-mail address for an electronic journal that publishes student work. Send e-mail and include your name, address, and phone number as well as your school's name, address, and phone number; it is used in *Paperless Publishing* (Chapter 7).

    JMM12@psuvm.psu.edu

Mathematics

The Geometry Center

A WWW site that presents a gallery of interactive games based on geometric principles; it is used in *Weaving the Web* (Chapter 9).

    http://www.geom.umn.edu/apps/gallery.html

Geometry Forum

The e-mail addresses of the coordinators of the Geometry forum; they are used in *Mission: Mathematics* (Chapter 3).

Annie Fetter: annie@forum.swarthmore.edu

Gene Klotz: Klotz@forum.swarthmore.edu

Math Archives Gopher

A Gopher with math software and access to other Gophers; it is used in *Mission: Mathematics* (Chapter 3).

`archives.math.utk.edu`

Math Association of America

A Gopher for math resources; it is used in *Mission: Mathematics* (Chapter 3).

`maa.org`

MathMagic

An e-mail address for MathMagic, a project that supplies new math challenges every three to four weeks; it is used in *Mission: Mathematics* (Chapter 3).

`cshooper@tenet.edu`

Miscellaneous

AIDS Database

A telnet site with AIDS information; it is used in *Contribute to Finding a Cure* (Chapter 4).

`debra.dgbt.doc.ca 3000` and log in as **chat**

AIDS Hypercard Stacks

An anonymous FTP site that contains AIDS Hypercard stacks; it is used in *Contribute to Finding a Cure* (Chapter 4).

`ftp.sunset.se` and select the path `pub/mac/misc/medical/hypercard`

AskERIC

An e-mail resource where you can get answers to specific questions. The WWW and Gopher addresses can be used to explore the ERIC resources. It is used in *Trivia Treasure Hunt* (Chapter 5).

E-mail: `askeric@ericir.syr.edu`

Gopher: `ericir.syr.edu`

WWW: `http://eryx.syr.edu`

For Sale Newsgroup

A newsgroup for people who have something to sell and for people who are looking to buy; it is used in *Hobbyist's Delight* (Chapter 5).

```
misc.forsale
```

Kidlink

A list server for kids; it is used in *International Survey, Virtual Excursions,* and *Polling for Answers* (Chapters 2, 6, and 8). To get a general description of the Kidlink project, send **get kidlink general** to the subscription address.

post to: `kidlink@vm1.nodak.edu`

subscribe to: `listserv@vm1.nodak.edu`

or `listserv@ndsuvm1.bitnet`

Kidsphere

An educational list server for kids; it is used in *International Survey, Virtual Excursions,* and *Polling for Answers* (Chapters 2, 6, and 8).

`kidsphere-request@vms.cis.pitt.edu`

Murray Elementary School

This is the WWW home page for an elementary school in Ivy, Virginia; it is used in *How Do I Use the Internet?* (Chapter 1).

`http://curry.edschool.virginia.edu/murray`

National Institute of Allergy and Infectious Diseases (NIAID)

A Gopher that contains AIDS-related information as well as the National AIDS Clearinghouse from the CDC; it is used in *Contribute to Finding a Cure* (Chapter 4).

`odie.niaid.nih.gov` and choose "AIDS Related Information" from the menu.

National Library of Medicine

An anonymous FTP site containing information from the National Library of Medicine; it is used in *Contribute to Finding a Cure* (Chapter 4).

`nlmpubs.nlm.nih.gov`

Seattle Metro Washington Park Zoo

A WWW site for the zoo in Seattle, Washington; it is used in *How Do I Use the Internet?* (Chapter 1).

```
http://davinci.vancouver.wsu.edu/zoo/zoo.html
```

UNICEF Gopher

This is the address for UNICEF's Gopher site; it is used in *Visions of the Future* (Chapter 4).

```
hqfaus01.unicef.org
```

The Exploratorium in San Francisco, California

This is the WWW site of San Francisco's Exploratorium; it is used in *How Do I Use the Internet?* (Chapter 1).

```
http://www.exploratorium.edu
```

Reference

The Almost-Complete List of MUSHes

A long list of multi-user simulated environments that provides addresses, short summaries, and links to appropriate FTP sites and home pages; it is used in *Playing in the MUD* (Chapter 9).

```
http://www.cis.upenn.edu/~lwl/muds.html
```

Archie

Telnet addresses to access Archie and Veronica services; they are used in *How Do I Use the Internet?* (Chapter 1).

```
archie.internic.net
archie.rutgers.edu
archie.ans.net
archie.sura.net
```

Current List of Active MUDs

An anonymous FTP site that contains a list of active MUDs; it is used in *Playing in the MUD* (Chapter 9).

FTP: `caisr2.caisr.cwru.edu` and look for `pub/mud`

subscribe to: `mudlist@glia.biostr.washington.edu`

Frequently Asked Questions (FAQ) about MUDs

An anonymous FTP site that contains a list of answers to many questions about MUDs; it is used in *Playing in the MUD* (Chapter 9).

`ftp.math.okstate.edu` and look for `pub/muds`

The HTML Documents: A Mosaic Tutorial

A WWW site to find out more about Mosiac; it is used in *Weaving the Web* (Chapter 9).

`http://fire.clarkson.edu/doc/html/htut.html`

Hypertext Guide to the Internet

A WWW site with a guide to the Internet.

`http://www.rpi.edu/Internet/Internet.html`

IRC Tutorial

An anonymous FTP site that has IRC tutorials; it is used in *How Do I Use the Internet?* (Chapter 1).

`cs.bu.edu` and look in `/irc/support` for the file named `IRCprimer1.1.txt`

Janice's K-12 Cyberspace Outpost

A WWW site for K-12 information; it is used in *How Do I Use the Internet?* (Chapter 1).

`http://k12.cnidr.org/janice_k12/k12menu.html`

K-12 Resources

A WWW site for resources for students and educators in grades K-12; it is used in *Weaving the Web* (Chapter 9).

`http://www.nas.nasa.gov/HPCC/K12/edures.html`

k12-euro-teachers

An e-mail address to help students find a net pal; it is used in F^3: *Finding Foreign Friends* (Chapter 2).

```
majordomo@lists.eunet.fi
```

Kids

An educational list server for kids; it is used in *Virtual Excursions* (Chapter 6).

```
kids-request@vms.cis.pitt.edu
```

Kids Newsgroup

A Usenet newsgroup just for kids; it is used in *How Do I Use the Internet?* (Chapter 1).

```
misc.kids
```

List of List Servers

A list of list servers; it is used in *How Do I Use the Internet?* and *The Main Event* (Chapters 1 and 6).

FTP: `ftp.sura.net`, type **cd /pub/nic** and then **get interest-groups.txt**

WWW: `http://www.ii.uib.no/~magnus/paml.html`

FTP: `crvax.sri.com` or `128.18.30.65`

Lynx Browser

An anonymous FTP site where you can get Lynx browser software.

`ftp2.cc.ukans.edu` and look for `/pub/lynx`

Middle School Newsgroup

A Usenet newsgroup for junior high school students; it is used in *How Do I Use the Internet?* (Chapter 1).

`k12.chat.junior`

Mosaic Browser

An anonymous FTP site where you can get Mosiac browser software for Macs, PCs with Windows, and Unix machines with X Window.

`ftp.ncsa.uiuc.edu` and look for `/Web`

NASA Ames Research Center K-12 World Wide Web

A WWW site for an extensive listing of K-12 and teacher resources; it is used in *Weaving the Web* (Chapter 9).

    http://quest.arc.nasa.gov/

The NCSA Education Group's OnLine Tutorials

A WWW site with online tutorials; it is used in *Weaving the Web* (Chapter 9).

    http://www.ncsa.uiuc.edu/Edu/Tutorials/TutorialHome.html

Newbie News

A list server to help new users.

    NewbieNewz-request@IO.COM

Omni-Cultural-Academic-Resource

A WAIS resource that has worldwide historical information; it is used in *Exploring the Past* (Chapter 2).

    Telnet to wais.com

Reference Desk

A Gopher service with many reference tools you would find in a local library; it is used in *Trivia Treasure Hunt* (Chapter 5).

    gaia.sci-ed.fit.edu and choose "Reference Desk" from the menu

The Scout Report

This site contains updates of new sites and resources on the Internet; it is used in *The Main Event* and *Weaving the Web* (Chapters 6 and 9).

    Gopher or telnet: is.internic.net and look in "Internic
    Information Services"

    WWW: http://www.internic.net/infoguide.html

    list server: majordomo@is.internic.net

Software Archives

An anonymous FTP site for the software archive at the University of Michigan; it is used in *How Do I Use the Internet?* (Chapter 1).

    archive.umich.edu

Telnet Site with IRC

A telnet address to access an IRC client; it is used in *How Do I Use the Internet?* (Chapter 1).

```
exuokmax.ecn.uoknor.edu 6677
```

Usenet Group List

An anonymous FTP site that has *An Educator's Guide to E-mail Lists.*

`nic.umass.edu`, look in `pub/ednet` and type **get educatrs.lst**

Viewing Software

An anonymous FTP site where you can download viewing software; it is used in *Gallery of the Future* (Chapter 7).

`bongo.cc.utexas.edu` and look in `/gifstuff`

WAIS Databases

These are two telnet addresses for WAIS databases. They are used in *How Do I Use the Internet?* (Chapter 1).

```
wais.com
```

```
quake.think.com
```

log in as **wais**

Sports and Hobbies

Neon-Sign Baseball Statistics League (Rotisserie Baseball)

A list server containing baseball statistics; it is used in *Hobbyist's Delight* (Chapter 5).

```
serv@sbccvm.bitnet
```

Professional Hockey Server

A WWW site containing World Cup information; it is used in *The Main Event* (Chapter 6).

```
http://maxwell.uhh.hawaii.edu.edu/hockey/hockey.html
```

Professional Sports Schedules

A Gopher containing professional sports schedules; it is used in *How Do I Use the Internet?* (Chapter 1).

> `gopher.bsu.edu` and look in `/Ball State University/`
> `Professional Sports Schedules`

The Running Page

A WWW site about running for exercise; it is used in *Hobbyist's Delight* (Chapter 5).

> `http://sunsite.unc.edu/drears/running/running.html`

Ask a Young Scientist

An e-mail service that scientific questions may be sent to (it may take up to 48 hours for a reply, and it is only available October through March); it is used in *Scientific Explorations* (Chapter 3).

> `apscichs@radford.vak12ed.edu`

Interactive Frog Dissection

A WWW site that includes text, 60 images, 17 QuickTime movies, and clickable image maps about the dissection of a frog; it is used in *Environmental Experiments* (Chapter 8).

> `http://curry.edschool.virginia.edu/~insttech/frog`

NASA Spacelink

A telnet site that contains information from NASA; it is used in *How Do I Use the Internet?* and *Scientific Explorations* (Chapters 1 and 3).

> `spacelink.msfc.nasa.gov`
>
> or `192.149.89.61`

National Student Research Center

An e-mail address that facilitates the establishment of Student Research Centers in schools across the country; it is used in *Environmental Experiments* (Chapter 8).

> `nsrcmms@aol.com`

Installing and Using NetCruiser

Welcome to Netcom's NetCruiser. If you've got a modem and a PC running Windows 3.1 or greater, this program is the only other thing you'll need to get up and running on the Internet. NetCruiser allows you to send and receive electronic mail; find interesting programs, pictures, and information; and, in short, do all of the exciting things you can do out there in cyberspace.

In this appendix, we'll show you everything you need to do to get NetCruiser running on your computer and then show you how to use each of NetCruiser's features. We'll provide examples and illustrations that will show you how simple using NetCruiser really is.

System Requirements

Before you do anything, you need to make sure that you will be able to run NetCruiser on your computer. To do so, you must have

- *An IBM-compatible computer with a 386, 486, or Pentium processor in it*
- *DOS 5.0 or any version more recent than that*
- *Microsoft Windows version 3.1 or 95*
- *At least 4 megabytes of RAM*
- *A modem that runs at 9,600 baud or faster*

If you've got all five of these things, you are ready to go.

Installation and Registration

Two things have to happen before you can start cruising the Internet: You have to install NetCruiser on your computer, and you have to set up an Internet account with Netcom. NetCruiser does these two things for you in one single procedure, which should take you about ten minutes to complete if you have the following information ready before you start (we've provided spaces so you can make yourself an easy checklist).

Your modem brand and model _____

Your modem's baud rate (speed) _____

The port your modem is on (COM1, COM2, etc.) _____

Your area code and telephone number _____

A user name for your e-mail address (make it up) _____

A password _____

A credit card number and expiration date _____
(ask your parents to help you with this)

Installation

Ready?

1. Make sure Windows 3.1 or 95 is running on your computer.

2. Put the NetCruiser disk that came with this book into your a: drive (or your b: drive if that's where it fits).

3. Start NetCruiser's setup program: Pull down the "File" menu on the Windows Program Manager and select the "Run" option. Then, where you are prompted for a command line, type **a:\setup** (or **b:\setup**) and click on "OK."

4. Click on "Continue" to have the setup program copy NetCruiser onto your hard disk. This takes only a few minutes, and the setup program displays its progress as it goes. When the copying is finished, NetCruiser is on your hard disk waiting to be configured, which you will do in the next two steps.

5. You must tell NetCruiser what kind of modem you have, its speed, and where it can be found. This is the information you entered on the first three lines of your checklist. Enter it now in the Modem Settings window shown in Figure C.1.

Figure C.1

The Modem Settings window

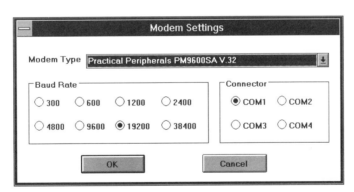

Select your modem brand and model on the Modem Type pulldown list by clicking on the arrow to the right of the Modem Type box. When you see your modem on the list, click on it once to select it. If you can't find yours, that's okay; just click on "Generic," the first entry on the list. Next, click on the baud rate or speed at which your modem runs. Note that there is no choice for 14400 nor for 28800. If you have a 14,400-baud modem, just select 19200. If you have a 28,800-baud modem, select 38400. Finally, in the Connector box, click on the "com" port to which your modem is attached and then click on "OK."

> If you enter this information incorrectly, don't cancel the installation. You can correct it later when you're done. Just start NetCruiser, pull down the "Settings" menu, select the "Modem Parameters" option to make the Modem Settings window reappear, and type in the correct information.

Note

6. In the last step before you set up an Internet account, you must select the telephone number that NetCruiser dials to access Netcom and get you on the Internet. Because you don't know the number and can't type it directly into the Phone Number window (which is on the screen at this point), click on "Directory" and select a number from the window shown in Figure C.2.

Figure C.2

Choose an Access phone number.

Choose An Access Phone Number
Dialing Prefix
Please make sure the following settings are correct before clicking the OK button. If you need to dial a 9 or some other prefix to access an outside line, please enter it in the box provided.
Prefix: [   ]   ☐ Require a "1" before the Number   ☐ Keep Area Code
OK   Cancel
Choose Dial-In Phone Number
⦿ Use local service number
○ Use NETCOM Dial-800
NetCruiser will direct-dial the number you choose from the list at right. Telephone company charges may apply.

503-626-6833 Portland, OR
510-274-2900 Walnut Creek, CA
510-426-6610 Pleasanton, CA
510-865-9004 Alameda, CA
512-206-4950 Austin, TX
602-222-3900 Phoenix, AZ
617-237-8600 Boston, MA
619-234-0524 San Diego, CA
702-792-9340 Las Vegas, NV

Scroll down the list of phone numbers given until you find one for your area code (which you noted on your checklist). Some area codes have more than one phone number. If there is more than one number in your area code, pick the number for the city closest to where you live.

If your area code does not appear on the list, it might mean that you need to call Netcom using a different area code, which could be long distance and very expensive.

> To get the current list of Netcom's local numbers (called *points of presence*) for Internet access, call Netcom at 1-800-353-6600.
>
> **Note**

If you find that Netcom's current list of access numbers doesn't have your area code either, Netcom provides a toll-free 800 number, which you can use by clicking on the "Use NETCOM Dial-800" circle.

> Netcom imposes a surcharge for using its 800 number. It is cheaper than long distance but not cheaper than local access; use a local-access number if one is available.
>
> **Note to Parents**

Finally, if you choose the 800 number or a number outside your area code, you will need to click on the "Require a '1' before the Number" and "Keep Area Code" boxes. When you're done, click on "OK" to return to the Phone Number window. The number you chose will appear there now, so click on "OK" to have the setup program create NetCruiser's icon and complete the installation.

Registration

Now that NetCruiser is on your hard disk, you need to set up your Internet account, so on the NetCruiser Setup window now on your screen, click on "Start Registration." This brings up a welcome message and a reminder about needing your name, address, credit card number, and so on. Because you've already prepared this information, click on "OK" to begin.

1. Type in your first and last names, and (from your checklist) your address, your home phone number, the user name you want, and your password (twice). Note that when you have typed in your user name, NetCruiser will show you your full e-mail address. It will look something like `<yourname>@ix.netcom.com` or `<yourname>@netcom.com`. When you have entered all the information, check it to make sure it is correct and then click on "Continue."

Note If you choose a user name that someone else already has, the setup program will give you a chance to pick a different one.

2. Type in a secret word. This is just in case you forget your password and have to call up Netcom for help. You can use your mother's last name, a pet's name, or anything else you will be sure to remember. Click on "OK" once you've typed your secret word.

Note If you have questions about installing or running NetCruiser, call Netcom technical support at 1-408-983-5970.

3. NetCruiser is ready to call in and create your Internet account. If you've got your parents' credit card information ready, click on "Continue" and then "OK."

4. When prompted, enter the credit card information and click on "OK." You are done with installation and registration. You may have to click on "OK" or "Continue" on a few more information windows, but when NetCruiser signs off, you've successfully set up your Internet account.

Upgrading NetCruiser

You can always access the most recent version of NetCruiser through NetCruiser itself.

1. From the main window, select "File" and then click on "Download New Version."

2. If you don't have the latest version, the "Download new version" window will appear. Click on "Download." (If the downloading process stalls at any point, click on "Exit" and try again later.)

3. After the files are downloaded, a message will inform you that the download was successful. Click on "OK."

4. Next, click on "Upgrade" and then click on "Yes" to close all running sessions.

5. Read about the upgraded version in the NetCruiser Upgrade window, then click on "Exit."

6. At the "Upgrade complete!" window, click on "OK."

For more details, see the NetCruiser Appendix in Sybex's Access the Internet! by David Peal. For ordering information, see the Note at the end of this appendix.

Logging Into NetCruiser

You are now able to do all the things on the Internet that you've heard about and have wanted to try, so let's go to it. The first thing you need to know how to do is log into NetCruiser; this is what actually puts you on the Internet.

Fortunately, NetCruiser makes logging in automatic; just start the program, type in your password (the first time you start up NetCruiser, you will have to enter both your user name and your password), and click on "Start Login." That's all there is to it. When you see NetCruiser's main screen, pictured in Figure C.3, you're on the Internet and ready to explore.

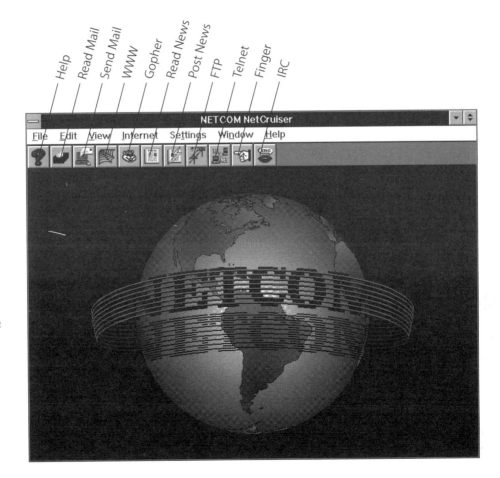

Figure C.3

The NetCruiser main screen

Electronic Mail

The first thing you might want to try is sending e-mail to your friends to tell them you've arrived. The next sections will show you the basics of sending messages and reading the ones you get in return. They will also show you some more advanced features, like sending the same message to more than one person at the same time and using an electronic address book.

Sending a Message

To learn how to compose and send an e-mail message with NetCruiser, work through the following steps. It's pretty simple.

1. On NetCruiser's toolbar, click on the "Send Mail" icon, the one that looks like an envelope coming out of a computer screen. This will bring up the Address Mail To... window, shown in Figure C.4.

When you want to know what a button on any of NetCruiser's toolbars will do, move your mouse so the pointer is over the button, then look at the bottom of your screen. You will see an explanation of the button's function on the left.

Tip

Figure C.4

The Address Mail To... window

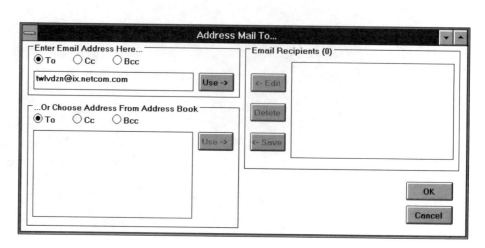

2. Type in the address of the person who will get this message. In Figure C.4, you'll see a message addressed to `twlvdzn@ix.netcom.com`. When you have typed in the address correctly, click on "Use->."

3. The address you typed now appears in the "Email Recipients" box. This means you're ready to compose your message, so click on "OK." This brings up the Send Mail window, shown in Figure C.5.

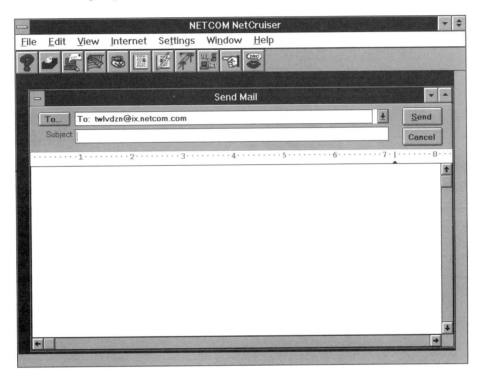

Figure C.5

*The
Send Mail
window*

4. The Send Mail window is where you actually write your message; notice that your message is properly addressed. At the subject line, type in one or two words that tell what the message is about, click on the large blank box under the ruler, and then type your message.

5. After you've checked your message for mistakes and are ready to send it, click on "Send." That's all there is to it.

> If you decide you don't want to send your message after all or want to start again from the beginning, click on "Cancel" and then "Yes."

Note

Building an Address Book

E-mail addresses are often difficult to remember. Many are long and difficult to type without mistakes. NetCruiser provides you with an address book that stores the addresses you use and saves you the trouble of typing them in each time you send a message. Here we will show you how to put addresses into your address book, and in the next section we will show you how to use the address book to send mail. To put an address into your address book, work through the following steps.

1. From the NetCruiser main screen, pull down the "Internet" menu and select the "Address Book" option.

2. On the window that appears, click on "New Entry." This brings up the window shown in Figure C.6.

Figure C.6

The Edit Address Book Entry window

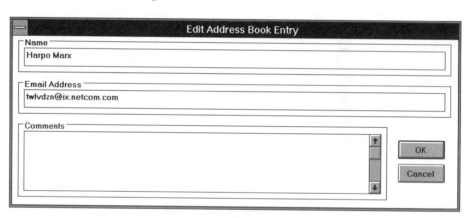

3. Under "Name," type the real name of the person whose e-mail address you are putting in your book, and under "Email Address," type the person's e-mail address. In Figure C.6, we've entered the e-mail address for someone named Harpo Marx.

4. Under "Comments," you can type a note or reminder about the person whose address you are editing.

5. When you have checked what you have typed and it is correct, click on "OK" to put the name and address into your address book.

6. Repeat the steps 3, 4, and 5 for each name you want to put in. When you are finished entering names, click on "Done." Now your address book is ready to use.

Sending Mail Using an Address Book

Sending a message using your address book is almost like sending a message without one. The only difference is that you don't have to type so much.

Did you know you can send e-mail to the president of the United States? His e-mail address is `president@whitehouse.gov`. As an exercise, put this address into your address book, and then work through the following steps to send the President a message.

Ready?

1. Click on the "Send Mail" icon in the toolbar. This brings up the Address Mail To... window, but notice now that your address book entries appear in the lower-left box, as in Figure C.7.

Figure C.7

Address Book entries in the Address Mail To... window

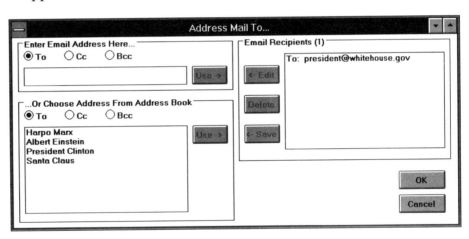

2. Click on the president's name from the list of people in your address book and then click "Use->."

3. The President's address now appears in the "Email Recipients" box, also shown in Figure C.7. Click on "OK," and the Send Mail window appears.

4. Enter a one- or two-word description of your message on the subject line and then type your message in the text area below the ruler. You might want to ask the president a question about the people he works with or tell him what you think of the job he is doing. Make sure to include your name and home address. You will get an e-mail message back from the White House acknowledging your message, but the president's office will respond to your message the old-fashioned way, with stamps and an envelope.

5. After you've checked your message for mistakes and are ready to send it, click on "Send." You've done it.

Sending One Message to Many People

Sometimes you'll find that you need to send the same message to more than one person at the same time; for example, to tell all of your friends that you now have an Internet account. There is no reason to type your message over again for each person; NetCruiser can send one message to an entire list of addresses and save you a lot of work.

To send a message to more than one person, do the same things you would to send a message to only one person, but repeat step 2. Either type in all the addresses or select the addresses you want from your address book. In Figure C.8, we have entered the addresses of three people whom we want to get a message.

Figure C.8

Multiple recipients of one message

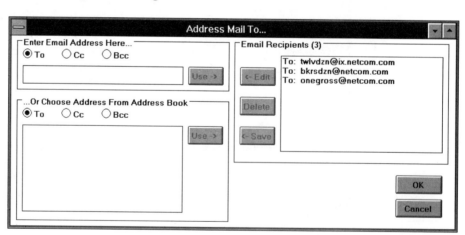

When you send your message, it will go to all of the addresses you specified.

Reading New E-Mail Messages

Once you begin to send e-mail, you will, of course, get some in return. This section shows you how to use NetCruiser to read the mail you get and then dispose of it in some way, such as deleting it, replying to the sender, forwarding it to someone else, or saving it to deal with later.

Reading new e-mail is very easy. To see how, work through the following steps.

1. Click on the "Read Mail" icon on the NetCruiser toolbar; it is the icon next to the question mark, the one that looks like an envelope popping out of a tissue box.

2. In the window that appears, click on "Inbox" and then click on "OK." This tells NetCruiser to check for new mail. NetCruiser then lists the header for each message you got, as in Figure C.9.

Figure C.9

A list of new mail messages

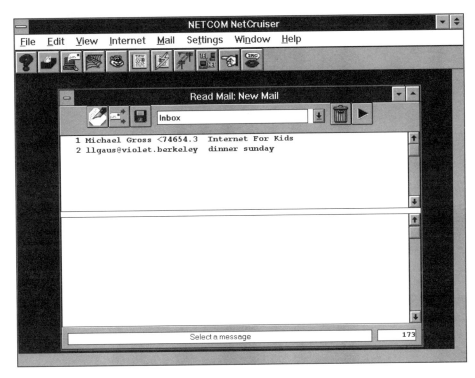

Note

If you have no new mail, NetCruiser tells you so in a message at the bottom of the window.

The message header gives you some idea of what to expect in the message itself. The header shows you the name or e-mail address of the person who sent the message and the subject of the message. In Figure C.9, for example, message 2 is from someone whose address begins `llgaus`, and the message is something about a dinner appointment.

3. Click on the header of the message you want to read and then click on the "Read" button in the top right corner of the New Mail window. It's the button that looks like a large triangle pointing to the right (or like the icon for the "play" button on a VCR). NetCruiser then displays the text of the message, as in Figure C.10.

4. When you're done reading your messages, close the New Mail window. That's all there is to it. Easy, yes?

Figure C.10

Reading a new e-mail message

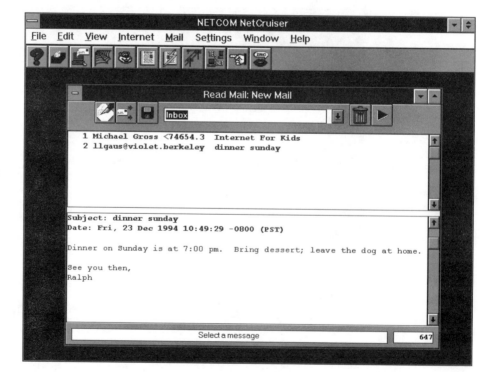

Dealing with Messages
Once You've Read Them

If you've closed the New Mail window, please reopen it now (follow the first two steps in the previous section) so you can learn to reply to, forward, save, and delete messages once you have read them.

Replying to a Message

Often you will want to write back to a person who has written an e-mail message to you. To do this, you could follow the steps we discussed earlier and write a message from scratch. If, however, you use NetCruiser's Reply feature, you'll save yourself some work because NetCruiser automatically puts the address and subject into your message; all you have to do is type the message text.

To reply to a message, double-click on the header of the message you want to reply to so that the message comes up onto your screen, and then click on the "Reply" button. It's the button all the way to the left of the New Mail window with the fountain pen on it. NetCruiser will ask you if you want to put the text of the message you just got into your reply. Click on "Yes" if you do or "No" if you don't. Now you are in the familiar Send Mail window; just type your message and send it.

Forwarding a Message

Sometimes you will want to send a message you received to another person. You could retype the whole thing, but that would be a big waste of time. Instead, NetCruiser allows you to "forward" a message by automatically putting the entire thing into a new message that you address and send.

To forward a message, double-click on the header of the message you want to forward so the message comes up and then click on the "Forward" button. It's the second button on the left of the New Mail window, the one showing the half envelope next to two small arrows. Now address and send the message as you've done before. Either type in an e-mail address or get one from your address book, type in the subject, add to the body

of the message some more text explaining what you are forwarding, and send it on its way.

Deleting Messages

Most of the time, e-mail messages are not worth keeping once you've read them. To delete a message, click on the header of the message you want to delete and click on the "Delete" button—you got it, the one with the garbage can. Then click on "Yes" to confirm the deletion.

Saving Messages

Sometimes you do want to keep your messages for a while. One way to keep a message is to do nothing after you've read it. The message will just stay in your Inbox for you to read (or forward, reply to, or delete) next time you read your mail. If you take this approach, you will soon find messages piling up in your Inbox, and you won't be able to find new messages in with all the old ones.

A better way of managing your messages is to save them. To save a message, double-click on the header of the message you want to save. When you see your message on the screen, click on the "Save" button, the one with the floppy disk on it.

Saving a message puts a copy of the message into a different mailbox, called the Saved Mail box. You can then delete the message from your Inbox and prevent clutter. To see how to work with messages you've put into your Saved Mail box, go on to the next section.

Working with Saved Messages

Working with old messages in your Saved Mail box is exactly like working with new messages in your Inbox, except that NetCruiser doesn't check for new mail when you open the Saved Mail box. You can read messages in the Saved Mail box, delete them, forward them, and reply to them in exactly the same way you do these things in the Inbox. The Saved Mail window looks the same, acts the same, and has the same buttons as the New Mail window discussed above.

You can open the Saved Mail box in two ways. If your Inbox is open, pull down the list in the top center of the New Mail window and select Saved Mail. Alternatively, click on NetCruiser's "Read Mail" icon in the toolbar and select "Saved Mail" from the list that appears. Using either method, you can now work with all of your saved messages.

Now you know how to use all of NetCruiser's e-mail tools. Close any windows that are open, and let's go on to the World Wide Web.

WWW

All right, get ready to hang on to your hats or your socks or whatever, 'cause in this section we're going to check out the World Wide Web (or "WWW" or just "the Web"). Without a doubt, the Web is the coolest thing going on the Internet. What makes the Web so cool is not just that there are huge quantities of stuff out there for you to explore but that the things you find are fun to look at, too.

The Web is organized into *pages* just like pages in a book. These pages contain not only text but also pictures—and sometimes even sound and video. What's more, each page is *linked* to other pages that contain related stuff—more text and pictures about the same subjects. All you have to do to get from one page to another is click on an *anchor* (one or more highlighted words) and off you go.

Note

Even though you can go directly from one page to another just by clicking on a link, pages may actually be located on different computers in different states or even in different countries on different continents.

The *Internet for Kids* Home Page

Start cruising the Web now by clicking on the Web icon on the NetCruiser toolbar; it's the one with the spiderweb on it. This will bring up Net-Cruiser's *Web browser* (a tool that lets you see Web pages), and the

Internet for Kids home page will automatically load up; it looks like the screen in Figure C.11.

> *Home page* is the term used for the main Web page at a Web site. Each site will usually identify itself on its home page and give some description of what's available there. The home page also contains links to related pages —these can be located either at the Web site itself or somewhere else.
>
> **Note**

Figure C.11

The Internet for Kids *home page*

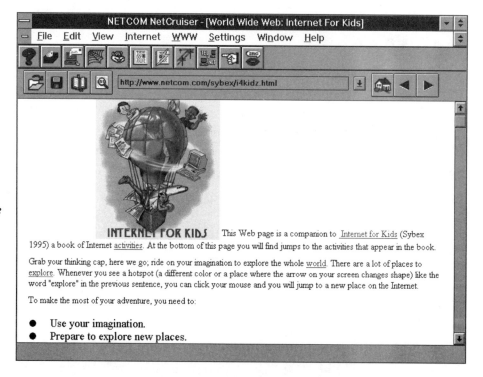

Let's take a minute to look around. Right away you see both pictures and text at the top of the page. See those underlined words (they're highlighted either in green or blue on your screen)? Those are the *anchors* or *links* that will take you to other Web pages (don't click on them yet; we'll do that in a minute).

Scroll down the page now—here and there you'll recognize Internet sites from the activities in this book. All the way at the bottom of the page, you'll see links to each chapter; by clicking on a link, you can do that chapter's activities using NetCruiser. Leave these 'til later—right now, to learn how to get around on the Web using NetCruiser, try the following example.

Basic Web Navigation

1. Make sure you have NetCruiser's Web browser open and the *Internet for Kids* home page displayed.

2. Scroll down to about the middle of the page until you see the anchor that reads <u>Janice's K12 Cyberspace outpost</u>. Click once on this anchor to go immediately to this new page, shown in Figure C.12. Moving from page to page is that easy!

Figure C.12

Janice's K12 Cyberspace Outpost

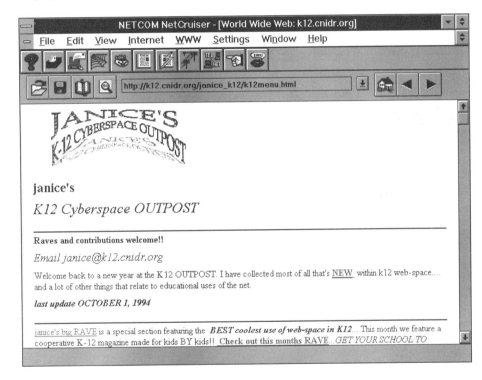

3. Take a minute to look and see what's on this educational Web page before we go on. Then click on the anchor that says <u>janice's big RAVE</u> to see a page with, as Janice says, great educational Web pages.

4. You should see the RAVE page now, and it looks like there's even cooler stuff beyond its anchors, but before we go there, try this. In the upper-right corner of NetCruiser's Web browser, click on the left-pointing arrow button. This is the "Previous Page" button, and it will take you back to the page you just came from.

5. Now click on the right-pointing arrow button. This is the "Next Page" button. Here it will take you back to the RAVE page you just left. To-gether, the "Previous Page" and "Next Page" buttons can take you backward and forward—one page at a time—through all the pages you've visited in a session.

6. Okay, now let's go on. From the RAVE page, click on the <u>ocean…</u> link. This takes us to a page that contains only one line, as well as an anchor to the <u>Singapore Ministry of Education</u>. Click on this anchor now. You've spanned the Pacific and are reading a page on a computer in Singapore, shown in Figure C.13.

Figure C.13

*The
Singapore
Ministry of
Education
Home Page*

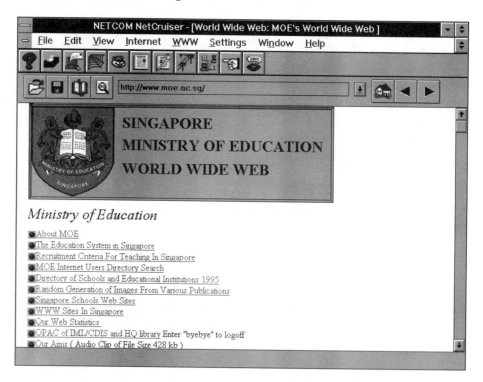

7. Now take some time to look around and explore the Web on your own. Follow anchors that look interesting and see where they lead you. When you're done exploring, click on the "Home" button—the one with the picture of the house on it next to the "Previous Page" button. This will take you to the first page we saw when we started, the *Internet for Kids* home page.

Note — You'll notice when you've been Webbing around a bit that some pages take a long time to load. This is because they've got a lot of large graphics on them. All of the data on a page, pictures as well as text, has to come over your modem, and sometimes this takes a while. If you get tired of waiting for a page to load, click on the "Interrupt" button that appears while pages are loading. It's the one with the Stop sign on it.

Bookmarks

If you've spent any time Webbing about, you'll see just how much there is out there on the Web. Most of it you'll only want to see once. Sometimes, though, you'll want to come back to a page, and what with there being so many of them and their addresses being so complicated, it may be difficult to find your way back. Fortunately, NetCruiser has built in a feature to take care of just this problem—the *bookmark*.

Bookmarks allow you to jump to a particular Web page from absolutely anywhere on the Web. To see how to create and use a bookmark, work through the following steps:

1. If you're not at the Singapore Ministry of Education page, go there now. This is the page we're going to bookmark.

2. Click on the "Bookmark" button—it's the one that looks like an open book with a bookmark between the pages. This brings up the Book Mark window shown in Figure C.14.

Figure C.14

NetCruiser's Web Book Mark window

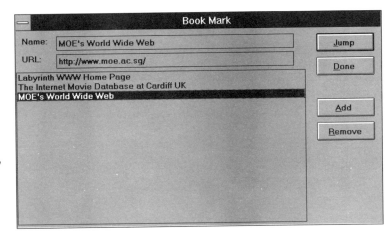

3. Notice that NetCruiser automatically fills in the name and address of the page you're going to mark. To create the bookmark, click on the "Add" button. As in Figure C.14, NetCruiser adds the name of the newly bookmarked page to the list of bookmarks it keeps in the large box. Now click on "Done" to close the Book Mark window.

4. Now go to another page anywhere else on the Web—click on any link on the current page and then on another link on the next page that comes up.

5. Now let's jump right back! Click on the "Bookmark" button to reopen the Book Mark window.

6. Click on the Ministry of Education (MOE) bookmark that you just created and then click on "Jump." Bingo! You're back.

The last thing you need to know about bookmarks is how to get rid of a bookmark if you don't want it on your list anymore.

Warning Be *sure* you want to delete an entry before removing it from the bookmark list. Once you instruct NetCruiser to remove it, you won't get a second chance to keep it—it will be gone for good.

1. Your Book Mark window should still be open; if you've closed it, please open it again.

2. Highlight the entry in your list that you want to delete.

3. If you're absolutely sure you want this entry deleted, click on the "Remove" button. The entry will disappear.

Well, there you have it. You've got the basics to really enjoy yourself on the Web. You can take some time now to explore the links on the *Internet for Kids* home page that take you to the activities in this book. If you'd like to do that some other time, go on to Gopher.

Gopher

Like the World Wide Web, Gopher gives you access to huge quantities of information located on computers all over the world. These computers are called *Gopher servers*. Unlike the Web, Gopher is not graphical. Instead of graphical pages, Gopher has text-based menus. Although Gopher isn't as strikingly good-looking as the Web, it is a lot faster to use.

NetCruiser's Gopher Viewer

Before we actually get going, here are a few words about what Gopher's menus will look like when you're out in Gopherspace. NetCruiser marks each menu entry with one of four different icons, according to the entry's content or function:

Icon	Entry
A folder	A submenu
A white document with blue "text"	A text file
A green document with 1s and 0s	A binary file
A tree on an island	A `.GIF` picture file
A magnifying glass	A *search entry* (an entry that allows you to search Gopherspace for a particular word or words)

By paying attention to these icons, you will have a better idea of what each entry on a Gopher menu contains.

Basic Gopher Navigation

To learn how to get around on Gopher and to get an idea of what is actually out there, work through the following example.

1. Start gophering by clicking on the Gopher icon (it looks like a cartoon gopher's face) on the NetCruiser toolbar. This brings up the Site Chooser, basically a map of the United States, shown in Figure C.15.

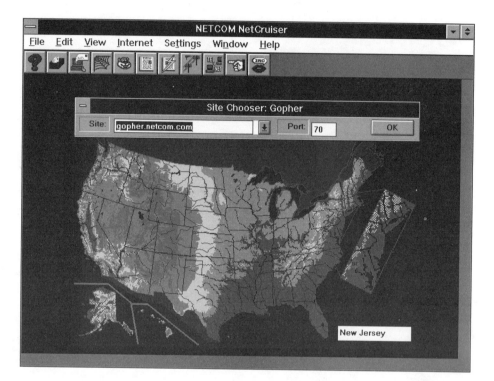

Figure C.15

The Site Chooser

2. The Site Chooser contains a list of Gopher servers for each state in the United States. We're going to go to a server in California, so on the Site Chooser, click on California and then pull down the "Site" list at the top of the Site Chooser window.

If you happen to know the name of a particular Gopher server, you can type it directly into the Site Chooser instead of using the map.

Note ··

3. Scroll down this list and click on `gopher.exploratorium.edu`. The Exploratorium is a hands-on science museum in San Francisco, founded by Frank Oppenheimer, a gifted teacher and brother of the famous physicist Robert Oppenheimer. We're going to its Gopher server. Now click on "OK." You should now be at the Exploratorium Gopher's main menu, shown in Figure C.16. Notice that the first item on the menu has a document icon next to it; it is the welcome message. All of the other entries are marked with folders; they are submenus.

Figure C.16

*The
Exploratorium
Gopher*

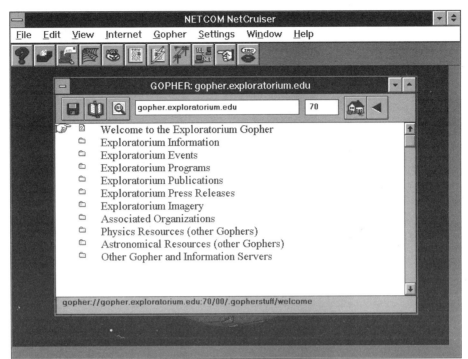

4. Double-click on "Exploratorium Imagery" to get to this submenu, shown in Figure C.17. This submenu contains an explanatory text file and many **.GIF** images.

5. Double-click on "Frank_O" to see a picture of the Exploratorium's founder. It's going to take a while for the entire picture to come across the telephone lines to your computer, so while we're waiting, take a look at the upper right-hand corner of NetCruiser's Gopher window. There are three buttons there; you use them to navigate in Gopher-space. The stop sign, which appears only in the middle of an operation, interrupts the current operation. Use it when it's taking too long for something to happen. For example, you could click on it now if you're tired of waiting for Dr. Oppenheimer's picture. The "Arrow" button moves you back to the menu you just came from. The "Home" button moves you to the top-level menu on the Gopher server, the one you saw when you first connected. Let's try these buttons out.

6. Click on the stop sign to stop the picture file (if it's already on your screen, enjoy). Now click on the "Arrow" button. This takes you back one menu level.

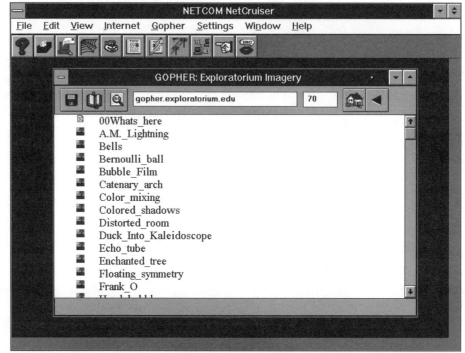

Figure C.17

The Exploratorium Imagery menu

7. Double-click on the "Exploratorium Information" entry, then double-click on "Facts_and_Figures" to get some basic information about the Exploratorium itself.

8. When you're done reading, click on the "Home" button. This takes you to the Exploratorium Gopher's main menu, where we were when we first connected.

Now you have the basic tools for getting around in Gopherspace. Take a while to explore some other Gopher sites. There are some listed in Chapter 1, or you could pick some randomly from the Site Chooser. When you're done, go back to the Exploratorium Gopher. We'll see one more very useful Gopher feature in the next section.

Gopher Bookmarks

No doubt you've got some sense by now of just how much there is to see out in Gopherspace and just how difficult it can be to get back to one particular menu that you like after you've gone to a handful of other

places. After a while, the **addresses of** all the Gopher servers start to jumble together.

NetCruiser's bookmark feature **is the** solution to this very problem. A bookmark allows you to **jump to** a particular Gopher menu from *anywhere* in Gopherspace. To **see how to** create and use a bookmark, work through the following steps:

1. If you're not at the Exploratorium Gopher, go there now.

2. Click on the Bookmark button—yep, the one with the book and bookmark pictured on it. **This brings up** the Book Mark window, shown in Figure C.18.

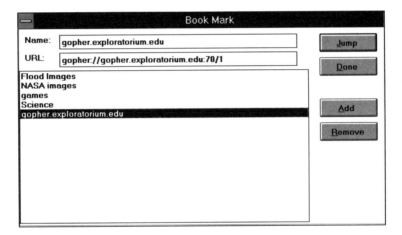

Figure C.18

Gopher bookmarks

3. Notice that NetCruiser **automatically** fills in the name and address of the Exploratorium Gopher. To create the bookmark, just click on "Add." As in Figure C.18, NetCruiser keeps a list of the bookmarks you create. Now click on "Done" to **close** the Book Mark window.

4. Leave the Exploratorium **Gopher and** go to another Gopher site anywhere in Gopherspace. It **doesn't matter** where, because we're coming right back.

5. Okay, are you out in Iowa **somewhere?** Click on the Bookmark button again to reopen the Book Mark window.

6. Click on the Exploratorium **Gopher** bookmark that you just created and then click on "Jump." Voilà! You're back.

That brings us to the end of Gopher. If, while you were exploring earlier, you found any Gopher sites you'd like to bookmark, go ahead and do that now. When you're done, close any open Gopher windows. In the next section, we'll see how to use FTP to copy files from the Internet down to your computer.

FTP

FTP (File Transfer Protocol) allows you to copy files from another computer on the Internet to your own. It is particularly useful when you need a utility file, for example, to fix a problem you have. It's also good for some fun, because there are many graphics files available that you can collect.

Note to Parents

A word about etiquette (or *netiquette*) here. Because FTP sites are located on computers used in business and universities, don't FTP to a site until after 6 P.M. local time for the site. Many FTP sites have been shut down because of too much public use during business hours.

NetCruiser is a particularly good FTP tool because it automates all the commands you would otherwise need to navigate between directories on an FTP site and to download files. To learn how to get a file using FTP, work through the following steps where we will get a picture of the space shuttle from a NASA FTP site.

1. Click on NetCruiser's FTP icon, the one with the telephone poles and telephone wires. This brings up the FTP Site Chooser, which looks and acts just like the Gopher Site Chooser.

2. Instead of choosing an FTP site from the map, we'll enter one directly this time. Type in `ftp.gsfc.nasa.gov` and click on "OK."

3. Click on "OK" to have NetCruiser log you onto the site as "Anonymous." This is the standard practice. When logging onto an FTP site, you log on as the user "Anonymous" and provide your complete e-mail address as the password. NetCruiser automatically takes care of these two steps for you.

4. When you connect to NASA, you'll get an introductory message. It's a good idea to read these messages because FTP sites often state their policies here. Once you've read the message, you can close the message window.

5. You should now have NetCruiser's FTP window on your screen showing you the root directory of the FTP site, as in Figure C.19. The display between the buttons at the top of the window shows you the name of the current directory. The top window displays the directories contained in the current directory. The bottom window displays the files contained in the current directory. File names are listed in the rightmost column. The center column contains file sizes.

In the top window, double-click on the **pub** directory. A window will appear with directory information; click on "OK" to close the window.

Figure C.19

NetCruiser's FTP window

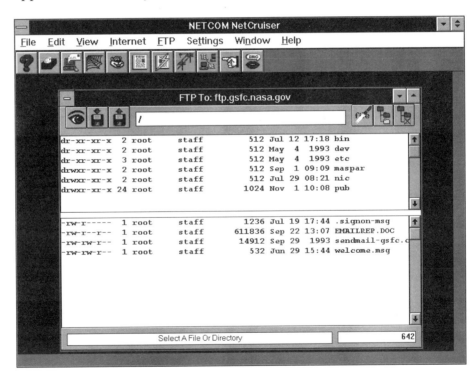

FTP sites often store available files under the **pub** directory.

Note ··

6. In the top window, double-click on **images**. Again, a window will appear with directory information; click on "OK" to close the window, then double-click on the following directory names in order: **gif** and then **shuttle**. You may have to scroll the window to find them. When you have done this, the FTP window should look like Figure C.20. The space shuttle **.GIF** picture files contained in this directory are listed in the bottom window.

7. The name of the file we want to download is **blastoff.gif**. Click once on the file name.

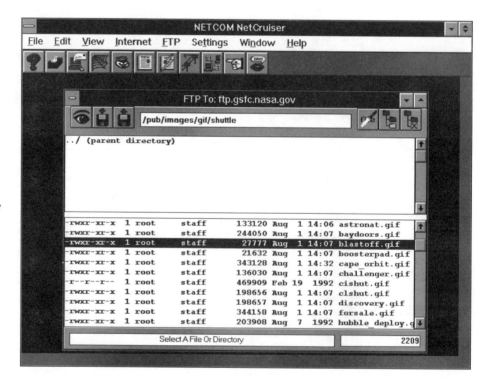

Figure C.20

Space shuttle .GIFs

8. Now that we've found the file we want, we can download it to your machine. Click on the "Download" button, which has a disk and a down arrow on it.

9. Select "Binary File" to tell both NetCruiser and the FTP site that you are downloading a binary file.

> You should select binary file even if you are downloading an ASCII text file.
>
> **Note**

10. In the window that appears, click on "OK." You are telling your computer the name to give the file when it arrives. If you don't like the name the FTP site has given the file, you can rename it here.

Once you have done all this, the file is downloaded to your computer. This process takes a little longer than others we've seen so far, but mostly because it takes a while to get to the directory containing the file we want. If you'd like to practice some more, start over at the beginning and get another file from this directory or from one of the other directories.

The hardest thing about FTP, though, is finding a site that has something you need or want. Some good FTP sites are listed in Chapter 1. You can find many others on Gopher. When you're done, close any open FTP windows.

Telnet

Telnet allows you to log into another computer and operate it from yours. Telnet is used to log into public computers and get information. To learn how to telnet to another computer and look around, work through the following steps. The process is similar to what you've done already with Gopher.

1. Click on the Telnet icon on NetCruiser's toolbar. This is the icon that is easiest to identify; it says "TELNET" on it. This brings up the Site Chooser, which you've seen before with Gopher and FTP.

2. We're going to Telnet to another NASA machine. Instead of selecting an address from the map, type `spacelink.msfc.nasa.gov` and click on "OK." This connects you to the NASA computer, which displays the NASA Spacelink welcome screen.

3. To log into Spacelink, enter **guest** at the "Login:" prompt and press Return. This displays another informational message. Note that NASA also has WWW, Gopher, and FTP addresses. Press Enter when you're done reading, and you'll see the Spacelink Electronic Library main menu, displayed in Figure C.21.

4. This computer arranges its information much like a Gopher menu system, so it shouldn't be too hard for you to navigate. We're going to find the journal entries of an Antarctic explorer. It's found under Spacelink.Hot.Topics, so press the ↓ key to move the dashed arrow to that menu choice and press Enter.

> ### When Telnetting...
>
> Welcome screens are very important; make sure you read them carefully. They state the policy of the site and they tell you if and how you can log in.

Figure C.21

The NASA Spacelink Electronic Library main menu

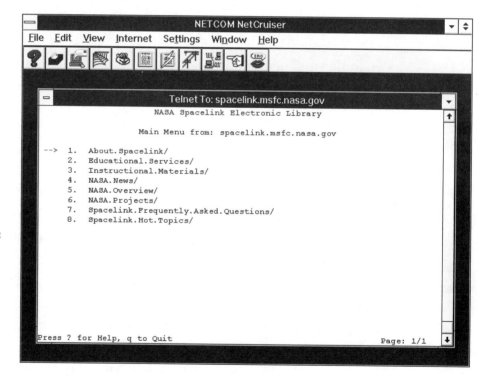

5. The journal entries themselves are buried a number of menu layers down. Select in order:

```
6. Live.from.Antarctica
6. Follow.the.Explorers...
6. John.Briggs
1. Life.at.the.South.Pole
```

This brings up Briggs' Antarctic Journal. Take a while to read it if you like.

That's all there is to it. Take a while to look around here or go to some other good Telnet sites listed for you in Chapter 1. Remember to read the instructions for logging in as a guest—which are posted at the site—and don't be discouraged if you find you can't get in somewhere. When you're done, close any open Telnet windows.

Newsgroups

A newsgroup is a conference dedicated to a single subject. Anyone who is interested can participate. Messages (or *Articles*, as NetCruiser calls them) posted on a newsgroup can be read by anyone who subscribes to the group. There are thousands of newsgroups out there; any number of them may interest you. In the next few sections, you'll learn how to join a newsgroup, read the messages posted on a newsgroup, and post your own messages.

Joining a Newsgroup

NetCruiser makes it easy to find and join newsgroups. Work through the following steps to join a newsgroup called `alt.kids-talk`, a newsgroup where kids talk about whatever is on their minds.

1. On NetCruiser's main screen, pull down the "Internet" menu and select the "Choose USENET Newsgroups" option. This brings up the Select USENET Newsgroups window shown in Figure C.22.

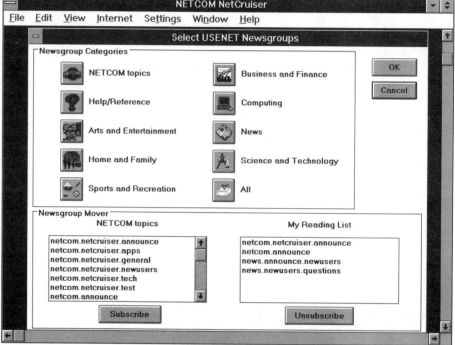

Figure C.22

The Select USENET Newsgroups window

2. Because there are so many newsgroups, NetCruiser groups them into categories, making any particular one easy to find. The `alt.kids-talk` newsgroup is in the "Home and Family" category, so click on that icon now. The list of Home and Family newsgroups now appears.

3. Scroll down this list until you find `alt.kids-talk`. Click once on the group name and then click on "Subscribe." The `alt.kids-talk` newsgroup is added to your *reading list*, which is what NetCruiser calls the list of newsgroups you subscribe to.

4. Click on "OK," because you're done. It's that easy to subscribe.

Reading a Newsgroup Message

Now that you know how to join a newsgroup, work through the following steps to learn how to read a newsgroup message. We'll look at some of the recent messages posted to `alt.kids-talk`.

1. On NetCruiser's toolbar, click on the "Read News" icon, the one with the newspaper on it. This brings up the list of newsgroups you subscribe to.

2. Click on `alt.kids-talk` and then click on "OK." This brings up the Retrieve Article Headers window, shown in Figure C.23, which you use to tell NetCruiser what messages you want to read.

Figure C.23

The Retrieve Article Headers window

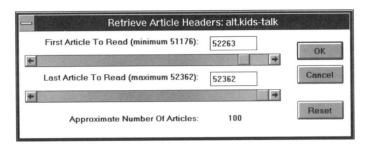

3. All newsgroup messages are numbered. You specify the ones you want to read by their numbers. The second number shown in the Retrieve Headers window is the last message posted to the group. The first number shown is the last message you've read. NetCruiser automatically sets the numbers this way, allowing you to read all messages posted since the last one you read. Here, however, you haven't read any messages, so NetCruiser arbitrarily picks the last 100 messages. We don't want to read quite this many now; 30 or so will do. Change the top number to a number about 30 less than the number of the last message and click on "OK."

4. NetCruiser grabs the headers for the messages you specified and displays them in the Read USENET window, as in Figure C.24. Newsgroup message headers contain the number of the message, its size, the e-mail address of the author, and the subject of the message. Scroll down the list of headers and click on one you want to read, then click on the "Read" button, the single arrow in the top right of the window. There you have it; the message appears for you to read. Continue on to the next section to learn how to read more than one message at a time.

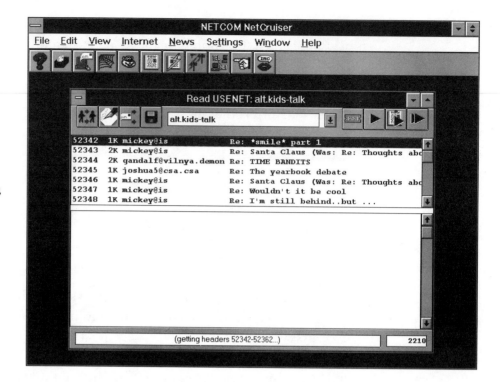

Figure C.24

*The Read
USENET
window*

Reading Selected Messages

Most of the time you are going to want to read more than one message,
but not necessarily all of the new messages posted. NetCruiser makes it
easy to be selective.

1. Select only those messages you want to read (do this by clicking on each
message header while holding down the Ctrl key).

2. Click on the "Read Next Selected" button, the one with a single arrow on
top of a newspaper. Click on this button again to read each message you
selected. That does it for reading newsgroup messages; nothing to it,
really. Take some time now if you want to join some other newsgroups
and read some other messages.

Other Read USENET Functions

Before we go on to posting messages, NetCruiser provides some other useful message functions located on the Read USENET window. We don't have space to describe them all in detail, but we do want to summarize them for you.

Reply by e-mail message	Instead of posting a message for everyone to read, you can reply by e-mail message directly to the writer. Click on the "Reply by Message" button, which has a fountain pen on it. The procedure is exactly like replying to an e-mail message.
Forward a message	Click on the "Forward" button (an envelope and two red arrows) to e-mail a newsgroup message to another person. This is exactly like forwarding an e-mail message.
Save a message	Click on the "Save" button (the floppy disk) to save a newsgroup message on your hard disk.
Unsubscribe	Click on the "Unsubscribe" button (it looks vaguely like a movie ticket) if you don't want to participate in a newsgroup anymore.

Posting a Reply Message

Half the fun of newsgroups is posting messages as well as reading them. Work through the following steps to learn how to post a message in response to a message you read.

1. Make sure the message you want to reply to is displayed on the Read USENET window.

2. Click on the "Follow-Up" button on the top far left; it has two arrows between two figures. This brings up the Post To USENET window, displayed in Figure C.25. Notice that NetCruiser has automatically filled in the newsgroup you're posting to and the subject of your message. Notice also that because you are posting a reply, the text of the original message is automatically included. You can delete it if you wish.

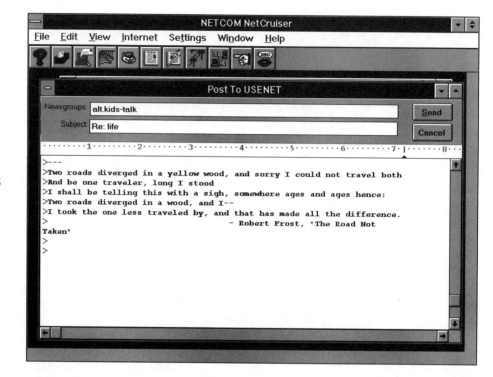

Figure C.25

*The Post
To USENET
window*

3. Type your message and click on "Send" to post it. Then click on "Yes" in the Tips window to confirm. Keep in mind that the message you post can be read all over the world. Make sure that you really want hundreds of people to read what you write. Close any open windows on your screen.

Posting a New Message

Sometimes, of course, you will want to post a brand new message, not a reply to someone else's. This is also very simple; the procedure is nearly identical to posting a reply. Work through the following steps to learn how.

1. On NetCruiser's main screen, click on the "Post News" icon, which shows a newspaper under a lightning bolt. This brings up the Post To USENET window.

2. When you are replying to a post, NetCruiser automatically fills in the newsgroup to post to and the subject of the message. Here, you must click on the Newsgroup text box and type the name of the group in

yourself, and then you need to click on the Subject text box and type in the subject of your message.

3. Type your message in the area below the ruler, then click on "Send" and "Yes" to confirm.

That does it for newsgroups. There are some popular newsgroups listed for you in Chapter 1, but it is a lot of fun to look around for yourself and find things that really interest you.

IRC

IRC (Internet Relay Chat) allows you to chat with other Internet users who are connected to the same IRC "channel" at the same time. It is like talking to a bunch of people on a CB radio. IRC is complicated, however, and a complete explanation is well beyond the scope of this appendix. What's more, if you want to talk to particular people, e-mail and newsgroups are more reliable means of communication; with IRC, you can never be sure if the person you want to talk to is online. To see how to have a private "chat" with another Netcom user, work through the following steps.

1. Click on the "IRC" icon on the NetCruiser toolbar; it's the button with the mouth saying, "IRC."

2. In the window that appears, you must choose the network on which you are going to chat. We will use Netcom's private IRC network. Make sure "NETCOM IRC Hosts" is selected at the top of the window, then pull down the list just below it and select "NETCOM private."

3. Enter the nickname you will use when chatting. If you don't type anything in here, NetCruiser will automatically use your user name.

4. Click on "Connect." This connects you to the private Netcom IRC network. Your screen should now display the window shown in Figure C.26.

5. Click on the "Query" button; it shows a head in profile saying, "Psst." Now type in the nickname of the person you want to talk to and click on "OK." This initiates the private chat. In Figure C.26, two Netcom

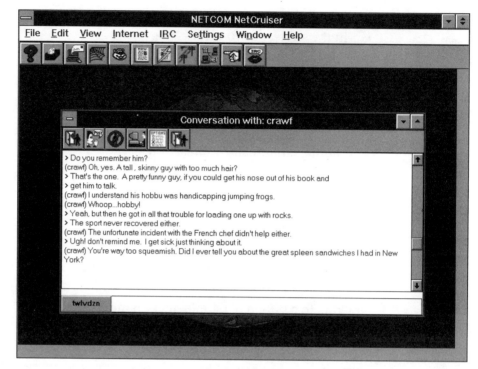

Figure C.26

*The IRC
control panel*

users nicknamed "twlvdzn" and "crawf" are chatting about a mutual acquaintance.

6. When you are done chatting, click on the "Disconnect" button, the button all the way on the right showing a figure walking out of a door, and then click on "Yes" to confirm the disconnect.

This should give you a feel for IRC chatting and for whether or not it is something you'd like to try out. For more information, check out the `alt.irc` newsgroup or get a good beginning tutorial by FTP from `cs.bu.edu`. The file name is `IRCprimer1.1.txt`, and it is in the `/irc/support` directory.

Finger

And now for something a bit different. Finger is a utility that gives you information about users on systems across the Internet. It gives you a person's real name, whether they've logged in recently, and even whether they have mail waiting for them.

Finger is most useful to you if you can remember what system someone is on but can't quite remember her user name. To learn how to find that person with NetCruiser's Finger utility, work through the following steps.

1. Click on NetCruiser's Finger icon, the one with the pointing finger. This brings up the Site Chooser. This time you can ignore it, so click on "OK."

2. At the "User" prompt in the Finger window, type the last name of the person whose address you are looking for.

3. At the "Host" prompt, type the address of the system where this person has her account, which is the part of the e-mail address after the "@" sign. For example, if you're looking for a Netcom address, type **netcom.com**. Now click on "OK."

4. If you score a hit, NetCruiser will display information about the person you fingered. Keep in mind that a lot of systems routinely have Finger capability turned off, so NetCruiser may come back at you with an error message.

5. You can repeat the second and third steps now to look for someone else. If you're done, click on "Cancel."

Getting Help

This brings us to the end of the NetCruiser appendix. We have tried to choose useful exercises and examples and be as clear as possible in our explanations. If you feel you need further help with some of the things we've shown you here, we suggest you try the following (in order):

1. Reread the relevant section and try again. Sometimes a little experimentation is all you need.

2. Use NetCruiser's built-in help system. Click on the "Help" icon on the NetCruiser toolbar, the one with the large red question mark on it.

3. Send a message to Netcom's technical support at the e-mail address support@ix.netcom.com. Be specific. Explain what you are trying to do, how you have tried to do it, and what didn't go right.

4. Call Netcom technical support at 1-408-983-5970.

Note

Sybex publishes a book called *Access the Internet!,* written by David Peal, that talks about NetCruiser in greater detail. You can find this book in your local bookstore or, to order it, call Sybex at (510) 523-8233 or (800) 277-2346 and ask for Customer Service.

Good luck, and enjoy!

Index

Note to the Reader:

Boldface numbers indicate pages where you will find the principal discussion of a topic or the definition of a term. *Italic* numbers indicate pages where topics are illustrated in figures.

GET A FREE CATALOG JUST FOR EXPRESSING YOUR OPINION.

Help us improve our books and get a *FREE* full-color catalog in the bargain. Please complete this form, pull out this page and send it in today. The address is on the reverse side.

Name _____   Company _____

Address _____   City _____ State ____ Zip _____

Phone ( ) _____

1. How would you rate the overall quality of this book?

❑ Excellent
❑ Very Good
❑ Good
❑ Fair
❑ Below Average
❑ Poor

2. What were the things you liked most about the book? (Check all that apply)

❑ Pace
❑ Format
❑ Writing Style
❑ Examples
❑ Table of Contents
❑ Index
❑ Price
❑ Illustrations
❑ Type Style
❑ Cover
❑ Depth of Coverage
❑ Fast Track Notes

3. What were the things you liked *least* about the book? (Check all that apply)

❑ Pace
❑ Format
❑ Writing Style
❑ Examples
❑ Table of Contents
❑ Index
❑ Price
❑ Illustrations
❑ Type Style
❑ Cover
❑ Depth of Coverage
❑ Fast Track Notes

4. Where did you buy this book?

❑ Bookstore chain
❑ Small independent bookstore
❑ Computer store
❑ Wholesale club
❑ College bookstore
❑ Technical bookstore
❑ Other _____

5. How did you decide to buy this particular book?

❑ Recommended by friend
❑ Recommended by store personnel
❑ Author's reputation
❑ Sybex's reputation
❑ Read book review in _____
❑ Other _____

6. How did you pay for this book?

❑ Used own funds
❑ Reimbursed by company
❑ Received book as a gift

7. What is your level of experience with the subject covered in this book?

❑ Beginner
❑ Intermediate
❑ Advanced

8. How long have you been using a computer?

years _____
months _____

9. Where do you most often use your computer?

❑ Home
❑ Work

❑ Both
❑ Other _____

10. What kind of computer equipment do you have? (Check all that apply)

❑ PC Compatible Desktop Computer
❑ PC Compatible Laptop Computer
❑ Apple/Mac Computer
❑ Apple/Mac Laptop Computer
❑ CD ROM
❑ Fax Modem
❑ Data Modem
❑ Scanner
❑ Sound Card
❑ Other _____

11. What other kinds of software packages do you ordinarily use?

❑ Accounting
❑ Databases
❑ Networks
❑ Apple/Mac
❑ Desktop Publishing
❑ Spreadsheets
❑ CAD
❑ Games
❑ Word Processing
❑ Communications
❑ Money Management
❑ Other _____

12. What operating systems do you ordinarily use?

❑ DOS
❑ OS/2
❑ Windows
❑ Apple/Mac
❑ Windows NT
❑ Other _____

13. On what computer-related subject(s) would you like to see more books?

_____

_____

_____

_____

14. Do you have any other comments about this book? (Please feel free to use a separate piece of paper if you need more room)

_____

_____

_____

_____

- - - - - - - - - - - PLEASE FOLD, SEAL, AND MAIL TO SYBEX - - - - - - - - - - -

SYBEX INC.
Department M
2021 Challenger Drive
Alameda, CA
94501

If You're Not on the Net Yet...

Everything You Need Is on This Disk

Use this customized software to get on the Internet and start having fun and learning right away. The software includes:

- A connection to the Internet via Netcom's **NetCruiser**, which connects you automatically through a local telephone number.
- A friendly **"Windows" face** so you can point and click your way around the Internet.
- A versatile and easy-to-use **e-mail system** so you can communicate with over 30 million Internet users.
- Two information-browsing programs—for **Gopher** and the **World Wide Web**—so you can search the world to find information you want fast.
- **Telnet**, so you can access computers all over the world from your own home.

What's It Cost?

Netcom's monthly rate is $19.95. This is charged to the credit card number you provide upon installation of the software and includes:

- 40 hours of prime-time access—between 9 A.M. and midnight.
- Unlimited access on weekends and between midnight and 9 A.M.

Additional hours are charged at the rate of $2.00 per hour.

Customer Support

For billing questions, call (800) 353-6600

For installation and technical support questions, call (408) 983-5970